The Green Good News

The Green Good News

—— *Christ's Path to Sustainable and Joyful Life* ——

T. Wilson Dickinson

CASCADE *Books* · Eugene, Oregon

THE GREEN GOOD NEWS
Christ's Path to Sustainable and Joyful Life

Cascade Books
An Imprint of Wipf and Stock Publishers
199 W. 8th Ave., Suite 3
Eugene, OR 97401

www.wipfandstock.com

PAPERBACK ISBN: 978-1-5326-8183-7
HARDCOVER ISBN: 978-1-5326-8184-4
EBOOK ISBN: 978-1-5326-8185-1

Cataloguing-in-Publication data:

Names: Dickinson, T. Wilson, author.

Title: The green good news : Christ's path to sustainable and joyful life / by T. Wilson Dickinson.

Description: Eugene, OR: Cascade Books, 2019 | Includes bibliographical references.

Identifiers: ISBN 978-1-5326-8183-7 (paperback) | ISBN 978-1-5326-8184-4 (hardcover) | ISBN 978-1-5326-8185-1 (ebook)

Subjects: LCSH: Creation—Biblical teaching. | Ecology—Religious aspects—Christianity.

Classification: BS680.C69 D43 2019 (print) | BS680.C69 (ebook)

Manufactured in the U.S.A.   12/06/19

To my mother, Suetta, for her unfailing love and encouragement,
and to my son Teddy, for his abundant joy.

Contents

Preface

GOOD NEWS CAN BE hard to find. Every day we are bombarded with horrors from around the world. The headlines speak of gun violence, deep political and cultural divides, floods, wildfires, and the abuse of power from politicians, business leaders, and even clergy. This daily deluge is so overwhelming that it can be difficult to find our footing long enough to even think about, much less address, the underlying problems. It is easy to miss how often these catastrophes find their source and are intensified by the historical plagues of racism, patriarchy, poverty, and militarism. And if these problems from our past that grip our present were not enough, the growing ecological crisis and emerging reality of climate change threaten to bring about a future that is much more difficult. As sea levels rise, weather patterns become more erratic, deserts expand, ecosystems collapse, and fragile balances on this planet are pushed off kilter, the news could become much worse. In fact, it already has.

The buried headline of the ecological crisis is the good news that this interconnected web of problems has a beautiful and joyful set of responses. It is possible that climate change could ultimately threaten the corporatized, consumerist, individualistic orders that are striving to colonize the entire planet. The privileged way of life that dwells in the suburbs and high-rises is unsustainable and inequitable. It would take more than five earths for everyone on the planet to consume as much as the *average* person in the USA.[1] But is the average privileged consumer even finding an abundance of joy, love, peace, and faithfulness in their lives? The possibility remains open in the unwritten news of the future that what we have to lose are our overfull work weeks, our isolated and compartmentalized daily lives, our unhealthy food systems, our rented storage containers, our long commutes, the constant barrage of assessment, our futile striving for happiness in prideful

1. Benton-Short et al., *Regional Geography*, 14.

success or selfish accumulation. The good news is that it is only by losing these lives that we may save our lives.

Jesus Christ guides us on a path of love that calls beyond our gated safe-houses into the space of risky but joyful community. We are not called to cast off our own chains and find a separate peace, but to work for the biblical vision of peace and justice. This is not a feeling that one could ever experience alone. It only emerges from a right relationship between our neighbors, God, and the land. We will save our lives and find lives of joy by giving them to others, by seeking to cultivate habitats where everyone and everything thrives.

The savior that offers us this hope may sound a bit different from the one that is preached about in many churches or that is vaguely known in mainstream culture. Yet, this message begins to leap from the pages of Scripture once we situate Jesus' life, ministry, death, and resurrection within the context of the Roman Empire. Jesus was a peasant who resisted the inequitable and destructive structures of the Empire that desecrated the land and left many in subjugation and poverty. Christ responded to this injustice with an inspiring vision and transformative practices.[2] He led a movement that sought to bring about an alternative kingdom and a new covenant. Jesus was anointed to renew and radicalize the simple and sustainable covenantal life of agrarian villages and cities to heal all of creation.[3] Fleshing out these contexts of resistance to empire and the renewal of communities built on radical justice opens up constructive connections between the Scriptures and our own lives.

In the Gospels Christ provides us with a vision (which we will explore in Part 1) and a set of social experiments, spiritual practices, and forms of relationship (which are charted in Part 2) that could guide us in our work for justice and sustainability. We can see this more clearly if we come to

2. While the point of emphasis in ecotheology is almost always placed on the cosmic Christ, the path of this book proceeds more by the way of a "Christology from below"—beginning with Jesus' life and ministry. I have fleshed out this vision for philosophical theology in greater detail in *Exercises in New Creation*.

3. Attending to this political, economic, and social horizon brings together issues of environment and justice that are often kept separate both in activist and academic circles. The primary focus in ecological hermeneutics, for example, has methodologically bracketed much of political and social life in its focus on the non-human elements of the Scriptures. In bringing the insights of scholarship on Jesus and the Empire and agrarian readings of the Hebrew Scriptures, together with work on environmental justice, political ecology, and constructive theology, I hope not only to fill a hole in the literature (an agrarian and environmental justice reading of the Gospels) but even more to foster connections between movements for justice and environmentalism. Because my focus is on this broader audience, I have bracketed issues of scholarly debate and limited my reference to contemporary scholarship to footnotes.

understand that the cross of Christ marks a path of nonviolent self-giving love. This path leads us beyond a vision of environmentalism as a special interest and enables us to see how the ecological crisis demands that we change our way of life (examined in chapter 1). The risen Christ is not a figure that escapes the earth, but, in the Scriptures, he is mistaken for a gardener. His purpose is to restore the goodness of creation and the human vocation to serve and preserve earthly life. Following Christ into actual gardens can help us find a starting point and a communal space to initiate this renewal (chapter 2). Christ implemented forms of organization and alternative economies in which people found abundance where others had only seen scarcity. The efforts of contemporary food movements offer avenues for similar forms of organization (chapter 3). Christ taught in parables that laid bare the cruelty, violence, and exploitation that hide behind the ruses of politeness and the gilding of status. We too must teach in ways that touch the imagination and speak to everyday life if we are to cultivate social change (chapter 4). Christ went to those who were broken and isolated by the social and political forces of the Empire and helped them find healing. Likewise, we are called to examine the rhythms of work and consumption that often damage our lives, so that we can mend our fractured communities and find wholeness (chapter 5). Christ brought together new communities through banquets and parties that tore apart social hierarchies and fostered a radical change in life, values, and relationships. Similarly, in our own houses we can begin to incarnate transformative meals (chapter 6). Christ modeled a life of prayer that sustains body and spirit for the labors of love and resistance, and we can begin to pray as he taught us, taking seriously that our hopes are set *on earth*, as it is in heaven (chapter 7).

To see this good news, we will have to find healing from our ignorance and numbness to the suffering of the earth. We have closed ourselves off for good reason. Without a vision in which we can hope or tangible actions and life-giving relationships that animate us, despair seems inevitable. The good news of Christ provides us with hope *and* a path.

This path leads in the opposite direction of the striving after success and status that dominates our world. The very use of the term "good news," a translation of the Greek term *euangelion* (which is also often rendered as "gospel"), points to this signpost marking diverging roads. In its common usage in the first-century Roman world, good news (*euangelion*) referred to public declarations of the good works of the Empire. Gospels were posted or proclaimed in public places as propaganda pieces that spoke of a military victory or of an abundant harvest (for which imperial officials wanted to take credit). The good news of the Empire whitewashed what I take to be its definitive characteristic: massive political, economic, and militaristic structures that protect the interests and lifestyles of the elite by *extracting* wealth from the labor of the poor and the fertility of the land.[4]

Jesus' public declarations of good news, by contrast, did not celebrate the power of the Empire, but announced the world-transforming power of self-giving love. The gospels of the Roman Empire were like our advertisements about the power of wealth to make you successful, sexy, happy, secure, and admired. Jesus, who was executed by the Empire, stained its glossy airbrushed images with the frightening reality of how empires really function. But the good news was that the Empire and its violence did not have the final word. Instead, all of creation was finding reconciliation.

The *green* good news, the path of new life leading out of the ecological crisis, likewise will require that we see the empire of wealth that surrounds us for the unjust sham that it is. Speaking of the exploitative corporate and national power structures of our time in terms of empire serves to unveil aspects of our world that we take to be normal, natural, or even praiseworthy. More importantly, this critical move frees us to travel down an alternative path to joyful, just, and simple life.

---

4. Boer and Petterson, *Time of Troubles*, xi–xii. Brueggemann, *Tenacious Solidarity*, 42–44.

Acknowledgments

THIS BOOK FEELS LIKE it wrote itself. This is because, in many ways, it is an expression of the communities and efforts of which I am a part. I thank Pat Clark, who handed me a copy of Herzog's book on the parables, in which I first saw the deep connection between so many different college classes, seminary modules, guest talks, Sunday school conversations, ministry initiatives, and communal changes I had been laboring on for years. I thank the friends and communities that have inspired and uncovered so much of what lies in these pages, especially the Green Christians Dinner Church, the Re:Generate Fellows, the Fig Tree Collective, the Religious Life Interns at Transylvania University, Twisted Trunk Community Garden, Green Chalice, the planners of the Young Adult Ecumenical Forums, and the WCC Stewards of 2003.

I am indebted to those who took the time to read over parts of the book and helped in the processes of refining and clarifying: the Lexington Theological Seminary faculty and staff (especially Leah Schade, Jerry Sumney, Emily Askew, and Loida Martell), Joe Blosser, Rachel Nance, Guy Waldrop, and Carly, Becky, and Suetta Dickinson. I thank Rodney Clapp for believing in and shepherding the project.

Most of all I am grateful for the shared life and love of my family: My brothers Bart and Jon, whose friendship keeps me grounded; my nephew Logan, who educates me about power grids and alternative energy and challenges me to rethink what the future might hold; my sister Becky and my mom Suetta, who are a constant source of encouragement, insight, and support; my wife Carly, who not only edits my musings on the good news but walks beside me and guides me back onto the path of love and joy; and my son Teddy, whose unfailing laughter, kindness, and brilliance gives me hope for what may come.

Part One: **A New Covenant**

1

Christ at the Crossroads
of Earth and Empire

MY PATH TO A green gospel did not begin in the conventional origins of environmentalism in the United States. While I enjoy a nice walk in the woods, if I postured as an outdoorsman, anyone who knows me would laugh. Though I like to fiddle around in the garden, my family left its roots in farming generations ago. I am a white guy from a small suburban town that remembers thinking as a kid: "How are there still mosquitos? Why haven't they solved this problem yet?" I come from a world in which it is intuitive to think that an entire species could or even should be eradicated because it irritates me. My turn to caring for creation did not demand leaving these neighborhoods or communities behind, but it is oriented by the hope of their redemption and transformation.

This journey started in and was guided by the church. I was raised by mainline Protestant communities, and my faith was deepened and expanded by the ecumenical movement—global networks of progressive Christian communities working for justice. This work with global Christians unveiled for me the destructive relationship between my white bread consumeristic life in the United States and the injustice of poverty, racism, violence, and ecological devastation that have colonized the world. For example, at the end of one meeting in Geneva, I bought some coffee from a friend from the east African nation of Burundi. In this simple exchange of coffee beans and money, we cut out the middle men of multinational corporations. Though I do not know the exact ratios of how much more money ended up in the hands of Burundian farmers, one study found that coffee, by the time it is sold in the United Kingdom, is marked up two hundred times the price paid to growers in Uganda.[1] This wildly imbalanced exchange has dire consequences for the people and the land. Burundi's economy is largely centered on the

1. Patel, *Starved and Stuffed*, 18.

cash crop of coffee, even though the country tends to fetch lower prices from international markets than neighboring African countries. The meager proceeds from this exchange largely end up in the hands of elites. The land that is used to grow coffee is often degraded by fertilizer use and shortsighted farming practices. While this industry provides little benefit to the average farmer, it puts further constraint on the land that is available to grow food and contributes to a situation in which the agricultural production of Burundi does not meet the needs of the population. This in turn has led to further over-farming, ecological degradation, conflict, and violence.[2] On the other end of all the stories my Burundian friend had told me about his ministry with struggling communities, desperate families, and hurting children, was the supermarket down the street from my house. The coffee that was cheap for me came at a high price for other people and lands.

I was initially resistant to facing such a reality. This problem is not limited to coffee. It is like kudzu—its tendrils and vines cover and choke everything. This waste and exploitation are woven into the social fabric, showing up in the disposable plates at a potluck and the clothes on my back. Struggling with systemic injustice is deeply unsettling as it shows the cracks in a cultural foundation on which I and most of the people I love have built our lives. To try to come to terms with such a reality is not just to challenge the norms of pleasantness and politeness, but it is to question the goodness of the systems in which one is, ostensibly, inextricably bound. And so, back then, and still today, I struggle to even acknowledge this reality.

The plodding and slow turning of my work to these issues initially filled me with criticisms and frustrations. I felt called to resistance, but I lacked a vision of joy, love, and peace that would make such acts sustainable and sustaining. When I encountered the Christian food movement, I found a chance to be *for* something rather than just *against* everything.[3] Hearing the green good news has been a bit of fresh air, or the movement of the Holy Spirit, that has breathed new life into my faith. Through community gardens, the support of alternative economic models, and joyful communities, I saw an opening to a beautiful alternative. While none of these acts were enough on their own, they provided nourishing first steps that inspired the imagination and cultivated alternative relationships and ways of life.

When I started reading the Scriptures with the concerns of food and environmental justice, I found deep wells of nourishing wisdom. Once the elements of creaturely life—fields, food, landscapes, bodies, lilies, illness, wine,

---

2. Oketech and Polzer, "Conflict and Coffee."

3. This phrasing is drawn from Bahnson, "Field, Table, Communion," 103.

birds, hunger—were no longer regarded as metaphors, but were figures concerned with the everyday, the Scriptures stopped seeming distant, confusing, or irrelevant. The green (or ecologically oriented) reading of the Scriptures shed a new (or green) light upon them, and in turn, opened a path to an entirely different way of life. The Scriptures and the gifts of faith communities, in turn, provided a more radical, holistic, joyful, and social way of addressing the ecological crisis than mainstream environmentalism.

Before we can embark down this path, in this chapter I want to address three stumbling blocks that could trip us up: mainstream environmentalism's focus on "*wilderness*," common understandings of Jesus' *cross*, and a narrow view of the title of "*Christ*." In addressing each of these stumbling blocks my point of emphasis will not be on criticizing forms of interpretation that I want to avoid; I will instead look for the green—which is to say new and life-giving—possibility at work in each.

Jesus Christ, Radical Environmentalist

In order to hear the green good news of Christ it helps to listen for his peasant dialect. Jesus was a carpenter, a lowly artisan, from the small agricultural village of Nazareth (which archaeologists estimate was composed of two hundred to four hundred people).[4] Historians propose that as a carpenter he would have worked in the nearby city of Sepphoris. Moving between these worlds, Jesus saw the exploitative ways of the elite from the vantage point of the sustainable peasant community where he was raised.[5]

In Sepphoris, the client ruler Herod Antipas was rebuilding a new shining capital of the region of Galilee in the Roman style. He was rebuilding the city because it had been burned by the Romans around the time of Jesus' birth, after an insurrectionist named Judas led a revolt and raided the armory there.[6] Judas was leading a resistance against a census the Empire was conducting. This imperial method of assessing the population and the land through a census would allow them to extract wealth in the form of taxes, and stood in tension with covenantal traditions whereby the land was God's and a source of commonwealth and mutual care.[7] Roman soldiers defeated Judas, crucified more than two thousand rebels, razed the city, and took many of its people off in slavery.[8] Herod Antipas was remaking

4. Crossan and Reed, *Excavating Jesus*, 32.

5. Oakman, *Jesus and the Peasants*, 167–73.

6. Crossan, *God and Empire*, 109.

7. Hengel, *Zealots*, 127–41, 331, 387–88.

8. Hendricks, *Politics of Jesus*, 51.

the ruins that Jesus grew up around in the image of the Empire and even renamed it "*Autocrator*," meaning Emperor or World Conqueror, the first title of Caesar Augustus.[9]

On his walk from his village to the imperial development, Jesus might have passed farmland that had also undergone radical changes.[10] Many smaller farms had been seized through cycles of debt and consolidated into larger plantations.[11] The large landholders sought to extract wealth from the fertility of the land and the labor of the people to support their opulent lifestyles and the system of the Empire, a long-standing problem that the prophets often lamented (Isa 3:14–15, 5:8–10, 24:5–6). Consistent with the tendencies of farming practices that grow large fields of a single crop for profit (monoculture agriculture), Jesus might have noticed a lack of care for the long-term health of the land.[12] In patterns somewhat similar to industrial agriculture today, growers interested in profit or forced by debt push the land and workers to increase the production of one crop for sale. This leads to the expansion of fields, a disregard for the contours of the land, and a loss of biodiversity, all of which contribute to the erosion of soils, the loss of soil fertility, and the spread of harmful blights and insects.[13] The consolidation of landholdings also contributes to the increasing divide between wealthy farm owners and impoverished and exploited farm workers, a dynamic Jesus constantly uncovers in his teachings, especially in the parables (and which we will return to in chapter 6). By contrast, village life organized around small land holders was animated by relationships of mutual support centered on the faithful *covenant*—relationships of love, care, and commitment between God, neighbor, and land (which will be a constant theme of this book, and explored in greater depth in chapter 3). Wheat, in the hands of a villager, was bread to be shared or seed to be stored. In the hands of a wealthy official, it was a commodity to be traded or an excess to be displayed.

The smaller farms were inclined to follow more sustainable and equitable patterns of life. On these farms, local families cared for themselves and their neighbors by growing a variety of crops throughout the year—wheat, barley, and legumes, planted during the winter on the flatter soils, and figs, olives, and grapes planted on terraced slopes and harvested in

---

9. Crossan, *God and Empire*, 102

10. Daly-Denton, *John*, 67. Fiensy, *Social History*, 55.

11. Freyne, *Jesus, a Jewish Galilean*, 45–46.

12. Freyne, *Jesus, a Jewish Galilean*, 46. Horden and Purcell, *Corrupting Sea*, 201–2.

13. Hughes, *Environmental Problems*, 122–27.

the early fall.[14] The covenantal communities of peasant farmers followed principles that maintained the soil—keeping to agricultural diversity and simple living, which subsisted well below the carrying capacity of their land.[15] The red soil of the region, which has a heavy clay content, and the reliance on rainfall (rather than irrigation) required the attention and care of wise farmers.[16] The hilly topography, which called for the labor-intensive construction and upkeep of terraces, and the processing of grains, olives, and grapes required a profound amount of communal cooperation.[17] The distant, extractive, profit-seeking ways of large landholders—who seized these former family farms—both fractured these communities and undermined their sustainable ways.[18]

In Sepphoris, Jesus would see the spaces where the commonwealth of village life had been funneled to support the lavish buildings and excessive lifestyles of the elite. This would be most clearly incarnated in the basilica, an administrative hub at the center of town that was visible from Nazareth.[19] Though we associate the word *basilica* with a church or cathedral, in Jesus' time it referred to the center of administrative activity in the Roman Empire.[20] The basilica in Sepphoris sat on a footprint of about 200 by 260 feet, which dwarfed the average peasant house size of about ten by thirteen feet.[21] As an epicenter of imperial power, governance, and economics, archaeologists think this basilica contained a market, a court, a dining area, conference rooms, and a small indoor mall for luxury items.[22] In the shadow of imperial opulence in the city, Christ would have seen the growing numbers of the desperate and dying poor in the streets. This physical architecture that loomed over the peasant village several miles away was the manifestation of the tentacles of empire that reached out to the land and consumed its bounty, and which bound up the people and extracted their labor. Can you imagine how Jesus' heart ached or

---

14. Adams, *Social and Economic Life*, 83–84. At the heart of these sustainable practices were crop rotation, with legumes playing a central role in fixing nitrogen, and fallowing. Horden and Purcell, *Corrupting Sea*, 201–2. Though Leviticus 19:19 prohibited sowing more than one seed in the same field, Rabbinic texts indicate a good deal of latitude and leniency on this matter. Adams, *Social and Economic Life*, 85.

15. Boer and Petterson, *Time of Troubles*, 72–73. Echlin, "Jesus and the Earth," 498.

16. Meyers, *Rediscovering Eve*, 45–46.

17. Meyers, *Rediscovering Eve*, 51.

18. Hughes, *Environmental Problems*, 122, 128.

19. Sawicki, *Crossing Galilee*, 178.

20. We should keep the basilica in Sepphoris in mind when we hear Jesus speak of a different order—the kingdom (in Greek, *basileia*) of God.

21. Reed, *Archaeology*, 118. Horsley, *Galilee*, 192.

22. Reed, *Archaeology*, 118.

his spirit was angered as he saw the roots of imperial development and success in the degradation of the land, the deterioration of social structures, and the exploitation of more and more people?

If Jesus is to have anything to say about environmentalism, it will likely not stop with replacing lightbulbs and buying certified organic products. Jesus' vision is more wide-reaching and touches on the entirety of life. It resonates with what is called the "environmentalism of the poor," or in the United States, "environmental justice" and "agrarianism." For those who live in neighborhoods (especially those populated by people of color) where toxic waste sites or heavy industry are located, or in regions that have been devastated by the legacy of mineral extraction, the links between nature and culture, the *environment*, and issues of *justice* are unavoidable.[23] Here, the soil is not ruined by natural processes or acts of God. Rather, neighbors develop cancer and water supplies are polluted through acts of boards—zoning boards and corporate boards that make calculations that render these places and people expendable. The perspective of *agrarianism*—a way of life rooted in the health of the land and the creatures that live upon it—clearly sees the social and political grounds of the ecological crisis.[24] Members of rural communities with deep roots in their place have seen policy changes and economic structures foreclose family farms, degrade soils, and hollow out entire towns. From this vantage point, environmental catastrophe is seen as deeply interrelated with the socioeconomic structures of production and consumption.[25] Environmental problems are not simply technical matters in need of experts or a separate issue that requires small consumer changes, but they are social and moral failings that demand a social movement and profound changes in our ways of life. While cultural and geographic differences often inhibit communities concerned with "environmental justice" and "agrarianism" from joining one another, perhaps they both can find harmonious resonance in the green good news of Jesus Christ. This shared challenge and the wisdom of traditions hold the possibility for the fusion politics of a moral and social movement.[26] Walking between Nazareth and Sepphoris, Jesus might have seen the fault lines that cause the tremors of ecological devastation—those between the rich and the poor, the conspicuous consumption of the elite and the exploitation of workers, the use of land for profit and the stewardship of land for subsistence.

23. de la Torre, *Doing Christian Ethics*, 126–36. Cole and Foster, *From the Ground Up*.

24. Davis, *Scripture, Culture, and Agriculture*, 1. Berry, *Art of the Commonplace*, 239–42.

25. Guha and Alier, *Varieties of Environmentalism*, 18.

26. Barber and Wilson-Hartgrove, *Third Reconstruction*.

The car-bound affluent environmentalist typically does not see these problems, insulated by the closed highway of their commute and the pace of their travel and lives. My initial awakening to environmental issues was centered on seeking to protect the forest I hiked in, or the national park with mountainous scenic overlooks that I would visit on vacation. While such places are certainly worthy of protection, a limited attention to them betrays a naïve and closed-off vision of what counts as God's good creation.

This narrowing of the natural world to "the wilderness" is strongly correlated with a notion that nature and culture function in different spheres.[27] On this account, one is faced with either virginal landscapes that are to be chivalrously protected or natural resources that are commodities for our use.[28] This view of certain types of habitats and land as "wilderness" obscures the human role in habitats. It draws our attention to the parks that are playgrounds for the rich and allows us to imagine that these spaces are synonymous with "nature." This limited understanding of the natural world keeps many people from seeing the environmental issues and needs of the neighborhood across town. Furthermore, it turns our gaze away from the habitats and creatures that surround us in our yards and offices.[29] We might resist the developer who threatens "wilderness," but fail to see the ways our lifestyles require this destruction and the squalid living conditions of many people. This environmentalism of the rich obstructs the deep interconnection between the care of creation and the demands of justice.

Furthermore, our love of wilderness—of nature removed from the corruption of human action—has paved the way for a wrong turn into a false "sustainability." Inherent in this ambiguous term is the question: the ability to sustain what and whom? Without seeing the connection between socioeconomic structures and ecological devastation, mainstream environmentalism has too readily adopted the myth of the Green Consumer Economy. This grand narrative tells us not to worry about climate change, that a green revolution in technology will actually lead to an economic renaissance. Because it has dressed itself in green garments, we have missed that what these merely technical solutions seek to sustain are not really ecosystems, habitats, or creatures, but the current economic order. If we are only familiar with our manicured lawns and the wilderness of our parks, we think that we live in a balance that could be sustained. But lost in this narrative are all the other people who *already* live in our sewage

27. Dickinson, *Exercises in New Creation*, 12–13.

28. Ruether, *To Change the World*, 64–66.

29. Cronon, "The Trouble with Wilderness." DeLuca and Demo, "Imagining Nature."

and habitats that have been irrevocably devastated. One does not achieve
health by sustaining a cancerous growth.

We cannot simply make the present order more efficient through a
turn to eco-business and pretend that we have addressed the worst effects
of climate change. The expansion of production and consumption is wildly
outpacing restraint or efficiency. Green consumption has not slowed down
consumers or the expansion of markets. The savings that businesses find
from efficiencies are reinvested into more factories, products, and stores.[30]
For example, various efforts have decreased the use of plastic bags. Regulation in China alone has decreased consumption by as many as forty billion
bags a year. The production of plastic, however, continues to increase as
manufacturers produce three hundred million tons a year, most of which
will end up in landfills and waterways. The oceans already contain at least
five trillion pieces of plastic.[31] There is a virtual continent of plastic in the
Pacific Ocean, where currents have collected 79,000 tons of plastic debris in
a patch three times the size of France, a collection that is increasing exponentially and is a small reflection of the estimated 8,000,000 tons of plastic
dumped in the ocean each year.[32] This is all to say nothing of the inequitable
distribution of these resources, and the suffering tied up in their production. The changes needed are not simple tweaks in our operations, but a
transformation of business models, the very logic of our economies, and the
values and structures that shape consumerist ways of life.

In Jesus' context the Roman Empire offered its own version of the green
economy that asked its elite to simply believe in the status quo and the virtue
of working hard within established structures. In the public square, through
poetry, through festivals and sporting events, on coinage and buildings, the
Empire declared that it had brought about a new age of peace and prosperity.
The Gospel of the Empire heralded Caesar Augustus, the son of God and
Lord, who had triumphed over the forces of chaos and ushered in a new creation. This golden age was to be an *eternal* empire built on an order that tied
together the fertility of the earth, hard work, support of the status quo, family
values, piety toward the gods, and military might.[33]

The good news of Jesus stands in stark contrast with the celebration
of the order of the Empire. He is a Lord that calls for the kingdom of God,
a new creation of mutual service and love rather than an army of slaves
who serve a few elites. Christ's good news does not look past the bodies

30. Dauvergne, *Environmentalism of the Rich*, 41.

31. Dauvergne, *Environmentalism of the Rich*, 124.

32. Mooney, "Great Pacific Garbage Patch."

33. Carter, *John and Empire*, 204–8.

broken by the Empire, or the communities and landscapes that have been decimated, but is addressed to them.

This book, however, is not addressed to peasants. Jesus' ministry, though it brought good news to the poor, was not limited to those who were impoverished. He also brought healing to the privileged by showing them how to turn their lives around. His strategies and visions were not limited to the politics of resistance; they were also directed toward the incarnation of joyful and sustainable ways of life. This is good news for the overworked, alienated middle managers of empire today. Christ's life provides us with a vision and ways of life that will help us to live and see otherwise.

They Paved My Old Kentucky Home and Put up a Parking Lot

These forms of living and seeing are brought into focus for me on a strip of God's good earth that I previously passed daily on my commute. This stretch of asphalt is almost indistinguishable from so many other places in the United States. It bears witness to both the numb amnesia of the good news of empire and the limits of simply wanting to preserve wilderness.

In the last decade, a number of stores have popped up on the west side of US 25 toward the southern edge of the city limits of Georgetown, Kentucky. Two dollar stores of different chains sit side by side, having opened within a few months of each other. Next to them is the new Pizza Hut, across the street from the abandoned building that housed the old one. Almost directly to the south is a pharmacy, which is across the road from a virtually identical pharmacy. For a certain way of looking at the world these developments mark convenience. Their signs announce the gospel of the abundance of empire. On my drive home, I can stop and pick up a prescription, some food, or a product I might want.

I have the gift of having a longer memory of this place. It is the town where I was born and raised and am now raising my son. For most of the people in this town, which has tripled in size since my youth, this space was never green and its loss is invisible. During my childhood this plot of land was a lush pasture, and the site of a sleepy family farm. In its place are the eyesores of consumerism. Loamy soil has been covered with blacktop parking lots and redundant stores that sell cheap products and unhealthy foods. Everything about this space is now built on buildings and products that are *designed* to be briefly used, easily discarded, and instantly replaced. The long arc of seasons and the renewing cycles of grazing and growing have been replaced with the ten-year business plan. Soon the Pizza Hut will likely abandon this building for a new one. Before too long I will need to return to the dollar store to replace the cheaply made box fan I bought there. But that soil will not soon return to fertile pasture.

The losses that these stores stand on are not simply confined to my memories of idyllic pastoral scenes or wilderness. Through the processes of globalization, these stores are linked to webs of production and transportation that wind around the globe. These stores are in the shadows of enormous factories, wastelands left behind from natural resource extraction, manure lagoons from factory farms, and bare monocultured fields. The fan I purchased in the store moves along obscure supply chains, stretching to southeast Asia—to factories where workers likely faced harsh conditions. It is made from plastic products derived from petroleum. Though I do not know the particulars of the human injustice or the ecological destruction upon which it was built, I can imagine.

I must imagine these paths of suffering so that my response does not stop short of thinking about deeper structural issues. The task is not simply to protect the green spaces that are still left (though we must do that). Nor is it to focus on my individual action as a consumer—which would leave in place all the deepest assumptions and structures of consumerism. The task requires that we seek to understand how our very ways of life are dependent upon and participate in this strange paved habitat.

Even more, we must look for ways and paths that allow us to live in a new manner. We do not just need to consume different goods, but we need to transform our economies. We need to transform our work lives and our relationships. We need to transform our ways of accounting, knowing, and seeing.

Christ's good news helps us do all of these. It follows the path of the cross, a path of nonviolent resistance that shows the cruelty of the dominant order and that cultivates compassion in his followers. The cross unveils both the beauty of creation that lies underneath the blacktop, and the web of suffering that the highways of consumerism weave. We begin with the cross because it is the aspect of Jesus' life that is most familiar to us. But underneath this suffering is a vision for another way of life that will help us to find justice, rest, joy, and love.

The Crossroads of the Imperial and Covenantal

Like the current ecological crisis, the cross of Christ marks the site of both catastrophe and new hope. For the Romans it was an instrument of execution that announced the defeat of their opponents, but for Christ it displayed the alternative path of self-giving love. The cross marks the conflict between two ways of living in the world—one that seeks to extract wealth from the land and exploit the people, and another that seeks to live on the land and with one's fellow creatures equitably and sustainably.

Though our familiarity with the cross as a golden symbol has smoothed its rough edges, it is important to remember that crucifixion was one of the most powerful acts of torture and propaganda that the Empire used. This public form of execution was the punishment reserved for slaves and political insurrectionists—people who dared to upset the hierarchy of the status quo. The cross was a billboard upon which the Empire displayed its power. For the disciples who saw their teacher brutalized and murdered in public, this was supposed to communicate that resistance was futile.

As an act of protest and nonviolent resistance, Jesus' death instead unveiled the desperate violence of the Empire.[34] While the good news of the Empire proclaimed that their systems of justice brought peace, Christ's peaceful and dignified demeanor in their trials showed its violence and cruelty. Therefore, the cross did mark a crisis, but it was the crisis of an entire way of life that needed to be repented of and transformed.[35] The path beyond this imperial catastrophe—which had forsaken the land and twisted the people—was illuminated by the power of self-giving love. As Christ would say at his last meal with his followers, "No one has greater love than this, to lay down one's life for one's friends" (John 15:13). The cross marks the dual movement of both resisting the injustice of the Empire, and living a life entirely dedicated to love regardless of the cost.

These dynamics of the cross are often lost because Jesus' death is abstracted from his life and context. In so doing we have lost the relevance that the cross has for our lives. Jesus was executed in no small part because he challenged the economic and social injustice of the Empire and unveiled the role that local elites played in this exploitation.[36] In our cultural context, however, we fail to make these connections because our understanding of "religion" often separates the life of faith from the economic, the social, and the political parts of life. It is probably necessary, therefore, to trace back through the Gospels some of the conflicts that precipitated Christ's execution. During the final week of his life, Jesus staged a number of protests, delivered teachings, and even occupied the center of power in first-century Israel—the Temple. In the midst of his work, the ruling elite sought to entrap

---

34. Gonzalez, *Luke*, 123–25.

35. I have explored these dynamics, especially in relation to Paul's account of Christ's cross in 1 Corinthians, in *Exercises in New Creation*, 69–80.

36. Brueggemann, *Money and Possessions*, 188.

Jesus by highlighting the subversive implications of his positive vision of re-newing sustainable communities and forgiving debt.

One saying of Jesus is often taken as a proof-text for the separation of politics and religion. But when placed in context, it points toward the conflict between the imperial and the covenantal ways of life. In the Temple, during his last week, Jesus declared: "Give to the emperor the things that are the em-peror's and to God the things that are God's" (Mark 12:17). This declaration is made in *response* to a question posed to him by "some Pharisees and some Herodians"—members of the royal court and some wealthy elites associated with the priesthood. These political *and* religious figures are interrogating Jesus because they hope to entrap him (Mark 12:13).

These elites ask Christ: "Is it lawful to pay taxes to the emperor, or not" (Mark 12:14)? In this question they want him to either state boldly and clearly that he is opposed to the occupying force—thereby committing a crime—or to show himself to be a coward and collaborator. The Empire regarded the failure to pay taxes as rebellion. At the heart of the Empire's economy and power structure was the demand for tribute and taxes. These taxes were *not* redistributed for the common good. Wealth flowed *upward* in the economic hierarchy and toward the center of Rome. These mecha-nisms radically redistributed wealth from peasants (who made up about 70 percent of the population) to the elites (the top 2 percent who controlled around two-thirds of the wealth).[37] The prosperity of the Empire was built on extraction—taking wealth from peasants, slaves from conquered peoples, and fertility and resources from the land. Like many imperial powers before them, the Romans used slave labor to transform the land. They drained swamps, cleared forests, terraced mountains, and cut roads to connect trade and build military power.[38] They transformed local sustainable agricultural economies into industries that produced a single crop that could be hoarded by a few and used for profit and trade.[39]

By contrast, the peasant village economies of Galilee and Judea tra-ditionally operated through mutual support and subsistence. They did not strive to produce an excess that could be sent elsewhere, but they worked to produce a healthy and sustainable balance whereby everyone had enough and the land remained healthy and fertile. Admittedly, village life was not without the presence of peasant landholders who would seek to gain power and hoard resources, but there were stronger mechanisms of shared

---

37. Herzog, *Parables as Subversive Speech*, 61.

38. Carter, *Matthew and Empire*, 14.

39. Crossan and Reed, *Excavating Jesus*, 62.

governance to challenge such impulses.[40] Archaeological evidence and Jewish tradition (though both paint a fragmented and contestable picture) suggest sustainable land use and limited hierarchical division.[41]

The imposition of taxes forced peasants to produce much more than was needed by the community. This shrank the bounty of the harvest, demanded more from the land, and made sharing difficult, which in turn tore at the social fabric.[42] One could no longer rely on one's neighbors. Given a hard season, a farmer might have to go into debt. This debt started a downward spiral with predatory lenders who ultimately foreclosed on family lands and consolidated their holdings.[43]

The Pharisees' and Herodians' question about taxes did not simply touch on a specifically political or economic issue, but on the conflict between two orders and ways of life. These orders—the imperial and the covenantal—organized people's lives, shaped their relationships, and cared for the land in starkly different ways. Christ highlights this with his question in return, asking if they will accept that everything belongs to Caesar or God. The answer to this question is a matter of faith, politics, and economics.

Much as in the case of the cross, Christ turned their efforts back upon them. He asked them to produce a coin, specifically the Roman denarius, and inquired whose image was on it. "They answered, 'The emperor's'" (Mark 12:16). By asking for the coin, Jesus performed an object lesson in the gospel of the Empire. The coin doubled as a piece of propaganda. The currency was minted with a picture of the Emperor and words that declared him to be the son of God and the high priest. As such, the coins were considered by many pious Jews to be idolatrous and to have them in the Temple was blasphemous. Yet, the elite who were trying to entrap Christ in the Temple were able to easily produce one.

They were able to produce this coin because the Temple was big business. It was, among other things, a central bank for Jerusalem. The Temple elite benefited from economic inequality and likely participated in cycles

40. Boer and Petterson, *Time of Troubles*, 68–69. To draw this contrast between the imperial and the local does not require that the latter was perfect. Even if competition, corruption, and inequality existed on this level, it is a false equivalency to say that all human systems are imperfect and, therefore, they are all the same. An Emperor with an extensive army, bureaucracy, and propaganda campaign is importantly different from a local crook or bully. Furthermore, Jesus was not simply trying to restore a forgotten romanticized peasant reality, or even a former Hebrew ideal, but he was seeking to radicalize them.

41. Horsley, *Galilee*, 204.

42. Oakman, *Jesus and the Economic*, 78–80.

43. Herzog, *Parables as Subversive Speech*, 204–7. Oakman, *Jesus and the Economic*, 72–77.

of predatory lending.[44] Christ was not simply showing that the Pharisees and the Herodians had committed a faux pas by bringing an idol into the Temple, but he brought out into the open the fact that the elite had made their loyalties clear. They were the agents of the Emperor and his exploitative and unjust practices. Christ, by contrast, is arguing that everything—except the idolatrous and destructive coins minted by the Empire—belongs to God. Ever so subtly, Christ calls upon people to give the coins (and the extractive, exploitative economy they brought with them) back to the Emperor and to live in a simpler, more sustainable covenantal relationship with neighbors, God, and the land. While this vision might inspire hope for some, the elite of the Empire knew that such a possibility meant rebellion, and so they responded with violence, using the only logic the Empire knows. They executed Jesus.

Jesus was killed because he challenged the ways of empire. The cross stands as the sign of a brutal order that builds its power on broken bodies. What the Empire calls peace and prosperity requires the destruction of habitats, slave labor, and broken communities. This brutality, however, is hidden by the pieties and propaganda of the elite. Christ's protest announces the crisis of the imperial order and points toward the path of another way of life. The cross of Christ asks us: to whom do we belong and which path will we follow—God's or Caesar's?

Occupy the Temple

Christ was protesting a crisis, much like our own, that was rooted both in the political and economic machinery of an unjust empire *and* the dominant moral and social visions of faithfulness and goodness. When he initially entered Jerusalem, Christ went straight to the Temple and even more directly challenged the ways that the religious and political elite collaborated with the Empire. We should not think of the Temple simply as a religious space. In addition to serving as a bank, it was also the central marketplace that bolstered Jerusalem's economy and the seat of the ruling council of elders and priests.[45] Though Herod Antipas was the client king of Galilee, the region to its south, Judea, was once again a Temple-state ruled by a council, called the Sanhedrin. Here, at the crossroads of religious, social, economic, and political power, Christ staged his first act of civil disobedience. He entered the temple and drove out those who were buying and selling things. He "overturned the tables of the money changers and the seats of those who

44. Herzog, *Jesus, Justice, and the Reign*, 136–37.
45. Thistlethwaite, *#OccupytheBible*, 42–45.

sold doves; and he would not allow anyone to carry anything through the temple" (Mark 11:15–16). In so doing Jesus brought the street-level operations of the Temple economy to a halt.[46]

While the ruling elite of the Temple wanted to claim that it was their actions that brought peace and prosperity, Jesus pointed to their oppressive structures as the cause of much suffering. The Temple and its priests held wealth because it too imposed taxes. According to the elite, these taxes were used to support a public sacrifice that was said to maintain the covenant with God and the fertility of the land. The excess from these collections meant that many of the priests and elders lived lavishly and amassed great wealth. Jesus wanted to highlight the connection between this excess and the exploitation of the poor. He specifically stopped those who were selling doves—the cheaper option of sacrifice that would allow someone to re-establish their purity, and therefore, their covenantal relationship. While still expensive, doves were the sacrificial option given to the poor, to women, and to lepers (Lev 12:6, 8; 14:22).

Christ insists that we should not be misled by the false piety of the elite, but see a direct connection between their status and wealth and the exploitation of the most vulnerable.[47] Jesus declares that we should look out for the elite "who like to walk around in long robes, and to be greeted with respect in the marketplaces, and to have the best seats in the synagogues and places of honor at banquets! They devour widows' houses" (Mark 12:38–39). Widows were extremely vulnerable figures, and the care for them was at the heart of God's covenant with Israel. The community maintained relationship with God by taking care of the widow, the orphan, and the stranger.[48] Christ joined a long line of prophets who declared that the veneer of sacrifice served to distract from the exploitation of taxes and fees. These monetary burdens injured the vulnerable and broke the covenant rather than renewing it. In Mark's account, this dynamic was incarnated in the Temple as Jesus spoke. Jesus saw a poor widow give all that she had to the temple. He lamented that "she out of her poverty has put in everything she had, all that she had to live on" (an image, unfortunately, that preachers dressed in

46. Myers, *Binding the Strong Man*, 301.

47. Hendricks, *Politics of Jesus*, 56–61.

48. During his occupation of the Temple Jesus cites the prophet Jeremiah's sermon delivered from the same place, in which he warned that the corruption of the elite, which turned the Temple into a "den of robbers," would lead to destruction (Mark 11:17; Jer 7:11). Jesus is evoking the wider passage, in which Jeremiah exhorts them to "act justly one with another" and to renew the bonds of the covenant between God, neighbors, and land. Jeremiah counsels that if they do not "oppress the alien, the orphan, and the widow" then God will dwell with them "in the land that I gave of old to your ancestors" (Jer 7:5–7).

fine robes at the front of worship all too often use as a prod to inspire people to give to the church) (Mark 12:41–44).[49]

For the religious, political, and economic elite, the Temple was both a practical and ideological tool that communicated that God was on their side. If the ancient Temple was a bank, would it be too much of a stretch for us to see contemporary banks as Temples—sites of moral value that orient our individual and collective lives? Banks and investment firms hold the treasures that we count on for our future security and well-being. We often use the treasure we build up there to measure our own value and success. The elite's vision of sacrifice and piety resonates with contemporary assumptions about the value of work and the focus on jobs. So long as we place our faith in the benevolence of the market, we are convinced that our hard work contributes to the prosperity of everyone. Furthermore, we supposedly owe this order and our livelihood to semi-divine job *creators*.

But Jesus' cross and ministry lays bare that this economy is exploitative and destructive. Its fruits simply fatten the elite at the expense of the land and the poor. Christ, by contrast, points toward a covenant where our care for the widow, the orphan, and the stranger is related to our care for the land. He shows that both the care of the vulnerable and of the land shape and emerge out of beautiful, reverent lives, which connect us to God. Jesus was put to death because he challenged the oppressive order of the Empire and the elite. But the path of the cross did not end in death. Instead, it marked the end of the Empire's illusions of peace and prosperity. It announced the hope of something new.

I wonder what feeling of joy might have rested over the crowd in the Temple the day it was shut down by Christ. It was certainly, at the least, an annoyance to those who benefited from business as usual, but for those who normally were made to feel marginal, invisible, and impure, the feeling of solidarity and hope must have been palpable. I cannot help but think of being part of a protest at the Kentucky State Capitol with the Poor People's Campaign—an effort that seeks to redirect the moral focus in the United States to the interrelated problems of systemic racism, poverty, ecological devastation, and the war economy. A crowd of clergy, activists, and poor citizens from the state were barred from entering the capitol building. There was a feeling of connection in the crowd standing outside the doors of power that were both literally and symbolically closed to us. We chanted in the call and response of: "Whose House?" "Our House!" In a political landscape that fosters cynicism and despair, there was a moment of empowerment and hope through speaking in one voice. This was deepened as the Rev. Dr. William Barber led

---

49. de la Torre, *Politics of Jesús*, 118.

us in prayer and spoke on the power that comes from ostensible weakness. My heart was lifted as we joined in songs. I felt all of this as a person with no romantic notions about the American political process or civil religion. What must it have felt like on that day with Jesus, when the thieves were kicked out of the Temple, and the building which was the microcosm of the vast macrocosm of creation once again became a house of prayer for all peoples (Mark 11:17)? For a day, Christ's disciples and the people of the land were able to envision something both restored and new.

Even with the gap of a couple of millennia, it is not too hard to hear resonances with the empire of wealth that shapes our lives. We also live in social structures shaped by different institutions and spheres of life—including what we call the "religious"—that collaborate to maintain radically unjust and inequitable distributions of wealth. The elite extract profits from the land and communities and they obscure their destruction with false pieties about hard work, merit, and equal opportunity. We live in the ecological ruins of a culture driven by unsatisfiable consumption and the agricultural transition from sustainable to industrial farming. These forces have led to the tearing and tattering of our social fabric.

Yet, we are even more insulated from the destruction of our ways of life. The highways once paved through the hearts of low-income neighborhoods now allow us to fly by without seeing them. The impoverished peoples whose bodies are broken to make our fast fashion or cell phones are kept an ocean or border away. The wastelands produced by mineral extraction are hidden and kept out of sight, even while they are large enough to be seen from a satellite image. Cooped up in our single-serving homes and homogenous social spheres, we are more apt to accept the good news of the empire of wealth. We might even think that everything would be solved if we simply put our trust in a different set of elites or if we worked a little differently within the empire of consumerism. And so, we need to face Christ's cross, and see its relevance for our lives.

The Wisdom of Connections

So long as different aspects of our lives are kept separate, we will not see the connections between problems and we will not have an integrated vision of an alternative path. If creation is limited to "wilderness," then it seems to have little to do with life in the city. If faith is given one day and contained in one building, then the cries for justice and peace echoing out of the Scriptures do not address all of our lives. If economics and politics play by their own rules, then they do not need to be concerned with morality or the limits of ecosystems.

To begin to see these connections is to begin to live into the wisdom of both ecology and Jesus. Ecology, by definition, is the study of connections and relationships. Taking the view of an ecosystem helps us to understand how different parts are dependent upon others (that mosquitoes, however irritating to suburbanites, are part of the food chain). In a similar fashion, Jesus' teachings, life, and death uncover connections. For example, in his protest in the Temple Jesus unveils the connection between the religious elite, the political and economic order of the Empire, and the plight of the poor.

I confess that I have been slow to see these connections. Wrestling with the causal lines between poverty in places like Burundi and the consumption of cheap coffee in the United States is difficult enough on its own. But if we dig deeper, we will see that the earth groans along with the poor. Oftentimes, the same systems that exploit farmers exploit the land. Globally, the production of coffee has increasingly mimicked the industrial production of crops like corn and soy. In these operations, coffee is not grown with canopy cover, but it is grown in full sun in ways that require fertilizer, greatly increase carbon emissions, devastate habitats, contribute to deforestation, limit biodiversity, and degrade soils.[50]

My initial alarm about climate change diverted my attention from issues of social and economic justice. I thought that these were competing movements dealing with separate problems. I was reluctant to see these connections because they implicated the very logic that organizes my life. As long as an issue remains a special interest, the proper response to it can be tied to a single policy. The task becomes organizing a committee whose work is achievable *and* does not directly affect our lives. The change, however, that comes from such an approach typically does not last, because it does not address the root problems.[51] The issues of environmentalism must be connected to matters of racial justice and the conditions of workers because they all emerge from the structures of empire.

When I was a student in divinity school I helped to start a grassroots organization that gathered young adult Christian leaders throughout the United States on issues of ethical importance. The event was planned by a group of young people that would reconstitute itself at the gathering each year (meaning that the main payoff was that it served as an incubator for young organizers). I returned to the conference after having rotated off the planning team several years before, when they were examining environmental

---

50. Jha et al., "Review of Ecosystems Services."

51. Salvatierra and Heltzel, *Faith-Rooted Organizing*, 28–30.

justice. In the space of shared worship, deep personal conversation, acts of service, and thought-provoking presentations, I got a glimpse of both the way that problems were connected, but also of the communal set of responses that they demanded. For example, the issue of deforestation and the impact this has on carbon emissions was brought home by a presentation from an organization that plants trees in low income neighborhoods. Adding canopy coverage over expanses of concrete and replacing overgrown shrubs in abandoned lots with trees serves to sequester carbon, improve public health, and even cultivate communal spaces.

The conference did not end with the critical work of drawing connections and raising awareness. These abstract insights were made concrete by the opportunity to get our hands dirty by planting trees in a carefully chosen spot. All of this work was revealed as holy and sacramental as we concluded with a hand-washing service, that mimicked Jesus' cleaning of the disciples' feet. These actions served to incarnate the joyful labor required to sustain the efforts of sustainability. The work of social and systemic change cannot be sent to committee but must be rooted in loving community.[52]

This emphasis on connections and community also means that there is work to be done in the neighborhood where I live. The work of justice and the care of creation is not solely located in some far-off place. Our different neighborhoods and ecosystems are connected. We might think of the relationships between the habitats of the elite and the polluted neighborhoods of the poor as a watershed or stream. Illness is rampant in the poor neighborhood not primarily because of decisions made there, but because it is downstream from the waste and pollution of the wealthy. The elite, however, do not exist on their own. Midstream are those who manage the empire. The middle managers often miss that their habitats are also polluted by the ways of empire because they are not so despoiled as those of the poor. Yet, those of us in the middle live in communities that suffer from epidemics of obesity, addiction, depression, isolation, and anxiety. We could respond to these different challenges as if they were separate. We could go on spending most of our time operating the mechanisms that are desecrating the earth. Or, we could begin to change our lives and communities to build the communal vision and power required for us to stand in solidarity with those downstream and move toward a more beautiful and joyful life in our places.

52. Salvatierra and Heltzel, *Faith-Rooted Organizing*, 93–105.

Christ, Anointed for a Task

The path of Jesus can be hard to see because the meaning of the title of Christ has been obscured. Christ is not Jesus' last name, but the Greek translation (*Christos*) of the term *Messiah*—the one anointed by God for a task of restoration and transformation. For example, the prophet Samuel (reluctantly) anoints Saul to be King of Israel, to *save* them from their enemies, and the spirit of the Lord rests upon him (1 Sam 10:1–8). Christ is not a last name or a title that demands our observance; rather, it is a mantle that signals the importance of the path of transformation.

We can better understand what the Gospels mean when they name Jesus the Christ by attending to the figures anointed in the Hebrew Scriptures. The Gospels repeatedly call Jesus the Messiah and tie him to the line of David.[53] Yet, the understanding of the Messiah, of God's anointed, that most strongly resounds in the Gospels is the vision painted by the prophet Isaiah. This resonance is worth further examination as it helps to highlight that Christ is anointed for the task of renewing just human relationships *and* healing all of creation.

The prophet Isaiah speaks of a coming king who will deliver people from darkness and break the rod of the oppressor (Isa 9:2, 4). The people will rejoice before this figure, "as with the joy at the harvest" (Isa 9:3). The prophet sings that to the oppressed a child of promise is born, "and he is named Wonderful Counselor, Mighty God, Everlasting Father, Prince of Peace" (Isa 9:6). This king will bring justice for the poor and "equity for the meek of the earth" (Isa 11:4). His wisdom and righteousness will bring a new creation where predation and conflict cease, and all will live in peace and intimacy. The poet proclaims: "The wolf shall live with the lamb, the leopard shall lie down with the kid" (Isa 11:6). Through the restoration of the covenant, which is to say the right ordering of human activity, "the earth will be full of the knowledge of the Lord as the waters cover the sea" (Isa 11:9).

The Gospel of Mark begins by speaking of Jesus as the anointed, the Christ, and immediately frames this in terms of the prophet Isaiah. Mark quotes Isaiah, saying that, "see I am sending my messenger ahead of you who will prepare the way, the voice of one crying out in the wilderness: 'Prepare the way of the Lord, make his paths straight'" (Mark 1:1–2/Isa 40:3). This ancient prophetic promise of preparation is identified with John the Baptist (Mark 1:3). John is the prophet who will anoint Jesus for the task of bringing about the kingdom of God. Therefore John baptizes Jesus, to anoint him for his task.

53. For example, they connect him to the Davidic line through his father's ancestry and his popular welcome into Jerusalem in the manner of an anointed king.

In the story of Jesus' baptism, Christ's task is framed in terms of a new creation and liberation. While the Spirit of the Lord descending and resting upon Jesus is standard fare for these anointing stories, and is repeated in the Gospels, the setting of the waters evokes the creation story and the opening passages of Genesis (Gen 1:2/Mark 1:9–10). Furthermore, Jesus' passage through the waters evokes the Israelites' journey through the Red Sea, which led them out of bondage in Egypt and into liberation (an echo underlined by Jesus' subsequent forty-day trial in the wilderness).[54] But most direct of all, the Gospels tell of a voice coming from the sky saying, "You are my son, the Beloved; with you I am well pleased" (Mark 1:11). This declaration draws upon the anointing of kings in the line of David (Ps 2:7–8), and Isaiah's account of the suffering servant.

From the context of exile, when much of the house of Israel was oppressed in Babylon and cut off from the land of the covenant, Isaiah pointed to the promise of a suffering servant. In Isaiah's poetic account, God declares, "Here is my servant, whom I uphold, my chosen, in whom my soul delights; I have put my spirit upon him; he will bring forth justice to the nations" (Isa 42:1).[55] This servant does not bring liberation like a mighty warrior, rather he is described as "a bruised reed he will not break." (Isa 42:3). The servant faces mockery and cruelty, saying "I gave my back to those who struck me . . . I did not hide my face from insult and spitting" (Isa 50:6). This response is an act of nonviolent resistance. His actions mark a different path that instructs and sustains the weary (Isa 50:4). This alternative power promises not only to sustain the servant and those he leads, but the prophet declares, "He will not grow faint or be crushed until he has established justice in the earth" (Isa 42:4).

This path of transformation through suffering resonates with the life and death of Jesus. He receives insults and mockery on the path of the cross with peace and dignity (Matt 27:27–31). But even more, in the Sermon on the Mount, Christ counsels his followers to pursue a similarly nonviolent path, telling them "if anyone strikes you on the right cheek, turn the other also" (Matt 5:39).[56] This response is not about submission or simply avoiding cycles of retribution. Rather, the striking on the cheek refers to the open-handed strike of a superior on a subordinate, and it is meant to humiliate. The response of offering the other cheek counters this debasement

---

54. This time in the wilderness "with wild beasts" invokes images of the peaceable kingdom (Mark 1:13/Isa 11). Clapp, *New Creation*, 78–79.

55. This wider passage (Isa 42:1–4) is cited again in direct relationship to Jesus' identity in Matthew 12:15–21.

56. Davis, *Biblical Prophecy*, 227–30.

with dignity. It appeals to a deeper power and strength, one which holds the promise of transformation outside cycles of violence.[57]

Jesus lays out the task for which he is appointed in the first sermon he preaches. In Luke's account, Jesus reads from the prophet Isaiah (Isa 61:1–2) at his home synagogue in Nazareth. Luke narrates that "He unrolled the scroll and found the place where it was written: 'The Spirit of the Lord is upon me, because he has anointed me to bring good news to the poor. He has sent me to proclaim release to the captives and recovery of sight to the blind and to let the oppressed go free, to proclaim the year of the Lord's favor.'" Upon finishing his reading, he declares that this Scripture has been fulfilled in their hearing (Luke 4:17–22). Jesus is anointed to bring good news to the poor, not the news of imperial victory and prosperity. He is sent to heal the broken and to free the oppressed. Far from being given a task divorced from social, political, and economic change, he is anointed to transform the world.[58]

Most significant in this passage is the prophet Isaiah's promise regarding "the year of the Lord," which refers to the year of Jubilee. The year of Jubilee was the highpoint of the Hebrew sabbath cycles (which we will return to in chapter 3). On the day of *atonement* every fifty years everyone was to be "released" from their debts (Lev 25:9–10). This meant wiping away monetary debts and restoring land holdings to an equitable distribution. This undermined the accumulation of wealth and the creation of plantations. The Jubilee meant structural change to the socioeconomic order.

All of this was grounded in the care of the land. In this covenant, God owned the land—everyone was simply a tenant (Lev 25:23). Returning land to equitable distribution served to maintain peaceful and joyful relationships between neighbors. It protected the relationship between God and the people (who, given too much land, might forget the place of the Creator and start to call themselves job creators). The Jubilee also meant the healing of the relationship between the land and people (Lev 25.18). As agrarian people have long known, a family that is reliant upon the land for generations will, at the very least, act to sustain its long-term fertility and flourishing more than an absentee landowner seeking profits of the next season.[59]

Jesus was anointed to proclaim good news to the poor, to release the oppressed *from* structures of empire *for* ways of delight, love, and justice. While his anointing echoed the calling of the Davidic line of kings, Jesus proceeded more in the way of the suffering servant. He was mocked and

57. Carter, *Matthew and the Margins*, 152.

58. Ringe, *Jesus, Liberation*, 36, 92.

59. Davis, *Scripture, Culture, and Agriculture*, 101–5.

brutalized by the powerful, but he followed the path of a different, nonviolent power. If we can see Christ as the servant anointed for this task, then we can also hear the call to follow his path of servanthood and love for the renewal of all creation.

Called for Green Good News

In the Good News according to Mark, Jesus is first called the Messiah by Peter. *On the way* to Caesarea Philippi, Jesus asked his disciples "Who do people say that I am?" After they gave a variety of answers, he asked, "But who do you say that I am?" To which Peter responded, "You are the Messiah" (Mark 8:27–29). The backdrop of this city seems significant, as it is both named after Caesar and the site of the opulence, corruption, and collaboration of the Herodian kings. Herod built a marble temple to Caesar Augustus there and his son Philip continued to enlarge and develop it in the Greco-Roman style.[60] Here, in a seat of imperial power, Peter is the first person to name Jesus the one anointed by God—typically a king who establishes justice.[61] Jesus quickly qualifies, however, that his path is not one of military glory, and he warns that he will "undergo great suffering, and be rejected by the elders, the chief priest, and the scribes, and be killed, and after three days rise again" (Mark 8:31).[62]

In this moment Jesus underlines that this path is not restricted to him. He tells both the crowd and his disciples, "If any want to become my followers, let them deny themselves and take up their cross and follow me. For those who want to save their life will lose it, and those who lose their life for my sake, and for the sake of the good news, will save it. For what will it profit them to gain the whole world and forfeit their whole life?" (Mark 8:34–36). Christ does not put himself on display to be passively admired. Rather he is the servant who charts the course for an entire kingdom of servants. To enter into this domain and to restore creation, a certain kind of life must be lost.

---

60. Carter, *Matthew and the Margins*, 322.

61. Myers, *Binding the Strong Man*, 241–42.

62. Mark has Jesus shift from the title of "Messiah" to the "son of Man" (Mark 8.31). This title was given to the figure who brings justice in Jewish apocalyptic literature and could be translated as "the Human One." As Ched Myers explains, the Human One/son of Man is a figure contrasted with the *beastly* figures who currently rule. For example, in the book of Daniel there is a stark contrast drawn between the *beasts* who rule empires and the truly *human* one who will come to restore justice. Myers, *Binding the Strong Man*, 243. In making this shift in titles, then, Jesus is trying to sidestep any imperial hopes the disciples might have for their teacher.

In the city of Caesarea Philippi—the place of power, wealth, and consumption—the loss is more pressing. And it is true that the privileged have
much that must be stripped away. But the green good news is that we all have
a world to gain. On the other side of this loss is a great hope. This is the hope
that the good news of the future will not be a report of a soaring Dow Jones
Industrial Average alongside a litany of violence and ecological catastrophe.
Rather we must begin to see the connections between these parts of the news,
between the empire of wealth and the wastelands left behind by its methods of
extraction. At the same time, we must begin to participate in the transformation of our ways of life to change these seemingly inevitable reports.

This coming kingdom will mean that we must lose some of the "peace"
and "prosperity" that the empire of wealth has promised us. We will lose some
of the piles of consumer goods that we have stored up in our ever-growing
houses. We will lose some of the prestige we have been able to find through
our jobs and titles. We will lose some of the comfort that comes from trusting
that a green economy will save everyone and everything.

But how many losses have piled up on the other sides of these gains?
How many lives, families, neighborhoods, cultures, habitats, and species have
already been sacrificed to maintain the order of this empire? How many of
our days, weeks, and years have we given over to this striving? How much of
our own identity has been warped by consumer culture and by professional
assessment? How many of our relationships have been strained, stained, and
lost in this race to nowhere? How much has this way of life made it difficult
for us to sit in silence, to pray to God, to really pay attention to the needs and
beauty of the creatures and the creation around us? What else would the loss
of one's life mean if not all of these injuries and absences?

The good news is that Jesus was anointed to release us from these
bonds. His green good news points to the path to restore creation. If we are
willing to lose our past lives, we too are anointed for this path to new just,
joyful, and sustainable life.

2

Cultivating Gardens

I AM A CHILD of processed food. As a kid I unconsciously assumed food came from a factory (which, in a way, mine did). Everything from breakfast to snack was supposed to come sealed in plastic. My stomach turned at the sight of dirt on a vegetable or piece of fruit. Rather than the source of life, fecundity, and growth, dirt was something to be avoided, swept out, and washed off. Though I have been accurately classified as a bit of a slob for much of my life, I still was shaped by this powerful norm and virtue of consumerism: cleanliness (some other primary ones being comfort and convenience).[1]

There were a few people in my life who tended gardens, those slow and personal schools that demonstrate the source of sustenance. A great uncle, and retired minister, took pride showing off the vegetables that he was able to encourage to spring forth from his sloped clay-covered backyard. He would smile and laugh with mischief as he led me through his verdant rows. I enjoyed being out there with him because of his enthusiasm, but I took no interest in the vegetables. I did not understand why he acted as though he were the keeper of a forgotten flame.

I also remember hearing stories about how people gardened *in the past*. My father had previously grown vegetables in a plot I now work behind our garage. My maternal grandfather, who I never met but was named after, was said to be a master gardener. But all of these acts of care seemed to be a non-cost-effective use of time to grow food that no family was accustomed to eating anymore, or hobbies that were discarded for more exciting options.

When I was not expressing my youthful disdain for the soil, I was disregarding it. This is the way of empire—contempt and callous consumption. And empires have long disregarded the soil to their own demise. The degradation and salinization of soil likely toppled the very first empires.[2]

---

1. Shove, "Converging Conventions."
2. Hillel, *Out of the Earth*, 78–87.

The Roman Empire collapsed in no small part because of deforestation, agricultural expansion, soil loss, pollution, and reckless consumption.[3] Perhaps we are facing something similar today. Humans have transformed one half to one third of the land surface of the earth.[4] Around a third of the earth's topsoil has already been lost, leading the deputy director of the United Nation's Food and Agriculture Organization, Maria-Helena Semedo, to lament that if we do not change our practices, we only have about sixty years of agriculture left.[5] That was in 2014. The clock is ticking.

Part of me misses the comfortable oblivion of my childhood of processed food. The bag that sealed my cereal served not only to mark its cleanliness, but also to separate me from the reality of its production. It held a commodity—not the fruit of the earth that was grown in a vast industrialized field. It compartmentalized a product tied to a web of life, and which required vast amounts of petroleum to be fertilized, harvested, processed, and shipped (about one third of global carbon emissions come from agriculture).[6] The logo on the box, or its friendly animal spokesman, served to mask the people who produced it and the farming communities decimated by the industrialization and corporate consolidation of farming.

Once the façade of the good news of the empire is ripped away, the place of privilege can be painful. There are plenty of numbing agents available to help us live with these open wounds, to go about our day as if they are not there. I fear this explains all too many of the hollow modes of entertainment and vacuous forms of community in our culture. But insofar as this discomfort is never faced, it festers into apathy, cynicism, demoralization, and despair.

The call of Christ demands that we face this truth. The exploitation of the poor and the desecration of the land produces injuries that we cannot wish away. In addition to the obvious injuries to bodies, creatures, and ecosystems, the structures of empire also serve to injure the webs of relationship. Poverty and racism break the bodies of the oppressed, and place wedges between communities and pervert the relationships of the oppressors. The culture that robs the land of its fertility and that causes the extinction of entire species also experiences the loss of connection with the beauty and goodness of creation. The creature that abuses the world as its private possession alienates itself from the Creator. And so, we must face this suffering. Even more, we must publicly and nonviolently resist the sacrilege of

3. Ruether, *Gaia and God*, 187. Hughes, *Environmental History*, 73–77.

4. Vitousek et al., "Human Domination," 294.

5. Arsenault, "60 Years of Farming."

6. Scialabba and Muller-Lindenlauf, "Organic Agriculture," 158.

the empire and its economy of exploitation and extraction. The call is to take up our cross and lose our lives.

But there is a life to be gained. This life is not so much one of heroic acts as of simple works of love. The suffering of the cross is not an intrinsic good, something that should be done for its own sake. Rather, the public suffering of Jesus unveiled the hidden suffering of oppression and extraction in the Empire and demanded a passion that overcame numb denial. Likewise, our compassionate suffering—our efforts to face injustice and walk with others—dissipates apathy and inspires solidarity.[7] The purpose of solidarity is not ultimately resistance, but the cultivation of beloved community.

The path of the cross winds back to life in the garden. Our new life is one of patient care and abiding joy, something we can witness if we follow a keeper of the forgotten flame out to his garden and listen for his laughter and whimsy. The path to Calvary begins in peasant fields and in wilderness feedings. Before we ever get to Golgotha, we must go to the garden at Gethsemane. After the resistance of the cross, there is new life in a garden, as a gardener.

Gardens, today, are experimental and experiential places where urbanites and suburbanites are once again rediscovering their creatureliness and their call to care and attend.[8] Whereas the wilderness was once the icon of an environmental movement directed toward conservation, the garden, and most especially the community garden, has become the icon of new movements that seek to save more than just the wild.[9] The garden marks a space radically different from the mountain hike. In the garden, creatures meet and acknowledge not their separateness but their interdependence, a space where people come not to find their authentic and true selves in solitude, but to overcome the isolation and individualism that plagues them. On a simple plot of land, nature and culture meet through cultivation. Here we must find the answer not to how we can escape the city, but answer the more difficult question: how can we live in the city and on the land justly, joyfully, and sustainably?

It was in the garden that I began to see a way forward from the ecological crisis. Previously I had hoped for solutions that would come wrapped in plastic—that perhaps we might be saved by consuming differently or through transforming technological processes. And while we will certainly need changes in those areas, we will also need to get our hands dirty. We

7. Soelle, *Suffering*, 70–74.

8. Bahnson, *Soil and Sacrament*. Langlands, *Cultivating Neighborhood*. Bass, *Grounded*, 46–49.

9. Jenkins, "Feast of the Anthropocene," 72.

will need to overcome our disdain and disregard for the soil. Working with
the land will serve not only to meet some of our material needs, but it could
also help repair our relationships. It can help us live into, as Jesus promised,
a new covenant. But before we can accept this new covenant, we must overcome our fear of a certain kind of loss.

Called to Be Gardeners in the City of Peace

The first disciples fled from the cross and feared that its suffering was final.
They did not understand that the path of the cross leads to a garden. In the
Gospel of John, Jesus is said to have been buried in a new tomb in a garden
(John 19:41). On the first day of the week after Jesus' crucifixion, Mary Magdalene went to the tomb, but found the stone at its entrance rolled away (John
20:1). Overcome with emotion, Mary wept at the sight. But as she looked
into the tomb she encountered two angels, two messengers of God (John
20:11–12). They asked her why she wept. She answered that "They have taken
away my Lord" (John 20:13). After saying this she "turned around and saw
Jesus standing there, but she did not know that it was Jesus. Jesus said to her,
'Woman, why are you weeping? Whom are you looking for?' *Supposing him to
be a gardener*, she said to him, 'Sir, if you have carried him away, tell me where
you have laid him, and I will take him away'" (John 20:15). In the garden Mary
could only see loss—perhaps because she still did not quite understand what
kind of Lord Jesus was. Even after encountering angels she did not recognize
Jesus for who he is. She correctly sees that the risen Christ is a gardener, only
she does not realize that a gardener could be Christ.

The path of the cross leads to a new creation. Humans were made to
keep a garden, and Jesus comes to restore our call and role as gardeners.
John underlines that it is on the first day that Mary goes to the tomb, evoking the creation story (John 20:1).[10] From the beginning of the Gospel, John
has been rewriting Genesis. He knocks us off our feet with the opening line,
"*In the beginning* was the Word, and the Word was with God, and the Word
was God" (John 1:1). Leading to his conclusion, he places the disciples on
their feet and on the path to the renewal of creation. Mary understands
who the gardener is when he calls her by name. He calls her "Mary." And
she responds by calling him "Rabboni," meaning teacher (John 20:16). By
identifying the gardener as her teacher, she once again takes up the mantle
of being a disciple, of being a follower of this risen gardener. He tells her
not to hold on to him, but to go forth and tell the disciples the good news:

10. Daly-Denton, *John*, 221.

she has seen the Lord—to which I would add, and he was not a king but a gardener (John 20:17–18).

The risen Christ renews creation, in part, by renewing the human vocation to "till and keep" the garden.[11] In the poetic imagination of the second creation story in Genesis, the creator responds to the lack of life on the face of the earth by forming a human from humus (the Hebrew is making a play on words as *adam*, the earthling, is made from *adamah*, the earth). God brings two forms of life into being together—soil and servant—to live in dependent caring relationship. God breathes life into this humanity and then plants a garden, placing the earthling in it (Gen 2:5–8). The earthling is put in the garden of Eden "to till it and keep it" (Gen 2:15). The verbs that mark this central task—the human vocation in creation—could also be rendered "to serve and preserve."[12] The garden and its plants do not provide products or fuel for other important human acts, but fundamental relationships of interdependence. The conditions of delight for humans, in this narrative, are not leisure or luxury but love and care.[13] We were made by God the gardener (who planted the garden) to be gardeners.

At the other book end of the Bible, the book of Revelation's vision of a new heavens and a new earth also imagines a return to this garden. Contrary to the imaginations of some contemporary Christians who expect to be snatched up to God, the apocalyptic vision of John of Patmos imagines God coming down (Rev 21:1–5).[14] God and the new Jerusalem come down to earth and renew it. And in the middle of this city, flowing out of the throne of God, is a river. This river feeds, on each side, the tree of life (Rev 22:1–5). The garden is restored as are its gardeners. This is the vision of salvation, reconciliation, and redemption: a garden in the city of peace.[15] The images of the garden expand our imaginations so that we can hope for the redemption of the city *and* the earth, rather than seeking to

---

11. Daly-Denton, *John*, 13–14.

12. Davis, *Scripture, Culture, and Agriculture*, 29–31.

13. Wirzba, *Food and Faith*, 47.

14. Wirzba, *Way of Love*, 207.

15. In its imaginings, Revelation is not attempting to give an eyewitness account of what will happen. Rather the Greek term for "revelation" means "unveiling." In the ancient world it fits within a genre of literature in which the false hopes and powers of empire are *unveiled* as beastly, and it proposes, in turn, a truly human vision of life—one in which our divine image and intimacy with the creator are restored. Wirzba, *Paradise of God*, 54–59. Revelation, then, seeks to transform our ideal images and hopes. It unveils the violent images of empire, of the political economy that promises power and wealth but deforests and denudes the countryside leaving a wasteland (Rev 17:16). Rossing, "River of Life," 492–94.

escape creation for heaven or evade the problems of the city through an idyllic pastoral setting.

This vision is radically different from the preoccupations of a great deal of mainstream contemporary American Christianity that is focused on the odyssey of an individual soul's journey to the afterlife. These biblical accounts of vocation and hope paint a picture of the life of faith that is about caring for creation, not the escape from it. To follow Christ is not to hold a private belief largely irrelevant to daily, practical, economic, and political activities, but it is the way of a simple, beautiful, and just life. Tellingly, in the artwork of the first thousand years of Christian community, there were no pictures of a dead Jesus. The focus was not on the atoning cross. The artistic and creative outpouring of the church was dominated by pictures of an earthy paradise that was a restoration of the garden.[16]

Similarly, this path diverges from mainstream American environmentalism through a vision of the earth as creation and its peoples as creatures, not as consumers. It is not as though the earth is divided into either nature, which is preserved, or natural resources that are managed. Rather, everything is a part of creation—including the human creatures and the rural and urban habitats in which they live. At the root of the crisis facing creation are broken relationships between those who eat, those who farm, and the land; perverse relationships between the elite, their middle managers, the workers, and those cast outside; severed relationships between the Creator and those who have forsaken their simple, dependent, and beautiful role as creatures.

If the challenges we face are grounded in relationship, then the manner of addressing these problems is social, and not simply technical or individual. We will not be saved by scientific breakthroughs, the greening of broken structures, or shifts in individual consumer habits. We will heal these broken relationships by forming new bonds and reviving old communities. To change our communities and ways of life we should look for places where we can cultivate deep connection and nourishment. Places where creatures nurture, care for, and depend upon one another, like in a garden.

Sowing Seeds and Words

Jesus' call to the garden—to a positive, joyful vision of earthly life—is too often obscured by our tendency to separate material, social, and spiritual domains. Jesus' teachings and actions are commonly taken to be only spiritual or symbolic. For example, my sister was recently reading the Gospel of

16. Brock and Parker, *Saving Paradise*, xii–xv.

Mark with her son and she asked me: "Bread keeps coming up. What do you think that symbolizes?" To which I responded, "This is one I can answer. The bread is about . . . bread. He is really concerned with feeding people." Now on a certain level, my sister is right, and my answer is obnoxious (a right I reserve as the eternal little brother). There is more at stake than just referencing single and specific loaves of bread from two thousand years ago. If that is all the story was about it would be quite stale. But, because of our habits of reading past the material and the social, it is worth underlining the importance of the incarnational, earthly stakes of Scripture.

Along these lines, though many Christians recite the Lord's Prayer weekly, if not daily, its material and agrarian petitions seem to have been lost. This is a prayer that asks for God's kingdom to come, for the Lord's will to be done "on *earth* as it is in heaven." It petitions for *our* daily *bread* and the forgiveness of debts (Matt 6:9–12). It is the prayer of a peasant Jesus for peasants that calls for the restoration of the covenant between God, neighbors, and land (a prayer we will return to in chapter 7). While this has spiritual consequences, it also calls for the incarnation of material and social change—that everyone be fed and that debts be released. Jesus is the Christ, anointed for the task of overturning the table of values and the extractive economy of the Empire that has left the people poor and the land stripped.

Jesus' constant appeals to agrarian life are often interpreted as illustrations used to reach the Palestinian peasants to whom he was speaking. On this reading, the real message is concerned with higher matters. From this it follows that when teaching in a different context one can discard the flowery images of the land for other more relevant metaphors. But when Jesus sets out to teach the crowds and the disciples about the kingdom it is no accident that he constantly refers to different ways in which people care for or exploit the land. In so doing, he weaves together the material, the social, *and* the spiritual.[17]

For example, in the chapter 13 of Matthew Jesus repeatedly speaks of the kingdom of God in botanical images rooted deeply in the field and the garden. He begins the series speaking of a sower who goes out and casts seed on different surfaces. (This was typical of Palestinian farming practices, where a farmer would sow seeds on a field *before* ploughing.)[18] Jesus tells a gathered crowd about a sower, who threw seeds over parts of the field that have been tread over, but birds came and devoured and consumed them. The sower cast some other seeds on a thin layer of earth just above rock. The seeds sprang up quickly but had "no depth of soil." When the sun rose,

17. Bahnson, *Soil and Sacrament*, 124.

18. Jeremias, *Parables of Jesus*, 11.

it scorched that earth and "they withered away." Still other seeds fell among thorns, and, even after being ploughed, the thorns grew back and choked them. But some seed was cast "on good earth and brought forth grain, some a hundredfold, some sixty, some thirty" (Matt 13:3–9).

Far from being an earthly story with a heavenly meaning, the parable was directed toward the political and economic situation of Jesus' hearers (we will return to the parables in chapter 4). The closest analogue to Jesus' little stories in our culture would be a political cartoon, in which an exaggerated fiction is drawn to lay bare a truth that is covered over by what we take to be real.[19] For instance, while an image of politicians in bed with oil executives might not be the most factual representation of the relationships that dictate policy in our time, it would be truer than video footage of one criticizing the other.

In this story, Jesus points to the abundance of the land and the violence of political and cultural obstacles. Whereas a Palestinian farmer might expect anywhere from a four to eleven-fold return from his seed, the good land without obstacles in Jesus' story yields grain ten times greater.[20] This image reminds hearers that the gift of God's land is one that should provide abundantly. But the violent verbs of the forces that inhibit this growth—of birds that *devour*, fire that *scorches* the earth, and weeds that *choke*—lead hearers to think about what really produces scarcity in the villages. The peasant, then, is left to draw the connection that God's land provides abundantly, but it is the violent ways of the elite that truly consume the harvest, leave their land barren, and choke out their community. The laborers know that while they may work fruitfully in the fields, the cycles of tax, debt, and foreclosure have led to scarcity and destruction in their villages. This simple story allows Jesus to say this in public, and it allows peasants to make connections that are obscured by the ruling order.[21]

It is much easier to make these connections if you have been in the field, or if you know that something is wrong.[22] If you are a landowner, living in the city and trying to draw an income from the land, you might not have any awareness of the scarcity that others face. If you are a steward who trades in the commodities of the fields, then perhaps you do not perceive the condition of the land or even your workers. Jesus explains, then, that for the elite the critique and promise of the kingdom will seem mysterious. Harkening back to the time of the prophets, and citing Isaiah, the powerful

---

19. Herzog, *Parables as Subversive Speech*, 87. Myers, *Who Will Roll*, 72.

20. Carter, *Matthew and the Margins*, 283.

21. Herzog, *Jesus, Justice, and the Reign*, 194–95.

22. See for example Cardenal, *Gospel in Solentiname*, 153–62.

will "listen but never understand" (Matt 13:13–14/Isa 6:9). For the wealthy the teachings of the covenant about sharing, sustainability, hospitality, and equity will all seem like obstacles that get in the way of abundance. Sharing will appear to undermine self-reliance, sustainability will devour growth, hospitality will thin things out too much, and equity will choke out the profit motive. The parable proposes to its hearers what is unthinkable in the dominant order: that the social structures of the extractive economy do not produce abundance, but scarcity and violence.

The parable's implied critique overturns the ways of the wealthy that want to render everything unto Caesar and trust that wealth produces abundance. The parable also points to a different domain of values: the kingdom of God and the abundance of God's good earth. In the Empire the rich get richer. But in God's kingdom, those who cultivate the good earth and value the relationships of the covenant will find that there is more than enough for all. Jesus undermines the Empire's gospel of prosperity with the good news of the kingdom of God where the poor and the hungry will be given more and live in blessed community.[23]

To his disciples—Christ's followers who take up his ministry and his forms of organizing—Jesus gave a further interpretation of the parable that underlines the social and spiritual obstacles along the path to the kingdom. Here the parable doubles to illustrate how our social and work relationships, the demands of our households, and the status symbols that we cling to for our identity will make the radical change required to follow Christ profoundly difficult. Jesus explains that the seed that falls on the path and is devoured by the birds is like the good news given to someone whose heart is deeply shaped by the powers of the Empire: they will simply not be able to understand. The seed that is sown on rocky ground, that springs up quickly, will be like those who might hastily move toward transformation, but at the first sign of conflict with the norms and powers of the world, go back to their old ways. The seed that is choked out by the thorns are those who hear the good news, "but the cares of the world and the lure of wealth choke the word, and it yields nothing" (Matt 13:18–22).

Christ is emphasizing for his disciples that our material problems are tied up with social and spiritual formations. Jesus warns that bringing about transformation does not simply require that one shares information. People shaped by empire, especially those with privilege and power, simply

23. Jesus is able to say in public that in the kingdom of God the wealthy will find scarcity. Only he speaks in code, allowing each hearer to plug in what they assume to be truly valuable: God's good earth or wealth. He says, "For those who have, more will be given, and they will have an abundance; but from those who have nothing, even what they have will be taken away" (Matt 13:12).

cannot understand because their hearts are shaped by a world that claims competition, growth, self-reliance, and wealth to be the governing values of nature. Others do not have the blessing of relationships and living situations that will foster moral courage in the face of resistance. To change how they eat, work, live, and relate goes against social norms that could mean their utter isolation. And still others are too tightly gripped by the immediate concerns of next month's mortgage payment or the distant hope of wealth to even contemplate a change. They might worry about what they will wear, about the loss not just of subsistence but of an identity if they no longer have *that* house, job, or lifestyle. I confess that I find myself stumbling over these obstacles all of the time. Simply learning the facts and becoming informed does not take these away. Rather, we need to be invited into a community that is already embodying a different way of life.

Jesus underlines not just the challenge that the disciples will face, but he notes that when they start to live in the ways of the kingdom, they will have abundance. He tells them, "as for what was sown on the good soil, this is the one who hears the word and understands it, who indeed bears fruit and yields, in one case a hundredfold, in another sixty, and in another thirty" (Matt 13:23). They will have more than they need, and from their abundance they can cultivate and nourish, serve and preserve God's good earth so that others may be invited and transformed.[24]

All one has to do to see a contemporary earthly version of the parable of the sower is to go to a suburban housing development that is newly constructed. The practices of the elite have turned over the earth with a complete disregard for topsoil and place. What is left is compacted soil, rocky places, and lots of thistles in clay-covered earth (these weeds grow in degraded soil because their roots can reach deeper into the earth for nourishment and nutrients). Without eyes to see, we fail to recognize the violent forces that have cut up this patch of earth and robbed it of its fertility. As people shaped by the empire, the only thing that is likely to register for us is the supposed abundance testified to by the houses created for the privileged. Such developments are not simply made to meet a free-floating consumer demand, but are habitats that fit in with the ecosystem structured by the distant work place, the rootless worker, consumer culture, and the market of prepackaged commodities. To counter the violence of the bulldozer, then, requires more than the protection of wilderness. It requires alternative social structures and goods—an entirely different way of life.

Jesus' parable is directed toward material, social, and spiritual transformation. It challenges the very earthly ways of extraction that lead to the

24. Myers, *Who Will Roll*, 167.

exploitation of people and the degradation of the land. But it is not only about getting the poor the calories they need. It is about renewing the covenant—the relationships that shape and animate life. The parable challenges the social structures that make these dynamics difficult to see for the poor. The teaching to the disciples further highlights the obstacles that those who are shaped by the empire of wealth will face in becoming agents of the kingdom of God. These are social and spiritual issues that lead people, even those who are informed, to hear the good news of new life and retreat into that which is familiar and secure—even if it is the security of a prison.

Christ's parable directs our attention to the ways that we care for the land and our neighbors. This confrontation forces us to ask: who do we ultimately serve, Caesar or God? We answer this question in the ways we structure our houses, direct our labor, shape our relationships, and dress our bodies. The ways of empire devour the commonwealth, scorch the fertility of the earth, and choke out loving community. Do we have ears to hear how the Scriptures point us toward the ways of the kingdom of God come to earth?

Gardens as the Site for Social Transformation

The parable of the sower concerns land and bodies. It draws a stark contrast between the poverty of the people and the abundance that should come from God's good earth. While its botanical images point toward the scarcity that may come from natural processes, its pedagogy critiques wider social structures. At stake are both the cultivation of the soil and the culture that shapes spirits. As Jesus explains, our social lives are *like* soil *and* are rooted in the soil. We are earthlings shaped by God and misshapen by empire to be consumers. Christ's word of good news offers the seeds of life that could transform both. He marks the path of the kingdom of God that promises the abundant harvest that comes from flourishing communities grounded in serving and preserving the soil and spirit.

If we want to begin to imagine what this kingdom looks like, we would do well to pay attention to places where these earthy, material, social, and spiritual connections are incarnated. For those of us that live in urban concrete deserts or in privatized suburban places where the closest thing we have to communal spaces are strip malls, community gardens can serve as just such an oasis. The garden marks a space where we can suspend industrial processes. Machines no longer provide ostensible control or render uniform products. Instead we work with the plants, the soil, the microbes, the weather, the topography, and hopefully not the wilt, for tomatoes that come when they may. In the garden we are no longer subject to invisible supply chains, faceless field workers, fertilizer runoff, depleted soils, and deep carbon footprints. Through the garden we can make a material and tangible difference.

Yet, the transformative potential waiting in the garden is not limited to the material harvest that can come from the land. The garden is also a school where we can cultivate new selves, relationships, and social visions about how our world can be structured.[25] In the garden we are no longer constricted into playing the role of the passive consumer (or even the exploited producer). Instead we are given an opportunity to become a member. Here we see that we are a member of a body that has an important function to play while at the same time being dependent upon the care and flourishing of others, just as hands are members of the body that play an active role, but that cannot exist without the rest of the body (1 Cor 12:21). Through this *member*ship we can build different kinds of relationships with our neighbors—human and nonhuman alike.[26] While its means and ends might be meager, at first, such efforts are most powerful in the ways that they show that alternative economies and communities are possible.

Christ proposed that the kingdom of God grew through such small efforts. In the midst of the aforementioned cornucopia of botanical parables, Christ taught that "The kingdom of heaven is like a mustard seed that someone took and sowed in a field" (Luke sets the seed in a "garden") (Matt 13:31/Luke 13:18). The mustard seed "is the smallest of all the seeds, but when it has grown it is the greatest of shrubs." (Matt 13.32). In the ancient world mustard was viewed as both something wholesome to be cultivated in a garden, and something invasive and subversive. When wild mustard set its roots in a grain field it could take over.[27] The kingdom, then, emerges through small acts that will both nurture our social bodies and subvert the logic that rules the monocultured fields.

The power and potential of the garden is amplified when it is pursued in community. The small seed does not make for much of a snack on its own. When a mustard seed is sown on a plot of land that is cultivated it can grow to great heights. As an individual effort pursued in solitude, a garden's harvest is modest. As a social experiment these shared spaces point toward the site of change that is too often missed in our culture—the local community. If the garden grows gardeners, and eventually garden cities, in addition to food, it can serve as the catalyst for greater change.

25. Jenkins, *Future of Ethics*, 56.

26. Wirzba, *Food and Faith*, 51.

27. Crossan, *Historical Jesus*, 278.

Too often we assume that there are only two levels of action: the individual and the systemic. We are seduced into this because the great myths of our culture proclaim that an individual is no small thing. Rather, individuals are supposed to be sovereign and autonomous, reigning through choices. But in concrete practice the choices that we have are often rather trivial. At the supermarket I can choose between an absurd number of breakfast cereals or crackers or cheeses, but I am largely dependent upon an impersonal, immoral, short-sighted economy to gain them.[28] I am left unable to make decisions that are socially responsible. I am largely just empowered to remain dependent and ignorant. What a strange paradox: to be told that you are free and independent, while in the space of the everyday to find that you are dependent upon broken systems.

Because I am told I am independent, and am desperate to cling to this illusion, I typically look toward my own individual action as the locus of change. I might try in earnest to change things. I might start buying food from the organic section. While this would be an improvement, many of the products are still produced by giant corporations that are governed by principles that will seek to game the system of certification. Farmers markets and Community Supported Agriculture offer a great deal more promise in building alternative economies (an opportunity I will return to in chapter 3).

Yet, in all of these efforts I am tempted to focus too narrowly on my own behavior. When I find that changing my choices does not seem to make much of a difference, I may feel helpless and settle into cynicism or apathy. Or, even if I feel successful, I might seal myself off from others, polishing my self-righteous zero-impact lifestyle as a treasure. But what good does solitary purity do in an ecosystem inundated with toxic waste?

The other option that seems to be available to us is to look for political change. This too is often limited to individual choice as political action is entirely circumscribed to the act of voting. Like the consumer in the supermarket, the citizen in the voting booth is apt to feel disempowered by the machinations of corporate interests. On both popular accounts of change our practical options are reduced to two rather passive forms of action: our buying a product or voting for a candidate. Both of these scenarios have outsourced action and labor to organizations and industries that represent us.

If we want political, economic, and agricultural change we will need to become more intimately knowledgeable about and involved with everyday processes, governance, and administration. This no doubt means communal activity through direct action and nonviolent resistance, protests and

28. Berry, *Art of the Commonplace*, 259.

boycotts. But it also means finding ways to embody and nurture alternatives.[29] Sustainable, joyful, and just communities, households, and neighborhoods can be both the means and end of change. From these grassroots, political will can be shaped and sustained.[30]

Admittedly, these social spaces are profoundly fragile and fallible. This is part of why Jesus spent so much of his time teaching about resistance and persecution. The work of the kingdom will lead to an abundant harvest, but we are working with degraded fields that are completely surrounded by the grinding machines of empire. We will need relationships to keep us going, the moral courage of others to embolden us, and a foretaste of a different kind of life to inspire abiding, subversive, and transformative hope.

From Graveyard to Garden

My first experience with a community garden began in a graveyard, or rather the plot of land that was designated as the old Episcopal Burying Ground in Lexington, Kentucky. The two-acre patch of earth is located near downtown, in the East End—a low-income and largely African American neighborhood. The burial ground is owned by a large, affluent Anglo church and is surrounded by a tall fence. Among the dead in the cemetery was the unmarked grave of a forgotten follower of Christ, a freed slave named London Ferrell. Ferrell was the pastor of the First African Baptist Church in Lexington for thirty-one years—a church claiming the largest membership in the state at the time. Ferrell was deeply loved by many in the town because of his daily service to his flock and the courage he showed during a cholera epidemic that struck in the city in 1833. Rev. Ferrell was one of three ministers who remained in town to care for the sick and bury the dead. Following the path of the cross, he went to the place of suffering and offered self-giving love.

The recovery of his witness and memory helped to spark new life in this closed off space, as the site was transformed into a community garden. Led by a new monastic community, members of the neighborhood, and the church, London Ferrell Community Garden was established.[31] Fruit trees were planted, individual plots were designated, and communal and open beds were sown.

Amid the many crucifixions of the empire—the destruction of land, the exploitation of the poor, and the great American original sin of structural

29. Bahnson, *Soil and Sacrament*, 129–30.
30. Berry, *Art of the Commonplace*, 81–90.
31. Bahnson, *Soil and Sacrament*, 248–49.

racism—London Ferrell's echo of Christ's self-giving love sowed seeds of hope. These were mustard seeds that held both the power of nourishment and subversion. And they were planted in the heart of the city with the hopes of both growing nourishing food and reconciling community.

I stumbled onto the garden after meeting Jeremy Porter, who worked for Seedleaf, an organization that serves a collective of community gardens in the neighborhood. I had been working at a liberal arts college a couple of blocks from the garden and had become increasingly immersed in issues of ecotheology, food, and sustainability. These interests had started to take over my teaching and thought. Only I could not find a place for action and integration. In fits and starts my wife and I started working at the garden, and I would occasionally take students there. Through tending to the soil and connecting with other people our despair was transformed into labors of love.

Spending time out in the garden, I began to realize the scope of the problems I was reading about. Growing food is difficult. The sort of intergenerational knowledge that had been passed on to my great uncle, grandfather, and father had been lost. If I wanted to maintain soil fertility, avoid disease, and engage in multiple growing seasons I needed a great deal more knowledge and experience.

My wife and I signed up for a "Master Community Gardner" class offered by Seedleaf. We had hoped to gain technical information so that we could be more effective gardeners. To our surprise and initial disappointment, on the first night of the training Ryan Koch, the executive director, handed us a book from the extension office and told us that most of the information we needed was in there. The training was more concerned with the community part of gardening. The training was focused on why and how people can be brought together and healed through working the soil.

Initially, I had wanted to gain knowledge to overcome my failures and limits. I had missed that this is precisely part of what the garden needed to teach me. Even with a great deal more knowledge, I am much too impatient, foolish, and otherwise committed to feed myself.[32] Furthermore, what good would it do if I found a separate peace by just feeding myself out of my backyard? Even if I set aside the hunger of others, it does little good to maintain the structural integrity of my own room if the rest of the building is falling in around me. Though we certainly need to be apprenticed in the crafts that will empower us to care for the land and each other, part of what these crafts have to teach us is to live and function within limits and through community.[33]

32. Wirzba, *Food and Faith*, 48, 52.
33. Wirzba, *Food and Faith*, 57–58.

Furthermore, many of the impediments to my gardening had little to do with knowledge and more with my inconsistency. The garden simply did not fit within the rhythms of my life. If I was lucky I could block out a time on Saturday morning to check in on things. Not only is this amount of time or frequency inadequate, it neglects the unpredictability of weather, the variant timing of plants, and the other schedules of the people with whom I should be working. The garden is a school but so is the workplace, the commute, the television, the store, and the social media feed. Not only are these training centers on different schedules, they are teaching conflicting lessons.

This inconsistency and incongruence with consumer culture is at the heart of why community gardens are often so short lived (and why the environmental movement has made so little headway). The rhythms of both caring for a garden and a community do not fit in with our other prepackaged, single-serving, and plastic-wrapped social structures. Oftentimes a community garden is briefly sustained by the initial excitement of doing something new and the whiff of authenticity that fills the air. But even in its first seasons, come the heat and irregular vacations of late summer, the garden is left to one or two faithful champions. After a couple of growing seasons, these champions frequently become burned out and the garden goes fallow as its gardeners sow seeds in other places—places where the seeds of joy are consumed, scorched through shallowness, and choked out by worry and anxiety.

The garden will provide us both with a mess of green beans and a lesson about how our to-do lists are often obstacles rather than instruments for doing the everyday work of planting, watering, weeding, and communing. The trip to the supermarket is easily checked off the list, but the garden is not. The service project that lasts two hours on Saturday is efficiently accomplished, the long messy work of justice and social change is not. The tension between the rhythms of the garden and the rest of our lives are instructive. The community garden can draw attention to the wider structures of our habitats—to the ways of life that dominate the unsustainable suburb and the exploited urban neighborhood.

In the garden I found the beauty of creation, the joy of contemplating the work of the creator, and the connection that comes from nourishing community. But its slow rhythms also helped me hear the exhausting uptempo drumbeat of the rest of my life. Time in the garden helped me hear the speed of my anxious beating heart as I spent time trying to claw my way up the ladder of success, as I fell in line to the marching beat of meetings and commutes, as I zoned out through the trance beats that helped me numb out in between. These rhythms were lulling me into a pace of life where I was racing toward my grave with little awareness of the joys I was passing over, and even more, the graveyards of polluted ecosystems, extinct species, and oppressed peoples that were left in the wake of my lifestyle. The path of the cross moves both toward the grave and to new life.

Through our time in the garden my wife and I also built relationships with people who moved outside of our suburbanite circles. We forged friendships by caring for the earth. We unconsciously learned from people who were making decisions that reflected a set of hopes and values that were quite different. Without really noticing it, what I thought was possible for my life was changed by coming into relationship with people who did not seem to be so concerned with career success, or whose hopes where not shaped by the more modest goals of a mortgage and a retirement account. I learned subtle lessons from my friend Sean Gladding, one of the leaders of the new monastic community that helped to start the garden. He would reply to the question: "What do you do for a living?" by saying, "I try to love my neighbor." This response honestly reflects how he has structured his life. The moral courage and alternative witness of people we shared time with in the garden slowly helped us to make change in our lives. The changes would be rightly characterized by the values of empire as downward mobility, but by the ideals of a different kingdom as the small seeds of integrity, joy, and justice. Through the actions of creaturely care, the observance of our limits and gifts, by slowly learning to move with other rhythms, and the work of alternative community the garden grows social change.

This form of social change is very different from the vision of service that often motivates the work that more affluent Christians initiate in poorer neighborhoods. Too often people of privilege assume that they are individuals with an abundance of material goods that need to be shared with people who have less. On this account it is not that social structures or that the spiritual nature of wealthy communities are internally unhealthy, it is just that too many people are excluded. This means that the task is simply to give the hungry food, or if we are being really proactive and following the ultimate American goal of autonomy, we might want to teach them to raise their own food. On this account, *we* are the ones who can help *them*. It is our social structures and the bounty that they produce that provides abundance and even salvation. Such a vision of Christian love leaves uninterrogated the economic, social, and political structures that produce these problems and the possibility that the wealthy also need repentance, transformation, and saving.

Community gardens are often fraught with these dynamics. Much of the local food movement is framed in terms of a white American social imaginary, where a return to the land is romanticized and seen as a space of freedom. This ideal image is less likely to inspire the descendants of slaves who were tied to working the land in bondage.[34] Furthermore, these projects are often not centered upon social change, but are organized around the neoliberal (which is to say consumerist and corporate) ideals of consumer choice, entrepreneurism, and self-improvement. The garden, on this account, does not set up an alternative economy or form of community, but it serves to produce products and train people to participate in the dominant marketplace.[35] At worst this renders the community garden the idol whereby white saviors worship themselves as the benefactors of those in need. In a more benign form, the garden fits within a hipster aesthetic that is still too individualistic (thereby missing the possibility of social and political change).

The power of the garden to grow something nourishing and subversive, little mustard seeds in the midst of the city, comes from the combination of cultivating food that nourishes bodies and community that transforms spirits. The garden can serve as a school that counters, rather than fulfills, many of the dreams of white America. My wife and I did not find that we were able to produce abundance in the so-called food desert of a poor neighborhood. Rather we began to learn that the problems in that neighborhood had their source upstream in our suburban lives. The consumer goods that fill our home are often made in low-income neighborhoods that pay residents inadequate wages while they also pollute their living spaces. We are fed by the army of underpaid workers who suffer from a lack of access to healthy food and resultant health problems. Our garbage often finds its way back to burden these same places. In seeing this connection and in finding a foretaste of an alternative, we began to learn that the work of change must take place in the habitats of the poor *and* the privileged.

Sweating in Solitude on the Soil

Through my time in gardens I have seen glimpses of the kingdom, but I would not characterize it as the experience of resurrection life. Rather, it fits the Christian pattern of the already, not yet. Something has happened and continues to happen out in the garden. Sometimes I experience abundance or I see ways that the field *could* produce one hundred fold from the small seeds of change, but that has not come to fullness yet. The garden

---

34. Carter, "Blood in the Soil," 45–46, 51–54. Carter proposes to address such associations with counter-memories of African and African American agricultural genius and tradition (58).

35. Guthman, "Bringing Good Food."

is as much a place of trial as it is of delight. Or, to be honest, it is more Gethsemane than Eden.

For the last several years I have turned my attention to a garden closer to home. Twisted Trunk Community Garden was started by the faculty, staff, and students of Georgetown College. After several seasons of flourishing it entered a fallow period (a pattern not uncommon, especially with college communities where there is frequent turnover with students and increasing overwork with faculty and staff).[36] It was revived by some former students, Sable and Kyle Snyder, who attended nearby Georgetown Baptist Church. I reached out to the coordinators of the garden in hopes of adding some new energy—an offer which they very openhandedly accepted. My hope was to renew the partnership with the college and to establish new relationships with other communities. The plot of land that the garden is on is small, but it is centrally positioned in the town in relationship to a number of schools and churches.

In my meager efforts I have found more isolation than community. The first growing season I picked a weekly evening to be present in the garden and would send out regular invitations for others to join me. No one would show. Much of this was undoubtedly due to poor planning on my part. I picked an evening that worked for *my* schedule and the invitations I sent were general and electronic rather than personal.

One evening early in the season I had hoped to lay down some paths between our rows to protect the soil, keep down weeds, and help give members access to plants. Turning to the materials that were on hand, I decided we would lay down some newspaper, wet it down, and cover it with straw. I gathered the materials and showed up with visions in my head of collaboration and laughter. My nominal attempts at organization, however, did not render any participants, and so I was left to try and start the project by myself.

It was a hot day. At first I welcomed the occasional gust of wind. But soon the breeze became my adversary as it scattered the newspapers I feebly tried to lay down. My efforts at wetting down the paper were equally quixotic as I initially scrambled to bring water from a rain barrel and then fought with a twisted hose. The straw that broke the camel's back was the actual bale of straw. It was so tightly packed that I could not pull any out without cutting the straps that bound it together. When I did cut them it virtually exploded all over the lawn. This mess of straw forced my hand into laying it all out, instead of just doing part of the project.

36. On the beginnings of this community garden, see Bryan K. Langlands's interview with Homer White in *Cultivating Neighborhood*, 47–63.

The frustration and heat built on each other. All of which was exacerbated by the pressure that I needed to get home to relieve my wife, who was caring for our sick son. I watered the garden with my sweat. But even more difficult, inside my spirit churned. "Why do I try?" I thought. This question echoed in my head not just about this night, or this garden, but it was magnified by the failure of so many of my efforts to cultivate alternative communities and to live sustainably. Feeling the pangs of isolation and the creeping of despair, I melodramatically wondered, "What is the point of trying to swim against the current of this suburban strip-mall covered town? Everyone is rushing around with schedules full of sound and fury, satisfying nothing." Light-headed from the heat, I was demoralized. Lost in my self-pity was the reality that I was often the one who failed to show up to the invitation of others. As the season wore on, I protected my time in the garden less and less. My response to the garden's needs diminished.

This past growing season we opened the garden with a work day. The organization was more intentional and the weather happened to cooperate. A crowd showed up. We began with a liturgy that paired Scriptures with the acts of tilling, sowing, composting, and watering. Children ran through the garden. People worked together and laughed. It was a beautiful day.

This is the plight of the gardener in empire. There are foretastes of the kingdom, but there are even more trials. Often when we try to make a change we will find frustration and isolation. The rhythms of our lives do not match up with the patient and unpredictable demands of either communities or gardens. The garden does not work as an add on, where we pencil it in for the one evening we have free for the whole month. The rain will splash water on that conceit. And so, if we are going to try to begin to move and dance to another song, to a joyful drum beat, we will have to resist and change the exhausting and syncopated steps of empire.

The Olive Press in the Garden

If we will look, we could encounter the risen Christ in the garden and rediscover our identity as disciples and gardeners. If we listen, however, we will also hear that prior to the cross there is another garden. In that garden Jesus faces the burden of resisting the Empire alone, and he weeps and he laments.

After his public demonstrations and before he was arrested and executed Jesus retreated to a garden (John 18:1). In Mark the place is named Gethsemane, meaning "the olive press." Jesus gathers with his disciples at the site of both cultivation and production. Olives were one of the primary staples of agriculture and diet in Israel (often listed along with wheat and wine). They produced oil that was nourishing, medicinal, and also served as fuel. Oil was a commodity used for trade (it probably does not take much imagination to draw out the implications of how empires treat oil in the Middle East). Oil was also used for anointing.[37] If we still cannot hear the political implications of this site, Luke places it at the foot of the Mount of Olives, the place where the Lord will stand on the day of judgement (Luke 22.39; Zech 14:4). Set at the garden of the oil press, it is clear that Christ's struggle is not simply a private matter. Here, Jesus Christ—the Anointed, the peasant revolutionary who brought a new covenant, prepared for his final conflict with the Empire.

Like the parable of the Sower—in which the abundance of the field refers to both the nourishing of bodies and spirits—the oil press in Gethsemane marks the site of resistance where both the means of production and forms of community are at stake. In this garden Jesus felt the weight of standing up to the Empire. The Gospels give us a snapshot of Christ's vulnerable prayerfulness. Like an olive press, the stones of pressure are added one by one—the first to the last, squeezing every last drop out even from the pit. First, Christ felt the pressure of anticipating the pain and loss he would face at the hands of the Empire. He withdrew with his closest disciples and sought to pray. He confessed that, "my soul is deeply grieved to the point of death" (Mark 14:32 NAS). He begged them to "remain here, and keep awake" (Mark 14:32). Turning to prayer, a second stone was added, as he felt the weight of despair, perhaps wondering if God had abandoned him. Calling God with the personal name *Abba*, Papa, he prayed, "for you all things are possible; remove this cup from me." Even with this tension, he continued, "yet, not what I want, but what you want" (Mark 14:36). Already bearing the stones of persecution from the Empire and the holy demand of the task that confronted him, the stone of alienation was piled on. He turned to his friends and found that they could not stay awake with him. They fell asleep again and again (Mark 14:37–41).

In the garden we sometimes find glimpses of the kingdom, sometimes we are able to sow seeds for change, but sometimes we face a time of trial. Going against the dominant culture does not always lead to something so spectacular and obvious as a cross, but it always comes with tensions and sufferings, however subtle. Sometimes the pressure to step back in line is issued in the form of ridicule, other times it comes through the pressures of jobs and bills that dictate the use of time. Trying to live and work for justice in structures bent on extraction, consumption, exploitation, and overwork

37. Rousseau and Arav, *Jesus and His World*, 220–23.

can often lead one to question if one has been separated from what is good and trustworthy. Perhaps most difficult, in looking for transformation we sometimes find ourselves isolated, or even worse, alienated from those relationships that are fundamental to our very being.

The scene at Gethsemane models two responses to these pressures, a negative and a positive. On the one hand the disciples go to sleep. At issue here is not that the disciples exercise some self-care and actually rest. Central to Christ's call and any hope of a joyful life is a good deal of sabbath keeping. The problem is that they fail to remain alert and present. This is a great temptation in the face of the tension with and within empire, to numb out—to put our minds, hearts, and consciences to sleep by distracting ourselves. We leave Christ's side with the dreams of empty entertainment, with the distraction of our to-do list, with the fantasies of success or prestige. We don't stay awake and address the real issues, but we put that part of our soul to sleep. (And consequently, this is one of the many reasons why I think it is difficult to get people to come to gardens and sanctuaries. It is not that they are boring, but that their silence brings into focus matters that people do not want to face.)

On the other hand, Christ bears witness to a vital spiritual exercise: prayers of lament. Jesus does not pray to God and piously say what he thinks he is supposed to say. He honestly gives voice to his vulnerability. He faces his suffering and moves through it. Through lament, Christ names this pain and brings it to the surface. By crying out to God he begins the first fumbling steps of moving after being numbed or asleep. He also turns to the support of others, not once, but multiple times. While such exercises are not sufficient, failing to engage in them can leave us apathetic, cynical, and despairing. Crying out and facing the suffering opens a path for further action. Even when the garden is a place of pressure, alienation, and failure, it can still serve as an opening for transformation.

Abiding in the Vineyard of Love, Friendship, and Joy

Jesus looked out into the fields and he saw conflict and crisis. He saw the devastation and exploitation that came from the ways of the Empire. While God provided abundantly, Christ knew that the harvest was being stolen by both explicitly violent and subtly exploitative means. It was devoured, scorched, and choked. The imperial extraction of commodities was like an oil press, squeezing the people and the land, and causing them to cry out. And so, he sought to organize and incarnate a different food economy and a different kind of community, initiating subversive acts that would, like mustard seeds, take over the wheat fields the Romans wanted to hoard for themselves.

Though Jesus often taught in parables and codes—so that the elite did not quite have the ears to understand the implications of what he was saying—he also taught, organized, and acted in more direct ways that unveiled his intentions and the violence and cruelty of the empire. His efforts in the agrarian communities of Galilee charted a course to Jerusalem and Golgotha. He pointed the peasants to the ideal of the garden knowing that it also led to a cross.

The destination of this journey was not the place of the skull beyond the city, but the renewal of the garden, where the relationship with God, neighbor, and the land is restored. Whereas the ways of the Empire will attempt to separate his disciples from each other, from God, Christ, and their new way of life, Jesus speaks of a botanical and cultivated space in which they are joined together in love, friendship, and joy.

In his last long conversation with his disciples in the Gospel of John, Jesus places his followers in a vineyard—a space that is both metaphorical and creational. Christ tells them, "I am the true vine, and my Father is the vine grower" (John 15:1). The disciples are not simply related to Jesus as individuals who believe in him in the depths of their minds, but they are a part of him and this encompasses their whole lives. He says, "I am the vine, you are the branches. Those who abide in me and I in them bear much fruit, because apart from me you can do nothing" (John 15:5). Throughout the passage Jesus repeats again and again that the life of discipleship is one that is centered upon the gift and requirement of "abiding" with him (John 15:4, 5, 6, 7, 9, 16). The operative activity is not belief that saves a soul but dwelling in the vineyard as a part of Christ. In this way of life individualism and independence give way to mutuality and interdependence. This is the condition in which one finds life and bears fruit.

The vineyard, furthermore, does not flourish out in the wild, beyond the pollution of culture, but these branches require cultivation.[38] Jesus declares that God, the vine grower, "prunes [*kathairei*]" the branches that bear fruit (John 15:2). Jesus continues, saying that they have already been "cleansed [*katharoi*]" by the word he has shared with them (John 15:3). Lost in translation is that the words *prune* and *cleansed* have the same root and are tied to the cleansing action that Jesus began his last lesson with, his making the disciples "clean [*katharo*]" by washing their feet in an act of love

---

38. Callahan, *Love Supreme*, 80.

and service (John 13:10).[39] To dwell with Jesus as a branch of the vine will require the loss of certain parts of themselves—the loss of their illusions of independence, the loss of the promise and security offered by the Empire, the loss of their numbing agents, the loss of the rhythms of their past life. But as both the images of pruning and cleansing underline, this loss is an addition by subtraction. It is a loss that makes possible fruitfulness and that is made possible by self-giving love.

Jesus incarnates the alternative rule of love in which the disciples now dwell, and he underlines the importance of the transformation of social relationships and communities through love. He counsels them, "as the Father has loved me, so I have loved you; abide in my love," and commands them to "love one another as I have loved you" (John 15:9, 12). Foreshadowing his coming crucifixion and underlining the trials that they will face opposing the ways of the Empire he tells them: "no one has greater love than this, to lay down one's life for one's friends" (John 15:13). At the heart of this vision is not suffering for sufferings sake, but a vision of friendship driven by joy. He says these things "so that my joy may be in you, and that your joy may be complete" (John 15:11). Through Christ's love and their love for one another they become friends of Christ (John 15:15). As such, his followers and friends are "appointed" to go bear fruit that will "abide" (John 15:16). How else can we understand the courageous actions of the disciples to leave behind what little security they had found in the Empire, than by imagining and feeling for ourselves the joy of abiding in the love of Christ?

As followers of the one anointed to renew creation we too are called to abide in love, friendship, and joy. This demands not simply our belief, but the transformation of our entire way of life. We will find this in community, through acts of costly love, patient attention, and careful cultivation. Will we be able to overcome our habits of numbing out, and instead give voice to lament? Are we open to pruning some of the parts of ourselves cultivated in the ways of empire? Are we ready to lean down to the dirty aching places of sore feet, wet soil, and humble service? Can we turn our efforts to the long, arduous, and beautiful work of pursuing social practices and alternative efforts that begin to cultivate a healthy, joyful alternative? The risen Christ calls to us. We will regain our vocation if we can follow Mary Magdalene's witness and see that the one anointed to bring the new creation could be a gardener and reply, "Teacher!"

---

39. O'Day and Hylen, *John*, 152.

3

Transforming Food Systems

FROM A YOUNG AGE I was taught lessons about food. I was taught by the blessings recited before a meal and the fast food jingles that were branded into my mind. But many of these lessons came without a word. I was educated by the kinds of foods I was given and the variety that were limited or prohibited, the times and tables around which we ate—the dinner table, the potluck table, the cafeteria table, the television tray. I was instructed through the rituals of helping my grandmother bake cookies or the lunch lady scooping out my food.

Some of the early messages I received about problems related to food were communicated to me in the images and pithy messages of commercials. The gaze of starving children in Africa who could be sponsored for less than a dollar a day is impossible to forget. I remember the woman who was able to stay fit just by eating a cereal that, to me, tasted like cardboard. In these little thirty-second instructional videos I was introduced to the problems of hunger and health, and they framed food largely around eating. These issues seemed to be the plight of individuals who either had too little or gave into too much.

These images and countless other subtle messages from my white bread culture served to abstract people from systems. They located the problem in the plight of one person. In so doing, they obscured institutions and systems of power that shaped situations. They made them seem like the background formations of a world that was simply natural and normal, limiting the possibility of change to the mechanism of consumer choice. The only avenues to transformation were dieting and charity. Obscured in these little parables was the unhealthy food system that connected those struggling in hunger and those failing their diets.

Wendell Berry helpfully gives us a broader perspective by pulling the camera back from the face of the eater and placing her in the backdrop of the farm when he aphoristically states that "eating is an agricultural act."[1] Every bite of food we take is rooted in a field. That bite of oatmeal I eat in the still of the morning came to my house through a whole team of humans: as it was shelved in a supermarket, shipped by a trucker, processed and harvested by workers, and planted by farmers. This is to say nothing of the sun and water that nourished it, the microbes in the soil that helped feed it, and the plants that grew these oats that nourish my body. Those oats are not just an atomized collection of calories, but they are entangled in economic, biological, political, and social systems.

This systemic perspective helps to show a more holistic picture that is larger than the individual consumer who might buy or eat food products. This systemic perspective shows us how our food connects us to other communities, other peoples, other species, other places, and to the land. The gifts and responsibilities connected to food are not limited to good tastes or our diets, but they have to do with the treatment of the land, animals, farm laborers, fair prices, and communal health. Food is not just nutritional, but it is also economic, political, and social.

The wider view of our contemporary food system complicates and expands the problems associated with food. Even if our eye is trained on eaters it is not difficult to see this brokenness, as it was estimated in 2017 that 815,000,000 people are undernourished in our world (a number that is on the rise), though there are more than enough calories to feed everyone.[2] Almost 2 billion people are overweight and 650,000,000 people are obese (a condition closely correlated with poverty).[3] Bringing farms into view, we will see the ruin of rural communities as family farms and lands have been foreclosed upon through cycles of debt (as farmers try to make up for shrinking profit margins by scaling up, buying more land, seed, and machinery through loans). These smaller farms have been consolidated into large corporate entities run like factories. Farm workers labor in life-threatening conditions through exposure to pesticides and herbicides, performing backbreaking tasks that typically pay very, very little.[4] As I already mentioned in chapter 2, these farming practices have led to the profound degradation of the land in the form of the clearing of forests, the loss of soil health, and the spread of pests and pollution.

Our current food system is rooted in the so-called "Green Revolution" of the second half of the twentieth century. The Green Revolution spread the

---

1. Berry, *Art of the Commonplace*, 321.
2. Food and Agriculture Organization, "State of Food Security."
3. World Health Organization, "Obesity." Patel, *Starved and Stuffed*, 9–14.
4. Gottlieb and Joshi, *Food Justice*, 13–22.

industrial methods of agriculture all around the globe, with the package of genetically engineered patented seeds, pesticides, and massive amounts of chemical fertilizer. It sought to "feed the world" through the mechanisms of expensive farm machinery, massive monoculture fields, unregulated markets, and powerful corporations.[5] It pushed agricultural communities away from sustainable polycultures that maintained the fertility of the land and nourished local communities. Instead, it championed monocultures—growing a single crop to be sold in global markets with little regard for local human or land health. A prime example of misleading branding, this "Green" Revolution tried to transform the earth into a factory.

While from a certain perspective this revolution greatly increased the amount of wheat, corn, and soy that was produced by the world's farmers, it did so in an entirely unsustainable way. The Green Revolution relies on non-renewable resources, especially oil.[6] It requires massive amounts of oil to produce the fertilizers that soak its fields—and which deplete soil fertility. It requires oil to run the machines that tend the fields. It requires oil to process these crops into cereal, chips, soda, and cookies, and then more to ship them all over the earth. Though these methods claim to operate by the values of efficiency and productivity, it takes anywhere from three to ten calories of oil to produce one calorie of food through the efforts of industrial agriculture. Sustainable polycultures can produce something closer to twenty units of food for one unit of energy.[7] Taken in from a global perspective all of this oil, this soil degradation, and the loss of cleared forests means that industrial agriculture is responsible for one-third of all emissions contributing to climate change.[8]

We will lose sight of all of these problems and connections if we remain focused on our individual weight. Furthermore, we will fail to challenge the institutions of power, the economic configurations, and the social practices that produce these problems if we are only able to see the hungry individual. Looking more systemically, thinking ecologically and economically—which is to say in terms of relationships—will call on us to work for wider alternatives. We are called not just to teach a man to fish, rather than

5. While often touted as simply the result of scientific innovation, Patel helpfully highlights the ways in which the "Green Revolution" was driven by economic and political interest and considers the "opportunity costs" of other paths not taken. *Starved and Stuffed*, 130–41.

6. Wirzba proposes that it is so soaked in oil that it should be termed the "Brown Revolution." *Food and Faith*, 77.

7. Shiva, *Stolen Harvest*, 13. Lott, "10 Calories."

8. Scialabba and Muller-Lindenlauf, "Organic Agriculture," 158.

simply giving him a fish. Teaching him to fish will not feed him for life if the lake is polluted and his community is decimated.

While many of us have been unconsciously trained to see food through the eyes of individual eaters, just as intuitively we know that food is a site of culture and community. From childhood we have witnessed meals as social, sacred, and sacramental places where relationships are nurtured. It is around food that alternative systems and economies are most clearly, imaginatively, and joyfully forming in our time.

Likewise, Jesus fed hungry individuals, but he did so much more. His preaching and ministry were addressed to people living in the ruins of an exploitative and extractive imperial food system. His call to discipleship was directed to people who worked at various levels of this system (lowly fishermen, the middle management of tax collectors, and even rich landholders). He lifted up a vision of a renewal and radicalization of the local sustainable covenantal communities of the Hebrew villages, and he led and organized people to incarnate and experiment with alternative social practices, economies, and systems. Jesus did not *just* give a man a fish, rather he pointed people toward a different way of communal life. He called them to be fishers of people.

Calling Fishers to Transform the Food Economy

The first followers that Jesus called to help lead his movement for renewal and transformation were integral members of the Galilean food system. Mark tells us, "As Jesus passed along the Sea of Galilee, he saw Simon and his brother Andrew casting a net into the sea—for they were fishermen. And Jesus said to them, 'Follow me and I will make you fish for people.' And immediately they left their nets and followed him" (Mark 1:16–18).

If we want to picture these fishermen, we should not have anything leisurely or quaint in mind. While there are fathers and sons out on the water together, these fishing trips are no rite of passage or forced quality time, but rather they look more like forced labor. In the Roman senator and gentlemen of Cicero's hierarchy of honorable occupations, fishermen were listed dead last (with aristocratic land owners at the top).[9] Therefore, the first disciples that Jesus rallied to his cause were profoundly marginal. We need not abstract these people from their contexts and relationships in shame. Rather it was precisely the location of these fishermen in the economy and

9. Carter, *Matthew and the Margins*, 121.

in the food system that made them receptive to Jesus' subversive word and vital agents of his work.

In Jesus' time, fishing on the Sea of Galilee had become especially trying as Herod Antipas had increased his efforts to extract wealth from the fruit of the sea. Fishermen were squeezed on both sides of their fishing trips, as they funneled their catch to the elite both in the form of paying an imperial official for the right to fish in the Emperor's lake and on the back end as they had to pay a toll on their catch. As with everything else in the imperial economy, wealth flowed upwards, with tax and toll collectors getting their cut in the middle, and Herod Antipas, Caesar, and other elites taking the bulk.[10]

Furthermore, fish were not simply used to feed local populations. They were made into commodities by being processed into, for example, kinds of fish sauces that could be more easily shipped to centers of power and privilege.[11] A fair amount of this likely happened in the Galilean village Magdala (the home of Mary Magdalene), as it was also called Tarichaeae, literally "Processed-Fishville."

While these economies of extraction frame this story, the Gospel writers also bring different forms of economic relationship into focus. Jesus will overturn the empire of the elite with the renewal and transformation of a set of relationships different from impoverished laborers, tax collecting collaborators, and wealthy owners. In Matthew and Mark's telling, for example, we can barely get through a sentence without being slapped in the face with several terms that remind us of familial relationships. For example, we are told that Jesus "saw two other *brothers*, James *son* of Zebedee and his *brother* John" (Matt 4:21).[12] This is no coincidence, because in the ancient world the household was the basic economic unit. Along similar lines, Luke connects the two households saying that James and John were "partners [*koinōnoi*]" with Simon, that is they were in a cooperative together (Luke 5:10). These poor fishermen navigated the treacherous waters of taxes and tolls through relationships of interdependence and mutual support. They mark two different kinds of systems, one that is imperial, wildly hierarchical, and extractive and another that is local, more equitable, and cooperative.

While answering the call to follow Jesus meant leaving their households as presently constructed, as we will come to see, Jesus was not trying to cast household relationships aside but he was seeking to renew and radicalize them. This was, in part, because these households had been so deeply shaped by the patriarchal and oppressive order of Empire, in which

10. Hanson, "Galilean Fishing Economy."

11. Crossan, *God and Empire*, 122.

12. Carter, *Matthew and the Margins*, 122.

they had internalized the propaganda of the elite. The fishermen think that the source of the stench and rot in the fishing industry is their own making. They have too often accepted the victim blaming of the good news of the Empire that declares the poor to be lazy drains on the system and the rich to be the virtuous job creators that make the world turn.

On Luke's telling of the calling of the first disciples, Jesus is teaching on the shore of the lake when some fishermen come in from a long, fruit-less night of work. Jesus gets into the boat with Simon and tells him to cast out in the deep. Hesitantly, Simon complies and catches so many fish that his nets start breaking (Luke 5:2–6). Upon seeing this abundance Simon feels the weight of Cicero's hierarchy. He thinks he is not a man worthy of such a blessing. He says to Jesus, "Go away from me Lord, for I am a sinful man" (Luke 5:8).

Jesus' response here is crucial. He does not guide these poor fishermen to take these fish and feed the poor for that day. He does not wink at this struggling fishing co-op and tell them that they have the seed money to last in the Antipas's exploitative economy. Rather, he promises to make them "fishers of men"—perhaps the most misunderstood line in Scripture. By telling them that they will fish for men Jesus is not recruiting them into the shirt-and-tie, door-to-door business of saving souls. Rather he is taking a repeated image out of the prophetic tradition and telling them that they are going to overturn the whole imperial order. In Jeremiah the Lord, in disgust at the idolatry and iniquity of the elite of Israel says: "I am now sending many fishermen, says the LORD, and they shall catch them . . . For my eyes are on all their ways; they are not hidden from my presence, nor is their iniquity concealed from my sight" (Jer 16:16–17). Those "who oppress the poor, who crush the needy" are told by the prophet Amos that the time is coming "when they shall take you away with hooks, even the last of you with fishhooks" (Amos 4:1–2). So to be made "fishers of men" is to be agents of justice who will fish out and remove the elite who have oppressed the poor and broken covenant with God.[13]

In short, Jesus tells Simon, the real stench does not come from you, but from those at the top. He calls these members of the fishing cooperative to help him change it. To follow Jesus was about a shift in relationships and collective action. How does this call of discipleship address us today? Is it addressed to us as bodiless souls, as well-educated experts and successful entrepreneurs, or as people living in the stench of imperial waste who have forgotten the beauty and power that comes from cooperating with creation?

13. Myers, *Binding the Strong Man*, 132.

Blessed Are You Who Are Hungry–The Reversals of the Kingdom of God

In Luke's account of the Sermon on the Plain, Christ makes this contrast between extractive and sustainable economies clear. He declares that in God's order things will be reversed from how they currently stand. Preaching to a multitude of people from across Judea, from the center of power in Jerusalem, and even from Gentile territory, Christ declares: "Blessed are you who are poor for yours is the kingdom of God" (Luke 6:20). By contrast he laments, "But woe to you who are rich, for you have received your consolation" (Luke 6:24). He consoles, "Blessed are you who are hungry now, for you will be filled" (Luke 6:21). On the other hand, he warns, "Woe to you who are full now, for you will be hungry" (Luke 6:25). Christ's vision flies in the face of conventional wisdom that sees wealth as a blessing. It addresses the false claims of this wisdom and the self-blame of the poor and the oppressed who have internalized this ideology. Jesus lets them know that in the kingdom or empire governed by God's justice they shall not suffer.[14]

The system that Jesus is anointed to bring is marked by reversal, but it is not animated by vengeance. Christ's kingdom is inspired by love. This is made clear as Jesus follows up the statements of blessing and woe with the charge to "love your enemies," and the instructions of nonviolence to turn the other cheek (Luke 6:27; 29).

Christ's call to love is illustrated by specific examples from village life. This is often missed as the passages are taken as general principles removed from context and addressed to individuals. Jesus counsels: "Give to everyone who begs from you; and if anyone takes away your goods, do not ask for them again" (Luke 6:30). And further, "If you lend to those from whom you hope to receive what credit is that to you? . . . But love your enemies, do good and lend, expecting nothing in return" (Luke 6:34–35). At the heart of village life were interdependent forms of sharing, serving, and hosting. The focus here is on building up the social fabric. Therefore, the scene is not of one individual with money giving a homeless beggar a few dollars, but it portrays social practices of care that would make the kind of town or village where the beggar does not have to live on the street. Here lending and helping served both the purpose of providing material support to those in difficult times and as social bonds that built up trust, care, safety, and love.

Jesus' teachings echo the covenantal community that characterized peasant villages (which we will return to in chapter 4).[15] The calls to lending

14. Horsley, *Jesus and the Powers*, 138.
15. Horsley, *Jesus and the Powers*, 90–95.

and generosity resonate with the covenantal language that animates the Hebrew law. For example, if a member of your community is in need, you are
instructed: "do not be hard hearted or tight-fisted" but you "should rather
open your hand, willingly lending enough to meet the need" (Deut 15:7–8).
These loans and gifts should be given liberally and ungrudgingly, as this is
the basis of the social fabric. This economy should be animated by blessing—which passes on the gifts that were given by God and that will return
through love (Deut 15:10). Jesus' counsel that "if anyone takes away your
coat do not withhold even your shirt," is advice to shame creditors (Luke
6:28). It would *lay bare* (because the person without coat and shirt would
be standing naked) the breaking of the covenantal tradition that prohibits
taking interest from the poor when making a loan. As it says in the Book of
the Covenant, "If you take your neighbor's cloak in pawn, you shall restore
it before the sun goes down" (Exod 22:26).[16] This places the focus on relationships and systems of lending that lead to poverty or communal health,
rather than the charitable responses of individuals.

Luke frames the sermon in these covenantal terms, as Jesus appoints
twelve new messengers and elders for his movement (Luke 6:13–16). This
figure of the twelve echoes the twelve tribes of Israel and points toward the
promise and hope of the restoration of the land and its equitable distribution
for dwelling and care (Num 26:52–56; Ezek 47; Luke 22:30; Matt 19:28).[17]
Furthermore, Jesus comes down off a mountain to address the people in a
staging that feels like donning a Moses mask (Luke 6:17).

The covenantal community of agrarian village life was built around
simplicity, sharing, and sustainability. The goal of the community was to
raise enough food to sustain one's household, to do so in a way that cared
for the land, and to spread any excess around to those who were in need and
to show hospitality.[18] It is this way of life that animates his charge to, "Do to
others as you would have them do to you" (Luke 6:31). Jesus is advocating
for a form of community that is governed by mutuality and generosity, telling them, "the measure you give will be the measure you give back" (Luke
6:38). These calls to mutuality and generosity are not vague principles but
part of how relationships should function in a given place.

The picture painted by the woes and the blessings and by this litany
of calls for covenantal renewal indicates that these are precisely the things
that are missing from the lives of the multitude. The poor *will* inherit the
kingdom of God and the hungry *will* be filled. But under the rule of the

16. Horsley, *Jesus and the Powers*, 139.

17. Wenell, *Jesus and Land*, 104–38.

18. Herzog, *Parables as Subversive Speech*, 204–5.

elite, people are suffering and struggling. They are living in a system that produces excess for a few. This has not only left many hungry and poor, but it has broken the covenant between God, neighbor, and land (and therefore what is at stake are not just hungry individuals but oppressive systems of power). Jesus' promise is not that the poor shall become rich, because the logic of wealth is at the root of the problem.

In his sermon Jesus is explicitly focused on issues related to debt (Luke 6:29–30, 34–35, 38). Debt was at the heart of the imperial economy that was fracturing village life. As we have already noted, agrarian peasants labored under the burdens of taxations, tolls, and tributes. Galilean peasants faced multiple layers of taxation that served to extract wealth to the elite that would take up to 35 percent of their harvest.[19] These layers of taxes meant that during a good year peasants would have just enough to support themselves. This made the practices of lending and hospitality increasingly difficulty. People could no longer look to the community and their neighbors for support, but these bonds of love, trust, and connection were slowly severed. More and more households were left to fend for themselves.[20] This meant that during a bad year, when the harvest was poor, and the elite still demanded their cut, a household might have to turn to an outside lender.[21]

It was in this moment of weakness for a household that wealth could be produced. If you will recall Cicero's hierarchy, on the opposite end of the pyramid from fishermen were land holders. Owning land was the lasting and respectable way to gain wealth in this world. The predatory lender, charging high interest, sought not just a return on their money, but they sought to gain property when peasants defaulted on their loans and had to hand over their ancestral lands.[22] From 80 BCE to 8 BCE roughly half the peasant families in Italy (around 1,500,000) were kicked off ancestral lands through this process, aided by the Roman Senate deregulating mechanisms of the commonwealth to extend private property. While these peasants were displaced to cities and colonies, Romans brought in two million slaves (some from Palestine) during this period.[23]

This was the mechanism whereby men became rich, and it went against the central tenets of the covenant that prohibited the charging of interest and sought to constantly reestablish equity, especially in relationship with the land. This problem predated the Roman Empire. The prophet Micah condemned

19. Herzog, *Prophet and Teacher*, 53.

20. Herzog, *Parables as Subversive Speech*, 207.

21. Horsley, *Galilee*, 219–20.

22. Goodman, *Ruling Class*, 56–58.

23. Horsley, *Jesus and the Powers*, 28.

"those who devise wickedness," as they "covet fields, and seize them" (Mic 2:1–2). Isaiah laments those who foreclose on the land of others and consolidate farms and houses, leaving the dispossessed to death and themselves to isolation (Isa 5:8). Isaiah anticipates that this form of hoarding will not yield abundance but, with an agrarian sensibility, warns that this economy of opulence will lead to the desolation of the land (Isa 5:10). This dynamic is described during the postexilic era as some are forced to "borrow money" on "fields and vineyard to pay the king's tax," and are losing their lands. The loss of land leads to the enslavement of children (Neh 5:4–5). Nehemiah calls an assembly (*ekklēsia*) and tells the people to lend freely, to stop taking interest, to give back ancestral lands, and to forgive debts (Neh 5:10–12 LXX).

The tension between these two economies and food systems form the background of another scene of the call to discipleship when a rich man approaches Jesus and asks about what he must do to attain eternal consolation (Mark 10:17). Jesus responds with the central teachings of the Book of the Covenant, notably the last part of the ten commandments that concern everyday, economic life: "You know the commandments: 'You shall not murder; You shall not commit adultery; You shall not steal; You shall not bear false witness; You shall not defraud; Honor your father and mother'" (Mark 10:19). On Mark's telling, Jesus has made an important substitution. In place of the prohibition against coveting he says "defraud." This Greek term typically referred to the holding back of wages from a worker, or the refusal to return goods that had been entrusted.[24] In so doing, Jesus highlights that this man's wealth was ill-gotten, that it was gained through breaking the covenant with predatory loans and foreclosed land.[25]

Yet, the man does not pick up on Jesus' correction, or seem to have any sense of the damage he has done. He claims to be among the great moral exemplars, having kept these commandments since his youth (Mark 10:20). Jesus responds with love rather than vengeance. Mark goes so far to write that, "Jesus, looking at him, loved him." (Mark 10:21). This is the only place in Mark where Jesus is said to have loved anyone.[26] But this love is not sentimental or easy, rather it is followed by an invitation to discipleship. Jesus says to him: "You lack one thing; go, sell what you own, and give the money to the poor, and you will have treasure in heaven; then come, follow me" (Mark 10:21). Jesus invites the rich man to heal the social, political, economic, and ecological damage he has done through his accumulation, and

---

24. Myers, *Binding the Strong Man*, 272.

25. Horsley, *Jesus and the Powers*, 141–142.

26. Myers, *Binding the Strong Man*, 273.

thereby not simply give the poor enough calories, but to begin to repair the relationships, institutions, and ecosystems that he has destroyed.

The rich man did not take Jesus up on his call to follow the path of the kingdom. This led Christ to say: "How hard it will be for those who have wealth to enter the kingdom of God! . . . It is easier for a camel to go through the eye of a needle than for someone who is rich to enter the kingdom of God" (Mark 10:23, 25). As the disciples have been shaped by the moral world of the rich, they still associate wealth with blessing and are befuddled how anyone could be saved if the rich are not capable.[27]

Peter, the fisher of men, who cast aside his nets and his livelihood and followed Jesus as his Lord, chimes in that they did leave everything to follow him. To which Jesus responds that those who left their household "for the sake of the good news" will receive houses and fields a hundredfold (Mark 10:28–30). This is not to say that they will be the new plantation owners. The covenantal communities will be renewed through a more egalitarian and sustainable way of life.[28] They will receive the hundredfold harvest of the parable of the Sower that will allow them to lend with generosity, and to feed the hungry. These households will also be transformed, as Jesus does not just offer a promise to the patriarchal heads of household, rather with God and Jesus as the head of a newly constructed household, the promise is offered to "brothers and sisters, mothers and children" (Mark 10:30).

The elite and wealthy, the old fathers, are accustomed to thinking of themselves as the owner of God's blessing and the source of virtue. Jesus warns, however, that their systems have broken fundamental relationships between God, neighbors, and the land. They have produced a world of poverty, hunger, and distrust. Christ calls followers onto a different path. In the kingdom of God, "many who are first will be last, and the last will be first" (Mark 10:31). Jesus underlines that poverty is a symptom of wealth. The reversal of the order of the wealthy does not idealize poverty and the poor and leave the only authentic followers of Jesus as itinerate *individuals* who have no possessions. The covenantal renewal and transformation at the heart of his ministry points toward an alternative vision of equitable, sustainable, and joyful *communal* life.

The Big Green Economy Will Not Save Us

Though the scholars are whispering in one of my ears to be careful about anachronistically comparing contexts and drawing out specious implications,

27. Myers, *Binding the Strong Man*, 275.
28. Myers, *Biblical Vision*, 26.

the prophets speak in a poetic agrarian cadence in the other ear, telling me that there are important connections (and the stories of Scripture are largely about making these connections).[29] The ancient economy was not nearly as complex as our own, and it operated through radically different instruments and institutions. But in both times, there are multitudes who are hungry, poor, vulnerable, and overworked. Furthermore, behind these individual gaping mouths is the similar drama of a stolen harvest—the extraction of wealth and labor from the many into the hands of the few. There are vast piles of wealth that have been formed through foreclosing on the commonwealth—which has meant both the loss of sustainable agricultural communities and ways of life that value equity, sharing, generosity, and caring for the land. One matter that is more pronounced and perhaps unique to our time is the scope of the damage that has been done to the land and the entire earth, where the gifts of creation are being taken from future generations.

Such cataclysmic concerns would seem to demand immediate reversals. Yet I confess that I have too often answered the call to discipleship with the confusion and reluctance of the rich man rather than with the decisiveness of the disciples. For example, my family's awakening to the deep and expansive problems of the industrial food system have not led to instantaneous transformation. Rather we have traveled a circuitous path that is a blend of struggle, experimentation, excitement, and disappointment.

Before my ecological awakening, I had become accustomed to thinking of my responsibility in the supermarket under entirely different virtues. I unconsciously thought I was supposed to exercise thrift (in spending as little as possible), restraint (doing what I could to watch my waistline), and wholesomeness (eating more fruits and vegetables). Every trip to the checkout lane revealed a combination of compromises—cheap sugary stuff balanced by produce and processed food with low-fat labels. Food was already fraught with all kinds of rules and self-blame, and the possibility of having to add another set of byzantine judgments to a part of life I already did not have time for was overwhelming.

Our first and most significant adjustment in our attempts to eat more sustainably was, in part, made possible by redirecting these three virtues to stop buying meat—which has the benefits of being cheaper and healthier. In terms of environmental impact, there are fewer things that you can do that will as significantly cut down your carbon footprint. Livestock contribute about 15 percent of global carbon emissions. In no small part because it takes a lot of grains to produce meat.[30] About a third of global

29. Brueggemann, "The Uninflected *Therefore*," 243–49.
30. Food and Agriculture Organization, "Key Facts and Findings."

agricultural land use is allocated to growing feed to raise livestock. So you can add to the 15 percent of annual emissions another 12 percent from the clearing of forest for agriculture.[31]

Our further efforts to change our consumption, however, forced us to struggle with thrift, as we bought the same food, only now we substituted the "lite" labels with the more expensive "organic" labels. This change in consumer behavior was no small task, which made my realization that it was entirely inadequate profoundly discouraging. The USDA regulations that grant organic certification are focused on the inputs that are used in the production of agriculture. To be certified, organic farmers (or the corporations that often run organic farms) cannot use synthetic fertilizers, herbicides, or pesticides. All of these inputs have significant impacts on greenhouse gas emissions from agriculture. They also contribute to the pollution of ground water and produce "dead zones" in water ways (there is a dead zone in the Gulf of Mexico the size of New Jersey).

The deeper philosophy and promise of organic agriculture is not represented by this big green packaging. Organic certifications do nothing to directly regulate other impactful practices, like limiting the processing, packaging, and transportation of food. Nor do they guarantee sustainable land management practices that would have the biggest impact, both in terms of sequestering carbon in healthy soils and in creating resilient farm systems. The limited demands of certification are cumbersome for small farmers. They are, however, more easily manipulated by large corporations that deal in the shrouded space of global supply chains—that might market organic sugar grown on problematic plantations planted in recently clear-cut rainforests.[32] The organic box of cereal I buy that is shipped from California is still processed, packaged, and shipped across the country like the conventionally produced cereal, and the farms that grow the corn are likely managed by large corporations in ways that are only different in terms of inputs, as they are simply trying to get to the premium price that the organic label yields.

The difficult and deeply inconvenient truth is that the supermarkets will not solve this for us. Now I confess that my family still often goes to the supermarket and tries to fill up our cart with organic labels. In our small town our alternatives are seasonal. When I am in the neighboring city, I do like to go to the food co-op there. This organization runs on a different model that treats its employees better, is not driven by profits, and is more attentive to its supply chains. I enjoy the prayerful task of getting on my knees in the bulk

31. Scialabba and Muller-Lindenlauf, "Organic Agriculture," 163–64.
32. Rogers, *Green Gone Wrong*, 43–66.

food aisle and filling up our reusable containers with organic grains, beans, and flour. During the summers our small town holds a farmers market where we can purchase produce grown locally and regionally. We also participate in community supported agriculture with a local farm. At the beginning of the growing season we buy a share of the harvest and receive a weekly bundle of produce, which means we share in some of the risk and bounty inherent in growing food. This serves to shorten the distance our food travels, to more directly support regenerative organic practices, and allow us to see the people who feed us face to face.

On its own, this patchwork of practices is not sufficient to reduce our emissions or to transform the food system. They are each small steps that are worthwhile. But we must remember that systemic problems are not solved by individuals.

Perhaps the greatest change we must make is to get beyond our fixation on *consumer choice* as our only locus for change. This is where the alternative food economy holds its greatest power. The relationships fostered in the supermarket limit food to being seen as a commodity and ourselves as consumers. The supermarket allows me to wander its aisles in passive dependent ignorance. The pastoral pictures painted upon its boxes allow me to dream of the green fields that feed me, and they hide the ecological and personal devastation that yielded this fruit. But the co-op, the farmers market, and community supported agriculture remind us of the peoples and places that grow and nurture our food. They provide us with ingredients that demand our preparation and cooking, and foods that incarnate the seasonal bounty of God's blessings. These practices and institutions help us to stop thinking of ourselves as consumers and to start thinking of ourselves as members with a function to play that is dependent upon the whole membership.

By continuing to think of ourselves as consumers we are leaving the institutions and structures of consumerism intact.[33] Instead, we need to rethink the economy. In popular parlance, the economy often feels like an abstraction of numbers. The economy is assumed to be the underlying natural and rational computer code that governs our world. But we would be well served to reframe the term by what it means etymologically. "Eco-" means the "house" or "household." *Ecology* is the study of the connections and relationships of our earthly household. The second half of the word, "-nomy" simply means "the rule of" (like auto-nomy, meaning self-rule). The economy, then, is simply the rule of the household. It is the way that

---

33. Myers, *Who Will Roll*, 348.

our lives and relationships are ordered.[34] The economics of consumerism is not simply the statistical and rational unfolding of natural processes, but it is the way of life that is produced by certain institutions, architectures, and practices.[35] If we want to change these systems and our ways of life, then we will need to do more than simply *consume* differently. We will need to leave the supermarket and support, form, and imagine other institutions. We will need to transform the ways our households are ordered. We will need to rethink our food cultures, in order to foster something more beautiful, nourishing, and responsible than opening a box.

As part of a food system, as members of a body, we are not autonomous deciders. Therefore, we need to be less focused on our individual choices. It was this realization that I found most discouraging with the shortcomings of organically certified foods in the supermarket. I have been trained to think that I, alone, can instantaneously change things, and when that is not possible frustration sometimes transforms into cynicism and despair (a symptom, no doubt, of consumerism but a malady even more strongly pronounced by the social structures of gender, race, and class).

The solutions to these problems will neither be fast nor will they allow me to imagine that they are under my individual control. Rather, the responses will take time, and the slow work of collective action. They will cost us the myths that we are autonomous consumers who are gifted with the absolute freedom of choice.

But this is also the good news. Our cultural myths about the freedom of consumer choice have covered over the systemic constraints that mark our lives, distracted us from our individual isolation, and served as a smoke screen to hide the real costs of our lifestyles. We cannot put new wine into old wine skins, or more efficient products into the same old packaging. What is needed is a new way of life, which will take time, cooperation, experimentation, and transformation.

The Sabbath Rhythms of Sustainable Life

An overly simplistic understanding of the reversals of Jesus' vision of the kingdom have often obscured Christ's positive vision for a different way of life. This has foreclosed the routes to change opened by the gospel. I have never heard, for example, a productive conversation about the story of the rich man in the privileged white mainline churches in which I have spent

34. McFague, *Life Abundant*, 72.

35. For simple ways to bring economic literacy home for First-World Christians, see Myers, *Who Will Roll*, 66–71.

most of my life. Every time I have heard it preached the economic issues have been spiritualized, equivocated, or completely ignored. In Sunday school classes, when the question of giving away wealth is directly addressed there is a fixation on the line that: "For mortals it is impossible, but not for God; for God all things are possible" (Mark 10:27). I think this is, in part, because the demand to give wealth away has been individualized and universalized. It seems to mean that no one should ever possess anything, that everyone should always give everything away.

This abstract reading of the text can be its own form of protection as it stops us from looking at its deeper implications. Making the story about individual choice and a seemingly impossible ethical demand where I should never have any food in my mouth but should always be putting it in the mouth of another stops us from seeing the deeper challenge to *systems* of wealth. It protects us from discerning the demands that might be more specifically applied to our contemporary unsustainable food system that steals the harvest from both the present poor and future generations, or the present cycles of debt that grind down the global south and build up the north, or the reparations required for the decedents of people who were enslaved in systems that produced the present wealth of these same white congregations, or the educational debt that is limiting the vocational possibilities of younger generations.

Jesus' communal vision of covenantal renewal brings these constructive and challenging proposals to the forefront. This is perhaps most clearly the case in matters related to the Sabbath. Strangely, Jesus is often seen as an opponent of the Sabbath laws, whereas a closer reading of the covenantal tradition and Jesus' teaching and activity reveals that he is holding to the social, political, and economic institutions and practices that accompany the gift of sabbath release. In order to show this positive vision, the rest of this section will flesh out the nature of the Sabbath in the Hebrew Scriptures.

The Sabbath plays a central role in the covenantal traditions. In the Ten Commandments the demand for a day of rest, reverence, and release is the hinge between those commands centered upon the relationship with God and those that are concerned with relationships with neighbors through household and economic matters.[36] In the command to keep the Sabbath in the book of Exodus the gift of Sabbath is tied to God's act of creation (Exod 20:11). In the first creation story, the Sabbath is the crowning of creation (Gen 2:2–3). God does not rest from exhaustion and numb out on the couch so that "he" can be recharged from the work week. Sabbath is not the exception to the rule of an otherwise busy universe, but sabbath delight—in a

---

36. Lowery, *Sabbath and Jubilee*, 106.

creation that is very good and beautiful—is the ruling center of creation that orients all the other days of our weeks.[37] Furthermore, the Sabbath is not limited to one day a week, but as we will see, it shapes life in creation.

Sabbath rest resonates throughout creation. Everyone is granted rest—sons, daughters, servants, livestock, resident aliens—so it is not a privilege reserved for the elite (Exod 20:10). This life-giving and orienting rest and delight is further extended to farm animals, to the ox and donkey (Exod 23:12). Sabbath is extended to the land, which is supposed to lie fallow once every seven years—a process that both renews the land and provides some extra sustenance to the poor and wild animals (Exod 23:11; Lev 25:4–7). The Sabbath command illustrates a deeper point that the covenant between God and people was integrally tied up with the earth and everyday economic activity.[38]

In the version of the ten commandments in Deuteronomy the Sabbath is framed in terms of God's *liberating* work: "Remember that you were a slave in the land of Egypt and the LORD your God brought you out from there with a mighty hand and an outstretched arm; therefore the LORD your God commanded you to keep the sabbath day" (Deut 5:15). Sabbath rest is about delighting in the wonderful rhythms of creation that are radically different from the ways of empire—in which workers are never given a rest. In the imperial economy the Egyptians were ruthless taskmasters who made the lives of the Israelites "bitter with hard service in mortar and brick and in every kind of labor in the field" (Exod 1:14). Pharaoh saw creation as a collection of commodities, whereas God is committed to covenantal relationships that foster flourishing and rest.[39]

In the covenant the Sabbath is about rest *and release*—it is an orienting set of practices that orders communal life with the nourishing rhythms of creation and that serves to disrupt the slave-driving drumbeat of empire. At the heart of daily economic and agricultural life there should be an open-handed orientation. In the Hebrew law families who work the land are guided "not to reap the very edges of the field, or gather the gleanings of your field" (Lev 19:10). They are instructed to leave part for those who are most vulnerable (Lev 19:11; Deut 24:19–22). Land ownership is not as strictly bounded as people may go into a neighbor's field and eat grain to satisfy their hunger (though they cannot carry any away in a container) (Deut 23:25). In order to maintain equitable relationships and prevent exploitation, the law prohibits collecting interest on loans, especially to the

---

37. Wirzba, *Living the Sabbath*, 32–34.

38. Wright, *God's People*, 23.

39. Brueggemann, *Sabbath as Resistance*, 6.

poor (Deut 23:19; Exod 22:25; Lev 25:35-37). More explicitly related to the Sabbath, debt that accumulates on the land is to be released every seven years (Deut 15:1-2). The forms of debt that bring people to slavery will also be released every seven years. In Deuteronomy, they are released with reparations (Deut 15:14-15). Most radical among the Sabbath commands of release is the year of Jubilee, which every fifty years (every seven sabbath cycles) fosters structural and systemic change, where land shall be redistributed to its equitable ancestral holdings and the fields are allowed to rest (Lev 25:8-13).[40]

Keeping the covenant and living in these sabbath rhythms leads to a life of blessing—an agrarian vision in which the mutual well-being of the land and neighbors is animated by the constant reverent reminder that everything is a gift from God.[41] As the chapter following the Jubilee in Leviticus promises, if the people observe the Sabbath and the commandments, God will bless them with "rains in their season, and the land shall yield its produce, and the trees of the field shall yield their fruit." The people are promised, "you shall eat your bread to the full, and live securely in your land. And I will grant peace in the land" (Lev 26:4-6). Even more God promises, "I will place my dwelling in your midst . . . And I will walk among you, and will be your God, and you shall be my people. I am the LORD your God who brought you out of the land of Egypt, to be their slaves no more; I have broken the bars of your yoke and made you walk erect" (Lev 26:11-13).

Breaking the covenant, exploiting the poor, tearing the social fabric asunder, and *refusing the land its rest* will, on the other hand, lead to ruin. Whether it is granted a sabbath by its caretakers, or if the land is simply vacated by civilizational collapse, it will "enjoy its sabbath years" (Lev 26:34). Yet, even if this covenant is broken, God will still remember it and the land (Lev 26:42).

The prophets decried the exploitation of the poor that so often went along with a minimalist interpretation of the Sabbath. Amos excoriated the rich who "trample the needy and bring ruin to the poor of the land." He underlines that these elites viewed the sabbath as a brief exception that proved the rule of unjust business practices. The rich (like "Sunday Christians") could not wait for the Sabbath day to be over so that they could "practice deceit with false balances," manipulating market systems for their own gain (Amos 8:4-6). Isaiah condemned those who "devoured the vineyard" and hoarded

---

40. For a pithy review of the evidence of the extent to which these were practiced, see Horsley, *Jesus and Empire*, 115. Even if the Jubilee was not practiced in the first century, the egalitarian ideal continued to influence peasant hopes and politics. Fiensy, *Social History*, 9-14.

41. Berry, *Art of the Commonplace*, 296-97.

"the spoil of the poor" in their houses, thereby "crushing" the people and "grinding the face of the poor" (Isa 3:14–15).

The agrarian sensibilities of the prophets allow them to see that these ways of life lead to the fraying of the social fabric and the languishing and withering of the earth. As Isaiah laments, "The earth lies polluted under its inhabitants; for they have transgressed laws, violated statutes, broken the everlasting covenant. Therefore a curse devours the earth" (Isa 24:5–6).[42] The rulers and elite have instead made a covenant with death and social isolation, seeking refuge in lies (Isa 28:15).

The prophets held out hope for a renewal of the covenant. Isaiah points to the promise of an everlasting covenant that provides nourishment (Isa 55:3). It offers the invitation: "everyone who thirsts, come to the waters; and you that have no money, come, buy and eat!" It inaugurates a different economy, to "buy wine and milk without money and without price." This covenant, furthermore, challenges the opulence and logic of the imperial economy of consumption, asking; "Why do you spend your money for that which is not bread, and your labor for that which does not satisfy?" The alternative to these ways is not dieting on gruel, but Isaiah declares, "Listen to me carefully, and eat what is good, and delight yourselves in rich food" (Isa 55:1–3). A still later tradition of Isaiah frames this promise in the terms of the day of Jubilee as the suffering servant (treated in chapter 1) is anointed to proclaim, "The Year of the LORD's favor" (Isa 61:1).

The Sabbath offered rest and release—for all people, animals, and the land. It was not limited to an individual's action on one day of the week, but it was an integral part of covenantal relationships that oriented the whole of life. Sabbath practices turned people away from the busy, exploitative, and wealth seeking practices of empire toward the beautiful ways of creation that passed on the blessings of the Creator.

Gleaning on the Sabbath–Jesus and Jubilee

Christ's positive vision for the renewal of the sustainable and joyful life promised by the covenant between God, neighbor, and the land draws deeply upon these sabbath traditions of rest *and release*. Sabbath observance is at the heart of a repeated conflict in the Gospels. Because the calls for release are often forgotten by contemporary readers, this conflict is too often interpreted as being between legalistic Pharisees and a free-wheeling Jesus (and so it appears that Jesus is an opponent of Sabbath observance).[43] What is at stake

42. Davis, *Scripture, Culture, and Agriculture*, 17–20.

43. I want to underline that the Pharisees in the Gospels should not be read as a

in these stories is a conflict with what Amos lamented—the elite's limitation of the observance of the Sabbath to one day of the week while they crush the poor in their daily lives. Even more, Jesus is critical of a manner of interpreting tradition with an emphasis on purity codes that make the rich seem like they are the ones being faithful to God and the poor are the impure source of the decline of social and religious structures. Jesus' work here is twofold: he is seeking both to uncover the ideology of victim-blaming and injustice that the elites preached *and* to enact alternatives.

Perhaps most telling in Jesus' identification with the promise of Jubilee release, is his framing of his messianic task in just these terms in his first sermon in the Gospel of Luke (as we touched on in chapter 1). Having returned to the peasant village in which he was raised, *on the sabbath* Jesus goes to the synagogue. In the first century, the synagogue designates less a place and more of a gathering of the townspeople. This gathering is not simply what we would call a religious group, but it was a place where social, economic, and political judgements were made.[44] Jesus stood up and read from the scroll of the prophet Isaiah (Luke 4:16–17). He read, "The Spirit of the Lord is upon me, because he has anointed me to bring good news to the poor. He has sent me to proclaim release to the captives and recovery of sight to the blind, to let the oppressed go free, to proclaim the year of the Lord's favor" (Luke 4:18–19).[45]

Jesus points to the year of the Lord's favor, which is to say the Jubilee, as more than just an idea. Rather he hands the scroll back to the attendant, a person that is often responsible for tax collection and enforcing rulings on issues of debt.[46] He declares that "Today this scripture has been fulfilled in your hearing." (Luke 4:21). In so doing Christ is announcing a new exodus

---

standing for later Rabbinic Judaism that is in conflict with the burgeoning Christian *religion*. These anti-Semitic readings have a long and bloody history. The Pharisees in these stories are elites and retainers of the Empire. I take them more as literary figures than accurate historical portrayals of the first-century Pharisaic movement.

44. Horsley, *Galilee*, 223–32.

45. This quotation is primarily taken from the previously cited passage of Isaiah 61, only spliced within it is a piece of Isaiah 58:6 ("to proclaim *release* to the captives"), which makes the liberative reference to the Jubilee even more clear. Ringe, *Jesus, Liberation*, 38–39. Perhaps not coincidentally this passage from Isaiah condemns pious religious observance that is divorced from the practice of justice in everyday life, saying that the fast God chooses is the one that looses "the bonds of injustice." The religious practice that God desires is not the personal righteousness of denying oneself food, but of sharing "your bread with the hungry" (Isa 58:6–8). The works of sabbath release and rest are what hold the promise of rebuilding cities and the flourishing of creation (Isa 58:10–14).

46. Horsley, *Galilee*, 230.

from the tyrannical rule of the Empire. This is the work for which Jesus has been anointed: for the renewal of creation and the covenant.[47]

Jesus comes into conflict with Pharisees because their interpretation of tradition is more focused on purity than justice, on strictly observing one day of rest rather than an alterative order of release. Though the first century role of Pharisees in Galilee is far from clear, in the Gospels they are portrayed as advocates for expanding the application of purity rules beyond priests into the household and they often play the role of surrogates for the Temple elite in the territories beyond Jerusalem. The Pharisees used these boundaries of purity to protect their own status and to explain away the suffering outsider status of others. We might imagine this today as the narrative about how people with wealth or privilege have obtained these resources and this status because they work hard *and play by the rules*, whereas the poor *break the rules* and are a drain on the system. Never mind that the game is rigged, that the "successful" were, as the adage goes, born on third base but think that they hit a triple. Or, in relation to the food system, it is the myth that it is the ingenuity and prudence of the corporations that feeds the world, and their modes of development that bring poor peoples out of barbarity.

The parts of the Sabbath code that the Pharisees emphasized were those focused on the individual observance of rest—thereby losing sight of the calls for mutuality, generosity, and release. Jesus, by contrast, leads the disciples through a grain field on the Sabbath, and they pluck heads of grain to feed themselves (Mark 2:23). Through this act of gleaning and taking sustenance, Jesus was enacting the economy of mutuality and generosity that bound village life together and cared for the vulnerable.[48] These covenantal relationships, however, had become frayed through the funneling of the harvest to elites. Among these mechanisms of extraction was the Temple tax (it is sometimes speculated that the Pharisees tried to collect the Temple tax in Galilee for the Jerusalem elite or even collected it for themselves).

When the Pharisees see Jesus and the disciples gleaning on the Sabbath, they challenge him for breaking sabbath observance (Mark 2:24). Jesus responds by criticizing their focus on purity laws to the neglect of sabbath release.[49] Matthew's account of the story brings the Temple even more

47. He is also radicalizing these traditions and opening them up. Immediately following this story, Jesus appeals to the work of the prophet Elijah on behalf of the landless and against Ahab's treatment of the land and its people in the ways of empire (Luke 4:25–26). Brueggemann, *Land*, 92–94.

48. Lowery, *Sabbath and Jubilee*, 128.

49. Christ points to the precedent of David entering the Temple on the Sabbath and eating the bread of the presence (Mark 2:26). In so doing Jesus points toward the holy nature of his ministry, paralleling it with David's act of taking food on his campaign as

to the fore, as Jesus notes that the priests *work* in the Temple on the Sabbath, and he cites the prophetic declaration that God desires "mercy not sacrifice" (Matt 12:5–7/Hos 6:6). In referencing the hypocrisy of the Temple, Jesus brings into focus the inequitable distribution of goods through the extraction of taxes by the Temple.

For the elite focused on purity, it was those who engaged in an economy of priestly sacrifice that maintained covenant with God and the fertility of the land. Peace and prosperity was owed to those who could afford to pay these taxes and maintain their purity. The social ills that society faced, by contrast, were said to be due to those who were not able to pay their temple tax and who were eventually declared impure. The great majority who were living at the level of subsistence likely could not pay the Temple tax, as they were already stretched thin by the taxes and tolls that were more directly exacted with the threat of violence. On the elitist account, it was the poor's neglect of the sacrificial priestly relationship with God—not the exploitation of the Romans or the degradation of monoculture—that was leading to the fraying of the social order and infertility of the land.[50] In his act of nonviolent protest by gleaning from the fields *on the Sabbath*, Jesus pushes back at ostensible legality to uncover the cruelty and injustice that has been declared good by the dominant order.

Directly following this action Jesus elevates his nonviolent action to the point of civil disobedience.[51] He goes to the synagogue and sees a man with a withered hand (Mark 3:1). This sets the stage for a further challenge to the Pharisees limited understanding of the Sabbath. The Pharisees are spoiling for a conflict as well, as they are watching him "so that they might accuse him" (Mark 3:2). Already in a public place and acting on the holy day, Jesus heightens the drama by calling the man forward, and pausing to make sure the stakes are clear. He asks them: "Is it lawful to do good or do harm on the Sabbath, to save life or to kill?" This renders the Pharisees silent (Mark 3:4). This question peels away the structures and pieties that are taken to be normal and natural. It interrupts the narratives of purity and self-aggrandizement of the elite and the self-blame of everyone who falls short. It turns attention to the injured body of a vulnerable and marginalized man.

God's anointed. Furthermore, it also underlines that Christ and his disciples are hungry and in need. Myers, *Binding the Strong Man*, 160. The bread of the presence in the temple was a sign of God's hospitality, a reminder of the daily bread that God provides, and the priest was a representative of the people hosted by God. Therefore, even in this act of temple observance, the Sabbath was about the renewal of relationships of care and nourishment. Lowery, *Sabbath and Jubilee*, 117.

50. Herzog, *Parables as Subversive Speech*, 180–84.

51. Myers, *Binding the Strong Man*, 162.

It is as though they have been ridiculing him for using his salad fork on the main course while he is feeding a starving man. Jesus brings back into sight the promise that Sabbath rest is tied to release.

Jesus' action highlights the spirit of the repeated phrase associated with the Sabbath and the covenant: the reminder that you were a slave once and God delivered you out of the hand of Egypt. In this story the pious elite are not on the side of Aaron and Moses. Rather Christ "was grieved at their hardness of heart," a term closely associated with the cruelty of Pharaoh. Christ—the deliverer who will heal the sick—restores the man's hand.

In seeking to restore the man's hand, to renew the vision of Sabbath rest and release, and the covenantal care between God, neighbor, and land, Jesus challenged systems of power, exploitation, and extraction. Christ challenged the rendering of the Sabbath that insulates the elite. The Empire and its collaborators want to claim that it is only their storage cities, their piety, and their structures that can feed and secure us. They rule by a societal version of Stockholm syndrome, where people identify with the plight of their captors rather than their own. This is in no small part inculcated in our hearts through interpretations of the faith that focus on boundaries of purity and individual works, so that we can know *we* are saved and *they* are damned. We come to feel the values of the empire in our bones when we dress up in nice clothes and engage in sacrifices and rituals that maintain the status quo rather than mercy that heals the broken and feeds the hungry.

Christ came to bring the "year of the Lord's favor," the year of Jubilee—the most structural and systemic of the Sabbath rhythms. Sabbath release made way for a different kind of economy and food system. It was one that would challenge the funneling of resources to the wealthy. It would prohibit the growth of wealth through the charging of interest and it would call for an equitable redistribution of the land. It would demand agricultural practices that saw the land as a blessing owned by God, which must be cared for and allowed to rest. It would mean the renewal of regenerative agricultural practices that raised a variety of foods (rather than a single commodity) to care for the community and for the vulnerable. It would mean the toppling of the pyramidal structure of empire.

The elite knew this. That is why the scene ends with the Pharisees immediately conspiring "with the Herodians against [Jesus], how to destroy him" (Mark 3:6). The rich consistently hear the call to give away their privilege and wealth as a threat. Yet, if one can see beyond the systems of wealth and extraction, then one can also see that what is being offered is restful, joyful, just, and sustainable life.

From Food Banks to Food Justice

What would a Jubilee version of the commercial of the hungry child in Africa look like? Perhaps the child would be shown to be a member of a place and a community with a history. Could a brief commercial segment talk about how the history of empire and colonialism sowed the seeds of poverty? Could it narrate the transformation of local agriculture through the "Green Revolution"? Could the camera pan out to show fields degraded and robbed of soil fertility through the use of synthetic fertilizers and inputs, the desertification of lands through climate disruption, and the public health problems produced by industrialization and urbanization? Would it be possible to pithily capture the plight of farm workers in the fields and the lack of access to food that is shipped out of the community and all over the world? Could the camera show a split screen of extracted wealth and devastated communities and ecosystems? Could the purpose of the advertisement be more than sponsoring an individual child? Could it instead argue for a redistribution of resources and land to cultivate sustainable regenerative agrarian communities? While I do not doubt that this sort of storytelling is possible, the best cultural resource I know that connects these dots is still the poetry of the prophets and the life and ministry of Jesus, though we too often no longer have eyes to see the systemic critiques and alternatives that they are offering.

By failing to see the roots of the problems of the unsustainability of industrial agriculture, its abuse of workers, animals, and lands, and access to healthy food, we too often turn to the very systems that are deepening these problems. And so, regenerative sustainable agriculture gets coopted by the same corporate systems that minimize sustainable practice, maximize profits, exploit workers, and keeps healthy food out of the hands of the poor.

In a similar manner, in our efforts to feed the hungry individual, we lose sight of the systemic issues that produce hunger. Because we take our institutions of power for granted as normal and natural we end up turning to the same systems that produce poverty. In the United Sates feeding programs largely rely on the food and financial support provided by the corporate sector.[52] Handing the hungry person a box of processed foods is a bit like the Roman Empire pretending they are feeding the fishermen by giving them back a small fraction of their catch in the form of fish sauce. These acts of charity that are taken to be the solution to the problem rely on the unsustainable food systems that are producing enormous ecological debt for future generations and are built on the backs of impoverished food

52. Fisher, *Big Hunger*.

workers. Furthermore, the very people who are fed by these food banks and feeding programs are the workers who make these economies possible because these corporations do not pay them a living wage or provide benefits. A recent study found that in the United States corporations like Walmart and McDonald's receive one hundred fifty-four billion dollars in tax payer subsidies because they pay their workers so little that they are forced to go on programs like food stamps (programs that end up pouring more money back into Walmart).[53]

Yet, feeding programs, often driven by church groups, allow these same corporations to pose as the philanthropists who are fighting hunger. The food bank allows the elite to pretend that it is their virtue and resources that are holding everything together. This obscures the ways that wealth is extracted from the fertility of the land and the labor of workers, who are now portrayed as the recipients of charity. This is a partnership with corporate America that is paralleled across the environmental movement.[54] Lost in these charitable efforts, which take the current system for granted, are the insights into the causes of these problems, a consideration of long-term solutions, the possibilities of structural change, and collective action.[55]

A number of initiatives often grouped together under the banner of food justice are working to bring about systemic transformation. Land is being redistributed and commonly held through land trusts.[56] Small scale agriculture is nurtured through community members sharing the risks of the growing season through entering into partnership with farmers and buying a farm share or through the direct connections of a farmer's market. This shift from monocultured commodities to sustainable polycultures serves to nurture the land and to restore local communities.[57]

The focus on small farms in the food movement, however, often loses sight of larger issues of justice. The agrarian imagination in the United States often retreats to an individualistic Jeffersonian politics that is skeptical of governmental change and collective action.[58] The ideal vision, on this account, is a nation of small privately owned farms that restore white rural America. Just like the forebearer of this politics—the deistic doubting Thomas who owned slaves, venerated white supremacist myths about Anglo-Saxons, brokered the Louisiana purchase, and championed private

53. Jacobs, "Americans."

54. Dauvergne, *Environmentalism of the Rich*.

55. Kivel, "Social Service or Social Change?"

56. Eberhart, *Rooted and Grounded in Love*, 63–69.

57. Gottlieb and Joshi, *Food Justice*, 163–70.

58. Guthman, *Agrarian Dreams*, 174–76.

property through the land survey system—the white agrarian imagination often leaves out the history of slavery, genocide, and the reduction of everything to private property in its veneration of rural life.[59]

Like Jesus and the prophets, the *food justice* movement, however, is seeking to renew and transform sustainable communities. Buying clubs allow people of varying means to pool resources, so that each can get what they need, not just what they can afford. This connects regenerative organic farmers to people who do not have access to fresh and healthy produce, rather than making food that is nourishing to people and the land a luxury for the rich. Many of these networks seek to address the ways that food is woven in with culture and values, building on the capacities of communities rather than imposing elite aesthetics upon them. Perhaps most importantly, food security networks and councils bring together a variety of initiatives, organizations, and constituencies. Bringing community gardeners, local farmers, young mothers, teachers, nonprofit directors, public officials, long-time local residences, food workers, and poor people around the same table changes the conversation. This organization of organizations serves to undermine cultures of competition, where people focus on their own efficiency and productivity rather than being primarily concerned with shared systemic and communal problems. In this space avenues for collaboration among burgeoning alternatives become possible, and so does the promise of collective action and policy change.[60]

Bringing about systemic change will likely take a very long time. The hungry cannot wait for the cultivation of new systems and so in the transition period food banks serve a vital purpose. This is not to say that we should settle for an incremental pragmatism that often loses sight of alternative values and structures in its effort to get things done. We must not take our eyes off of the systemic issues. If we are simply triaging those injured by empire, our efforts cannot possibly keep up with their efficient and productive mechanisms of destruction. But nor can we spend our lives staring down the beastly structures of the elite, as we will crumble under cynicism, apathy, and despair.

We need to find social practices and local communities that will begin to incarnate these differences, and which will sustain this work for the long haul. In these social spaces we can find creative and shared ways in which

---

59. Douglas, *Stand Your Ground*, 11–14. Jennings, *Christian Imagination*, 225–26. The covenantal distribution of land is not the equal distribution of private property, as the relationship with the land is not seen as limited to the desires and needs of an individual but one's relationship to the land is fundamentally determined by one's relationships to God, neighbor, and the needs of the land. Brueggemann, *Land*, 177–83.

60. Gottlieb and Joshi, *Food Justice*, 201–6.

our lives are deepened and added to by something new and nourishing, rather than simply finding an aspect that must be cut out. This is the difference between a diet and a lifestyle change of less sitting, more joyful moving, and healthy foods. I have found glimpses of this in community gardens (chapter 2) and in dinner churches (chapter 6). These social experiments serve to sustain our moral courage, to give us a reprieve from the propaganda of empire and self-blame, to find material means to forge alternative food ways, and to channel collective energy that is too often dissipated in the solitude of an individual. These are not the answers, but they are practices and experiments that will sustain us in our long work.

Wilderness Feedings and Community Organizing

So long as the alternative food system does not blossom forth all at once, we will need to engage in the extended work of challenging the moral imaginary and creating social experiments. The imperial food system operates through material machinery—through the architecture of large silos, tilled fields, interstate systems, large food processing plants, enormous box stores, and barges and ports connecting economies all over the world. This landscape and habitat shape the hearts and minds of people who look at themselves as consumers, thinking their power is in individual choices. To challenge and transform these systems we will need to begin to build alternatives in limit spaces where the imperial grasp is not quite so firm. This might mean the urban farm in the abandoned lot, or in the Christian community that recenters itself around the study of its central texts and the sustenance of its subversive spiritual practices.

In the Scriptures we see Jesus engaging in this work of teaching, healing, and organizing in households and in the wilderness.[61] While Jesus does teach, heal, and demonstrate in the public place of the village assembly (the synagogue) and eventually even in the streets and Temple of Jerusalem, most of his work takes place in other spaces—on the plain, by the seaside, in the house, out in the wilderness. His work in these spaces is subversive and constructive, as he tries to restore people into sustainable, just, and joyful communities.

When Jesus empowers the disciples to take on his work of teaching and healing, he sends them out to the households of the surrounding villages two by two (Mark 6:6–7). He sends them on a ministry of healing and hospitality to villages to restore covenantal community. He instructs them to take nothing for their journey "no bread, no bag, no money in their belts"

61. Myers, *Binding the Strong Man*, 125–26; 149–51.

(Mark 6:8). Rather they are to rely on the hospitality of local households. They are to heal the bodies broken by empire, to proclaim transformation (*metanoia*), and to rely upon the economy of covenantal generosity in the villages (Mark 6:11–13).

The subsequent sending out of the seventy-two messengers and organizers in the Gospel of Luke more fully describes this process of healing and hosting. Jesus sends out the disciples as community organizers who both say and incarnate whenever they enter a household: "Peace to this house!" (Luke 10:5).[62] They are agents who are bringing not just the cessation of violence, but as the Hebrew notion of *shalom* holds, the fullness of life (like the largest vision of sabbath that is not just rest but restoration and delight).[63] This peace is realized in the renewal of the economy of mutuality and generosity as the seventy-two are counseled both to give to others and to rely upon them. Christ instructs: "Whenever you enter a town and its people welcome you, eat what is set before you; cure the sick who are there, and say to them, 'The kingdom of God has come near you'" (Luke 10:8–9). The disciples are showing the way of God's kingdom. The disciples bring the gifts of their ministry *and* they bring material needs that demand people practice covenantal generosity. The elite would see their action as humiliation. The rich prefer to play the role of host so as to make clear they are the ones that provide. The privileged like to conspicuously display their status. The disciples, by contrast, show that the humble path of simplicity fosters peace. Their reliance upon others does not lead to scarcity, but cultivates community. How often does our own pride get in the way of our being hosted by others, gaining from their wisdom, and cultivating a sense of mutuality and interdependence?

In the Gospel of Mark, the sending forth of the disciples in simplicity and relying on hospitality is immediately contrasted with an excessive birthday party of Herod Antipas. This banquet pulls together not just Herod's family but the "courtiers and officers" and "leaders of Galilee" (Mark 6:21). While Jesus' operatives move about the region organizing and renewing households and communities to realize the kingdom of God, the elite agents of empire gorge themselves on the stolen fruits of the region. If the violence implicit in the lavish banquet of the wealthy was not clear enough, Herod Antipas ends up cutting off the prophet John the Baptist's head and placing it on a platter (Mark 6:27–28).

Herod's food economy, which is built on the backs of peasants, is contrasted with the covenantal economies of mutuality and generosity and

62. Horsley, *Jesus and the Powers*, 136.
63. Heltzel, *Resurrection City*, 22–24.

connected to the oppressive ways of empire that have plagued the people of God in the past. The Baptist was introduced in the Gospel as a figure that prophetically cried out against the violence of empire, echoing other prophets that led the people out of bondage and into the wilderness (Mark 1:2–3). In his attempt to silence him through execution, Herod and his network of collaborators are tied to the kings who killed the prophets.

The setting of the next scene in the wilderness, where the hungry are fed, heightens these associations, as the current order of empire is aligned with the archetypal imperial food economy of Egypt. Immediately after escaping the armies of Egypt the Israelites are led into the wilderness where their moral imaginations are reshaped and their community is transformed through a different kind of food economy. Every day the Lord rains down manna from heaven for them to eat (Exod 16). But again, at stake are not just hungry individuals being fed. The Israelites in the wilderness were food workers who were charged with two tasks in Egypt. They built the storage cities of Pithom and Ramses and performed all sorts of work in the fields. They grew grain and then built the silos that stored this grain—the labor of production and the means of distribution in the food system (Exod 1:1, 14). The silos were the source of Pharaoh's power, as they allowed him to centralize the location of food and dole it out on his terms. This produced a pyramidal hierarchy with a few well-fed elites at the top, some middle managers in between, and hordes of slaves at the bottom. The lasting effect of this system was that the people came to trust in Pharaoh for their sustenance, and they internalized the moral economy and food system of Egypt (Exod 6:6–9).[64]

The people are led out into the wilderness to escape both the physical and spiritual slavery of Egypt. Their hearts and relationships are slowly reshaped through different forms of production, consumption, and distribution. Rather than slaving away in the fields, in the Exodus narrative the Israelites are told to *glean* the food that God provides each morning (Exod 16:15–16). While the verb here is often translated "gather," the Hebrew word means "to glean," and it is repeated to excess in the passage. The act of gleaning involves picking up the leftovers in the field. In Egyptian cave drawings it is clear from the bent over bodies of those charged with this task that they were at the bottom of the hierarchy.[65] And as we have already noted, in the Hebrew law, the gleanings of the field were to be left to provide for the most vulnerable. In these wilderness feedings, the Israelites were freed from the bondage and oppression of their Egyptian taskmasters, but they were not

64. Davis, *Scripture, Culture, and Agriculture*, 69–73.

65. Davis, *Scripture, Culture, and Agriculture*, 75.

to take this freedom to mean that they were now autonomous consumers. The act of gleaning reminded them of their dependence and vulnerability, *to* cultivate compassion in their hearts. Gleaning, in this food economy, did not serve as a boot to the head of the poor to remind them of their lowly place. Rather it put everyone in a position on their knees to be close to the earth, to be reminded that its bounty was not their possession, *so that* everyone could have enough. "Morning by morning they gleaned [the manna], as much as each needed" (Exod 16:21). This emphasis on sufficiency was further reinforced in the practices of eating and distribution that accompanied the manna, as each was given according to their need.[66]

This equitable food economy served not only to sustain the bodies of the people in the wilderness, but also to reshape their hearts. Throughout the story the people protest, initially lamenting that they ever left Egypt and its food system (Exod 16:2–3). The slaves have been taken out of Egypt, but Egypt has not been taken out of these former slaves. Therefore, the people are tested and trained with the rhythms of daily bread (Exod 16:4–5). Furthermore, this is the first place in the biblical story when people are given the gift of sabbath rest (Exod 16:22–30). These rhythms of sabbath rest and daily bread serve to transform this community so that it can be capable of caring for the land they will eventually enter.

Similarly, Christ leads his disciples out into the wilderness after they have returned from their first mission to the villages to restore covenantal community. He takes them across the sea to the wilderness so that they can "*rest* a while" (Mark 6:31). When they arrive, they see a great crowd that has gathered and is waiting for them. Jesus has compassion upon them and teaches them (Mark 6:34). But as it grows late the disciples become concerned about how the people will eat. They suggest that they send the people away to the surrounding villages so that they can "*buy* something for themselves to eat" (Mark 6:36). Jesus responds by telling them, "you give them something to eat." To which they rejoin, "Are we to go and buy two hundred *denarii* worth of bread, and give it to them to eat" (Mark 6:37)? In this exchange the disciples show that they are still looking to the economy of the Empire to feed and sustain them. They are looking to its marketplace to buy food and are still even thinking in terms of the imperial coinage of denarii.[67]

What they don't seem to see is that surrounding them are the producers of food. Galilee was the breadbasket of Israel. Luke sets the story at Bethsaida, which means literally, "house of fish" (Luke 9:10). Christ directs their

---

66. Davis, *Scripture, Culture, and Agriculture*, 76.

67. Carter, *Matthew and the Margins*, 306.

attention to the people and asks them to "go and see" what food they can find. In their first survey they find five loaves and two fish. Jesus then gives them instructions to organize smaller groups of around fifty people. Christ takes, blesses, breaks, and gives the food. These sacramental verbs designate the actions whereby objects are shifted from being commodities to be sold, to blessings to be shared. Rather than an instance of supernatural multiplication, this is a story of community organizing that directs the people of the earth to turn away from the imperial forms of distribution and to once again turn to each other and find sustenance in the sustainable ways of sufficiency, mutuality, and generosity.[68] Through these acts trust is shifted from the Emperor, whose head was imprinted on the denarii, to the Creator of the good earth. This leads not just to enough, but to an abundance that will sustain them. They gather up twelve baskets full of leftover bread and fish (a basket for each tribe that will be restored to the land) (Mark 6:43).

The contrast between systems, economies, and moral imaginaries is underlined by Jesus' initial response to the people. He has compassion for them, "because they were like sheep without a shepherd" (Mark 6:34). This is an image in the biblical imagination that points to the underlying political context that has caused the suffering of the people. In the Ancient Near East kings were often spoken of as shepherds (just search your memory for Egyptian art where the Pharaoh is portrayed with the crooked staff of a shepherd). The prophet Ezekiel famously condemned the elite of his time as bad shepherds. They first fed themselves, whereas good shepherds "feed the sheep" (Ezek 34:2). The elite do not strengthen the weak, heal the sick, or bring back the lost, instead the sheep are scattered and slaughtered for their banquets (Ezek 34:3–5). By contrast the Lord will serve as shepherd and will gather the sheep and bring them into rich pastures (Ezek 34:14–15). The Lord will make a covenant of peace with them and restore the fertility of the land and will break the bonds of oppression (Ezek 35:25–27). Jesus, likewise, has the disciples organize the people to sit "in groups on the *green grass*" (Mark 6:39). He leadeth them to green pastures and by still waters.

This wilderness feeding was a direct challenge to the imperial system and way of life. Simply gathering 5,000 people was considered sedition in the Empire and was punishable by crucifixion. The number Mark indicates of 5,000 men is, not coincidentally, the size of a battalion.[69] In the Gospel of John's account of the story, these political aspects are directly addressed as Jesus withdraws because he realizes they are about to "take him by force to

68. Myers, *Binding the Strong Man*, 206. Robert C. Linthicum draws strong parallels between Jesus' methods of ministry and the tactics of broad-based community organizing, especially around relational meetings (*Transforming Power*, 132).

69. Hendricks, *Politics of Jesus*, 183.

make him king" (John 6:15). Jesus was not that kind of messiah. Rather, he was anointed to bring about a different kingdom through nonviolent experiments that will restore and transform communities and all of creation.

Feed My Sheep–Renewing the Church

Up to this point I have said very little about the church. This is, in part, because I am reading the Gospels and the word *church* only occurs there three times (all in Matthew). This late appearance is also because the categories and structures connected with churches in the United States can serve as serious impediments for our understanding of Christ's teaching and the role that it could play today. American churches often limit their work to the domain of belief, which abstracts individuals from their bodily, communal, political, and economic life. The word translated as "church" in Greek (*ekklesia*) commonly refers not to building that is set apart, but to an assembly of people called together in a public place for the common good (which came up earlier in relation to the public gathering Nehemiah called of the people of Israel). The popular contemporary understanding of "church" might cause us to miss the call to fishermen, who labor at the bottom of the economic hierarchy, to fish out unjust elites.

In the United Sates churches are typically seen as voluntary organizations whose activities are synonymous with what goes on in *one* building. Such limitations obscure the reversals of the kingdom that lead to the renewal of mutual and generous covenantal life in the household, the marketplace, the field, and the community. Congregational life often compartmentalizes the holy to the time of Sunday, a vision of the Sabbath that conveniently edits out the demands for the redistribution of lands and release of debts. Furthermore, this emphasis on purity baptizes the managers of the status quo who show up to the sanctuary in their Sunday best, and turns our attention away from the wilderness spaces where the power of the people is bringing forth the sustenance of sustainable ways of life.[70]

Many manifestations of the church in our context operate in tandem with the ways of empire, as they are focused on individuals and even govern themselves on the same logic that seeks to monetize everything (setting priorities around budgets and membership numbers). Within this system and moral imaginary it is too easy to see the issues around food in terms of individual eaters who either eat too much or go hungry. Because structures of power are taken for granted as normal and natural we turn to these same systems to solve these problems—organizing food banks,

---

70. Berry, *Art of the Commonplace*, 309–13, 318–20.

or if we are truly radical, encouraging people to change their light bulbs and buy big green organic food. This leaves the unsustainable structures of monoculture industrial agriculture and unjust forms of unfettered corporate capitalism intact and unchallenged. Furthermore, it obscures the possibilities of food justice, where we can shape different collectives and inspire new social imaginaries.

But I have also waited to talk about the church in hopes that we can renew and reimagine it. The church, along with the family, is one of the few limit spaces left where the empire has not completely tightened its grip. In churches and at home people still have experiences of community that are driven by different values, and where practices of mutuality and generosity can serve as the rule rather than the exception.

The church could be one of the central places where this transformation happens. Groups like the Black Church Food Security Network, based out of Baltimore, work to empower black communities and economies by viewing the land holdings of black churches as an already existing land trust and connecting growers and churches up and down the Eastern seaboard.[71] Many churches are finding ways to repurpose their buildings to partner with their surrounding community to bring about healing and health to individual and social bodies by providing office space for nonprofits, meeting spaces for communities, hubs for artists, and facilities and volunteers for after-school programs.[72]

The church provides not only the network, the physical architecture, and the grounds where food can be sold and grown, but also a space where alternative, sacramental, and sustainable community can be cultivated. At church people can connect over the higher common purpose of sharing God's love and working for justice. In a world of tailgating and spectatorship, where we must numb and dumb ourselves down to a lowest common denominator, the possibility of sharing our whole selves in fellowship and communion is revolutionary. While we may be unpracticed at being together in this way, the rituals and hymns of worship, the spiritual disciplines of tradition, and the stories of Scripture provide us with ways to liberate our hearts from the values and habits of empire.

The church could also be moved to be centered around other spaces. Christian communities are currently forming around pieces of land rather than buildings, centering their shared life around a garden or a functioning farm. Other communities are reviving ancient models of

71. Banks, "Black Church."

72. For a collection of contemporary examples of such work see Jha, *Transforming Communities*.

fellowship—meeting in people's houses, worshiping through a shared meal, or creating intentional living communities.[73]

A more systemic perspective challenges the compartmentalization of faith into the conscience of an individual or a single building. It opens the possibility for expansion. In some ways, we might need to start seeing creation as a church, but in other ways we need to look beyond the church.

Toward the end of the Gospel of John Jesus repeatedly tells Peter that if he loves him he will tend and feed his sheep (John 21:15–17). This seems like a good place to start: ministries of feeding that see the sheep, the field, and the good shepherd. We can start with the slow transformative work of alternative, loving, compassionate, life-giving social experiments.

---

73. For a directory of such ministries see http://christianfoodmovement.org/.

Part Two: **Practices of the Kingdom**

4

Teaching in Parables

There once was a teacher who traveled to a neighboring city for a gathering about the ecological crisis. The teacher arrived hoping to find new practices, living models, and lasting relationships. On the first night of the gathering everyone packed into a room and watched a renowned climate scientist show graph after graph of radical if not cataclysmic change taking place on a planetary scale. The facts mounted, they piled, they weighed down the room. At the close of the lecture, the decorated expert had nothing more to offer than a series of contradictory platitudes and false fixes: "People are ultimately good and fundamentally self-interested. I think we can switch to electric cars pretty soon." The teacher was stunned. She had heard the same lecture decades ago. Neither the content nor the pedagogy of the movement had changed. As the gathering went on, the people continued to find themselves captive to experts and talking heads, all long on facts and short on imagination and action. The teacher returned home, convicted of one thing: the experts will not save us.

THERE IS A NARRATIVE or a story that shapes liberal approaches to education and politics that I now flatly reject: the idea that you simply need to give individuals the facts and trust them to make their own decisions. This narrative is inadequate because it avoids the systems and structures that shape our lives, it overlooks collective action, it has misdiagnosed the problem, and it is, well, a lifeless pedagogy.

And yet, this narrative of the need to inform the public has driven much of the environmental movement. Hence, we get the experts to present on the facts of the matter to a passive audience and then conclude by suggesting how individuals can change their habits of consumption. Such an effort *assumes as given* the very structures that are premised on unsustainable growth, endless consumption, and rising emissions. Rather than questioning or reforming the structure of the supermarket, this approach assumes it as inevitable.

Instead of criticizing corporate institutions that put profits over people, that are rewarded for externalizing their costs to ecosystems, workers, and future generations, it turns to them. This approach places the locus of action on individual choice, which in a habitat driven by corporate power, is actually very limited. Even when successful, in this context, the result is an informed individual who is formed by a world moving with all its might in the other direction. While the action steps of alternative consumption are often offered as an achievable baby-step that will empower individuals (the glimmer of light in the doom and gloom), they instead function to make people feel responsible for matters that are completely out of their control. Instead of offering hope this is a recipe for avoidance and denial.

One of the reasons that this pedagogy has been so prevalent in efforts to tackle the climate crisis is that it sets up the problem so that the informed and the experts are in the right and the onus for change is on others. This model of informing the public is deeply related to the colonial assumption that problems are largely based on dark chaotic ignorance.[1] The assumed problem is the dark other. In this scenario, what is needed is the educated, enlightened savior who brings the facts to bear on the situation. The (white) light of our gleaming city on the hill simply needs to be expanded so that others can be included in our order.

We are constantly taught that the central tension in our world is the light of civilized reason struggling with the dark forces of chaotic ignorance. The news reinforces this on a twenty-four-hour loop as it reports on the threats of the Islamic terrorist, the mentally ill gunman, the dark criminal, or the chaotic forces of natural disaster. All of these threaten the informed, reasonable order of our world. Missing from these stories of shootings and arrests are contexts of exploitation and poverty, the erosion of social and civic support systems, the hopelessness of broken homes. Lost in the story of the record hurricane are the warming waters of anthropogenic climate change, the destruction of wetlands, and the paving of earth that could weather the blow. This framing allows us to assume that the real problems are external to us and our ways of life.

Similarly, in matters of climate change, the problem is framed as the ignorant conservative skeptic who refuses to acknowledge the facts. Yet, what are we to do with of the fact that since the question has been tracked, most Americans have remained at least fairly concerned about climate change?[2]

---

1. Keller, *Face of the Deep*, 6. I have explored these dynamics of the relationship between pedagogy and climate change in more detail in Dickinson, *Exercises in New Creation*, esp. 11–17; 59–62.

2. Saad and Jones, "U.S. Concern."

Even more Americans consider themselves to be environmentalists. Yet, many fewer find avenues to action.[3]

While skepticism is a real problem in the United States, and perhaps one of the few true domains of American exceptionalism, the lack of political will and structural change seems to go much deeper than ignorance about the facts. There are layers of denial. One can be in denial that climate change is happening or that humans play a role in it. One can also be in denial about the *implications* of climate catastrophe.[4] It might be more logically coherent to deny that humans play a role in climate change and go about business as usual, than to look at the facts regarding warming temperatures, melting ice sheets, expanding deserts, ocean acidification, extreme weather patterns, species extinction, strains on agriculture, geopolitical instability, spiking refugee populations, and decide that we need to use canvas instead of plastic bags. Both the skeptical and the convinced seem to be unable to make the kinds of radical and collective changes needed to address such enormous problems.

This is in part because the problem is not dark ignorant chaos, but *the problem is unjust order*. Global emissions do not result from some collection of mistakes, but are the result of the smooth functioning of systems, institutions, structures, and apparatuses. These systems are intertwined with cultural values that shape our ways of life. Individuals, then, might *know* that their consumer choices at the supermarket will ultimately bring suffering to the poor, other species, and their children and grandchildren, but their lives are shaped by certain habits and time pressures, by economic limits, by social and familial expectations, and desires slowly shaped by culture and media.

There is an entire order (or really a complex web of orders) that is pushing all of us toward ruin. This is an uncomfortable realization because it means that we will need to do more than educate others so that they can change. It means that our very ways of life must change. But, as is the fundamental premise of this book and the gospel, this is the good news whereby we lose our lives so that we can save them.

To do this work we will need a pedagogy that can challenge and transform those who think they are already informed but who have been formed by unjust order, rather than a pedagogy that seeks to fill up the empty minds of the ignorant. We will need pedagogies that unveil the structures and visions that surround us, but that we take for granted as normal and natural. And we will need habits and practices that will

3. Peterson, *Everyday Ethics*, 111.

4. Norgaard, *Living in Denial*.

transform our minds, hearts, imaginations, and relationships so that we can live into new ways of life *together*.

Christ's use of parables gets some of this work done. The parables turn our attention to everyday spaces where imperial power hides in plain sight. Often our attention is trained on the spectacular—as we focus on stories of heroes and villains. The news draws our attention to exceptional places and cosmopolitan centers of politics and commerce. These narrative structures make it seem that the real issues are distant from our lives. Jesus' vignettes and miniature tales force us to look with new eyes at the order that surrounds us. Through little stories that are sometimes humorous, sometimes horrible, and often a bit absurd, Jesus brings our gaze closer to home and unveils the violence that lurks behind the veneer of the tailored suit and the signs of success that the elite don. In so doing we are forced to confront the unconscious ways in which we have come to regard wealth and success as synonymous with virtue, and poverty and hardship as signs of vice. Instead, we begin to see the ways that economies of extraction and exploitation are built on predatory lending, the reduction of land to commodity, and the exploitation of labor. All of this is covered up by the trappings of false generosity in which the displaced, the poor, and the destitute are fed with scraps from the tables of the rich, scraps from what was and should be the sustainable and joyful commonwealth of God's good creation. These parables serve to transfigure the ordinary and to enliven the imagination so that we can begin to see paths of resistance *and* transformation.

The Pedagogy of Parables

Many of us have been trained to read the parables in ways that abstract them from social settings and everyday life. This way of reading makes the parables into allegories in which the material and communal elements are easily cast aside for a kernel of meaning concerned with the afterlife. Or it is as though Jesus is the pedagogue of the children's story that explicitly says: "the moral of the story is: don't worry, be happy." By reading for the moral we peel away the story, its ordinary, material, social, economic, and political elements, so that we can get an abstract principle. We hold this moral, stand apart from the world, and apply it.

Jesus liked to tell little stories, but they were not allegories with a heavenly meaning. His parables were earthy stories addressed to agrarian and communal life.[5] As we touched on in chapter 2 with the parable of the Sower, Jesus was speaking to peasants. The stories he tells are not so thin

5. Herzog, *Parables as Subversive Speech*, 3.

on bodily life and social relationships that we can look *through* them to the kernel of an idea. Rather, these stories are thick, and so we should not look past their engagement in embodied, everyday, and economic concerns.[6] These are stories that we are supposed to inhabit. They interpret us, rather than us interpreting them just for an abstract principle. As we put ourselves in these stories we find that what we have taken to be ordinary is strange and we begin to see the ways that it could be transfigured.[7]

For example, Jesus' parable of the Good Samaritan is especially helpful because it comes from a scene in which Jesus is explicitly engaged in the give and take of teaching. The Gospel of Luke sets the scene, writing, "And see: A Torah Scholar stood up and posed a question to test him: Teacher, what must I do to have life in its eternal fullness?" Jesus replied, "What is in the Torah? How do you read it?" (Luke 10:25–26).[8] The scholar replied with the classic Hebrew answer of the *Shema* (Deut 6:5) on loving God, and its further interpretation to love one's neighbor (Lev 19:18). Jesus affirmed this answer, but the scholar wanted to defend his question, and he pressed further, wanting to know, "Who is my neighbor?" (Luke 10:27–29). Anti-Semitic readings of the Gospels have often supposed that this exchange is about a conflict between Jesus and Torah. But nothing in the story indicates that Jesus is rejecting the Hebrew Scriptures. Instead he is lifting up their radical vision. The parable that follows, then, is not a thin illustration that is centered on providing an abstract principle of universal love that exceeds the limits of the Jewish vision of love. Rather, Jesus tells the parable to render concretely what love looks like.[9]

Jesus tells a parable that places the hearers in the action, *and* that points toward some political and economic problems that are not often recognized. He tells of a man who was traveling on the road between Jericho and Jerusalem and who was beaten and left for dead by bandits. Two temple elites, a priest and a Levite, pass him by, but a Samaritan stops to help the man. He binds his wounds and takes him to an inn—paying for his stay and care and vowing to pay more when he returns to check on him (Luke 10:29–37).

To understand what loving God and neighbor, what the fullness of life looks like, we have to see the parable in its social, economic, and political framing. From the perspective of the elite, bandits arise from the vice-ridden poor, but for those with a wider view, banditry is a symptom of societal

6. McFague, *Speaking in Parables*, 4.

7. McFague, *Speaking in Parables*, 71–72.

8. Translation from Schottroff, *Parables of Jesus*, 131.

9. Schottroff, *Parables of Jesus*, 132–34.

decay. First-century Judea had been devastated by war and layers of taxation from Rome, the Herodians, and the Temple. As people were displaced from family farms, as the bonds of life-giving relationships broke down, and many were cast out into the vulnerable space of abject poverty, they often turned to the only forms of power that remained. The people who rob the man and beat him are both violent *and* desperate. The bandit is not a figure of individual corruption but is a member of a broken social and political body.[10] The bandits that beat the man on the road to Jerusalem are, in a way, the children conceived by the corruption of the Temple rulers—with their banking practices and their taxes. Not only do the priest and the Levite not bother to get their hands dirty with the blood of the battered man, but they are the more powerful and wealthy part of the syndicate that has left him for dead by the side of the road.

What does keeping the covenant and loving one's neighbor look like? The parable proposes it looks like a Samaritan, who, in the midst of a crumbling society of riotous poor and callous elite, sees those who are suffering and engages in the merciful act of binding wounds, in the time-consuming work of getting involved, and in the resource-demanding efforts of generosity and hospitality. Furthermore, the blessed life of love incarnated by the Samaritan through acts of care and interdependence in the foreground, brings back into focus the buzzing and beautiful world of God's blessing that is always lurking in the background, but which empire obscures.[11] This story takes the teachings of love and brings them close. Rather than standing apart, we find ourselves standing amid the troubles. Standing on this dusty road next to a Samaritan that we might not normally think of as virtuous unveils the structures of exploitation around us and turns us to look at our own actions and involvement.

The parable serves to reframe the ordinary. Jesus is trying to teach peasants a different way of seeing the world. Unjust order obscures its brutality, callousness, exploitation, and corruption by clothing itself in virtue and reason. The dominant order shapes the hearts of the people through narratives, rituals, songs, holidays, and iconography to make its ways seem normal, natural, good, right, and rational (the reason why today the national anthem is a matter of protest and extreme reaction). The parables allow us to stand at a different angle so that we can see past the glimmer and sheen of this social fabric and get a glimpse behind the curtain. Jesus' parables stage ordinary situations in such a way that those who are in power are not aligned with virtue or the light of civilizing reason and the causes

---

10. Horsley and Hanson, *Bandits, Prophets, and Messiahs*, 48–59.

11. Berry, *Blessed Are the Peacemakers*, 64–65.

of the problems are not necessarily ignorant dark chaos. Rather he gives his hearers the vocabulary to name the ways that the present unjust order is constructed. Showing the present order as something that is actively made opens the possibility that the current order is not natural, but it is part of specific histories and institutions, and therefore it could be otherwise.[12] The bandits' violence is a symptom of the callous greed and exploitation of the elite. But the hope lies in the renewal of covenantal relationships whereby we love our neighbor and, in turn, love God. (The political aspect of the Samaritan's mercy and hospitality should not be lost, as they are not simply nice, but they are emergent acts that could have the cascading effects of cultivating solidarity and building the bonds necessary for collective action and sustainable life.) The pedagogy of the parable locates our lives in the contested space of different social, political, and economic formations rather than simply presenting us with information.

Forming Hearts and Ways of Life

One of the last things my mom said to me when she dropped me off at college was, "You are going to learn so much, and some of it might even happen in the classroom." A tiny part of this comment might have been a jab at my academic performance up to that point (I was a poor student who had mostly slept through my high school education). But I think her primary point was to acknowledge that the residential experience of living with other young adults would be life changing. Sharing rooms, meals, daily rhythms, life stories, uninterrogated values, jokes, dreams, conflicts, rituals, and celebrations (also known as parties) would be more educational and formative than anything I learned in the classroom.

My mother's admission, or perhaps even counsel, was rather remarkable given that she and my father were both teachers in the traditional sense. They had, for certain parts of their lives, devoted themselves to the promise of the classroom. Yet, she was able to recognize that education is not just about information that is stored in one's mind, but that it is formation that shapes the heart.[13] When I returned to teach and minister to the same college many years later, this truth was profoundly clear to me as I struggled to raise issues of justice and sustainability in a habitat that was shaping creatures for futures of corporate work and country club living. (Though, as with any institution, there were many lively and powerful alternatives that struggled with this dominant force.) If we want to counter unjust orders we would

12. Herzog, *Parables as Subversive Speech*, 28.
13. Smith, *Desiring the Kingdom*.

be well served in thinking of education as broadly as possible—seeing the stadium, the supermarket, and the social media feed as schools that are shaping our hearts, relationships, and lives.

This broader understanding of education can also help us see the obstacles that prevent people who supposedly care about the environment from acting upon those concerns. For example, one study found that suburbanites who are more educated, affluent, and informed about environmental issues are *more likely* to use harmful chemical fertilizers, herbicides, and pesticides on their lawns. To repeat, the people who know that it is harmful to themselves and public health are *more* likely to use these inputs on their lawns.[14] The *fact* of public harm and the desire to change are outweighed by the public pressure to maintain one's lawn, to maintain a certain manicured aesthetic, to keep up property values, to follow local ordinances, to conform in neighborhoods anxious about difference, and to incarnate certain visions of the good life and the American dream.[15] In this instance, a brief lesson on water pollution and hazardous waste is counterbalanced by a lifetime of tests and assessments on identity, conformity, and success.

To begin to organize and mobilize the informed masses, and to make ways of life that others can be invited into, we need to begin to challenge these institutions, habitats, practices, values, and relationships. But before we can even do that, we must see them for what they are. Part of what gives the mechanisms of consumerism so much power is their invisibility. As with gender roles (and in no small part through gender roles), the suburbs shape us in ways that are taken as natural. For example, I might think of myself as a man who is (naturally?) defined by strength, which means protecting and providing for my family in certain ways. Even if one were to grant this highly questionable premise, I doubt the providing and protecting of the mythical cave man looks much like what is brought home to the suburban garage. Should the drive for the shiny car be chalked up to natural impulse *or* social convention and billions in advertising? As with racial identity (and in no small part through racial formations) the organization of time and the stratification of class of the dominant order are taken as normal. As white people who do not think they have a particular culture because their culture is dominant, and therefore transparent, the habitat of consumerism is invisible because it is so close and ever-present.

We need a pedagogy that does not look past the details of our everyday lives—a pedagogy, like that of the parables, that brings the culture of work, the organization of the household, and the ambitions and dreams of creatures

14. Robbins, *Lawn People*, 2–3.
15. Robbins, *Lawn People*, 3–16.

into focus. Situating learning in this ordinary space brings the learner in closer. It brings to center stage *figures* as persons not just as statistics. It dramatizes habits and it paints our social settings in exaggerated relief to foster empathy, action, gentleness, judgement, and passion. This pedagogy does not bracket out community, contexts, economics, and politics. Rather it seeks to do the critical work of showing the unjust scandal of what we take for granted, and to do the transformative work of changing hearts, mending wounds, and making new. There is so much that we still have to learn about sustainable and joyful life, and some of it might even happen in the classroom. Much of it will happen in community and in everyday spaces.

Unveiling Unjust Orders

Many of Jesus' parables serve to unveil the unjust order that surrounds us, but remains unnamed and unacknowledged because it is dressed up in fine robes and religious vestments. We often miss this aspect of the parables because we too are trained to identify power and success with virtue. This tendency coupled with our habit of reading the parables as allegories for heavenly belief or abstract principle, leads to particularly perverse interpretations. Whereas some of the parables are told to reveal the cruelty of the elite, we read the malicious plantation owner or violent king as a stand-in for God. Yet, these parables are told for the opposite purpose. God's kingdom is held up as *antithetical* to the all too familiar and lamentable scenario that is being narrated. This contrast is often obscured in translation, as *homoioun* is rendered "like" (implying sameness) rather than opening some of the parables with, "you should *compare* the kingdom of God with" the following story.[16]

This antithesis between God's justice and the unjust order of empire is often acknowledged in the parable of the Unjust Judge.[17] Jesus tells of a widow who repeatedly brings her claim before "a judge who neither feared God nor had respect for people" (Luke 18:2–3). The widow demands justice, but the judge will not even hear her case. Eventually he relents, not so that justice may be done but so that she will leave him alone (Luke 18:4–5). In this parable the antithesis is unavoidable, the incarnation of the justice system (the judge) is confronted by the incarnation of those who are to be protected by God's justice (the widow) (Exod 22:21–24). The parallel with contemporary political cartoons that unveil the corruption and inequity of the justice system is striking.

16. Schottroff, *Parables of Jesus,* 104.
17. Schottroff, *Parables of Jesus,* 192.

The judge exemplifies the retainer class that played an important role in the Empire. Between the elite and the mass of peasants and workers were bureaucrats, scribes, priests, and soldiers who maintained the order that kept power and wealth flowing upwards. The judge's role was to twist the traditions of law, Torah, and justice so that the machinery of exploitation and extraction not only continued to function, but so that it would appear to be in line with the will of God.[18] The imperial cities needed to keep these engines of extraction turning, as even a smaller city like Sepphoris (Antipas's city rebuilt near Nazareth), to keep afloat, required at least 1,600,000 kilograms of grain, 2,000,000 liters of wine, and 100,060 of oil per year, or 115 donkey loads per day.[19] Sepphoris was a city of 8,000, so just imagine what it would take for the million or so inhabitants of the city of Rome. All of this far outpaced rural surplus. After extraction and other necessary demands, it is estimated that peasants had between one-fifth to one-thirteenth of their harvest on which to subsist.[20]

Jesus underlines these antithetical kingdoms by contrasting the ways of the worldly judge with God. God will grant justice to those who cry out to him and it will be swift (Luke 18:6–7). Yet, Jesus does not simply place God into the same system and say that God would act differently. Instead he concludes by turning the tables on the hearer and turning over the tables of the present order by asking about God's judgement. He asks: if God's judge, the Son of Man, comes to earth, will he find faith? (Luke 18:8). The Son of Man, or a better translation would be the Human One, is a title from Jewish Apocalyptic literature designating the one who would bring about the utopia of a just world by overcoming the beasts of empire.[21] As the book of Daniel describes the fourth beastly kingdom, "It shall devour the whole earth, and trample it down, and break it to pieces" (Dan 7:20). The image of Christ returning as the Human One, to overturn the beastly order of empire, demands that the hearers of the parable think of justice not simply as each getting what they are owed. This figure calls upon prophetic justice, in which the vulnerable, the oppressed, and the injured are restored throughout creation in the peaceable kingdom. The parable unveils the unjust order of the so-called justice system, commends the resistance and persistence pursued by the widow, and points to a transformative alternative vision.

Other parables that describe this anthesis are often interpreted as describing the ways of God. The parable of the Talents, for example, tells

---

18. Herzog, *Parables as Subversive Speech*, 224–225.

19. Boer and Petterson, *Time of Troubles*, 82.

20. Boer and Petterson, *Time of Troubles*, 146,

21. Bieler and Schottroff, *Eucharist*, 35.

of a rich slave-holder who gives his slaves money to manage. The slaves function as retainer class stewards (the middlemen of the Empire) and are managing great sums of wealth as the master travels. The titular "talent" is an exorbitant sum of money that would have exceeded the comprehension of peasants. Two of the steward slaves invest the money and double the amount. The third, out of fear of the harshness of the slavemaster, buries the money so as not to risk facing his master's wrath. The slavemaster praises the first two slaves, inviting them to his banquet and giving them greater responsibility. He condemns the third slave and casts him out into the darkness, to live a life of abject poverty that will likely be very painful and brief (Matt 25:14-30).

This parable is often taken as commending the entrepreneurial spirit of the first two slaves and framing wealth as a blessing given by God. Yet, if we are to accept this reading, we will have to ascribe to God the qualities of this cruel slavemaster. The master does not deny the accuracy of the slave's description of him as "a harsh man, reaping where you did not sow, and gathering where you did not scatter seed" (Matt 25:24). Indeed, the master verifies it with his actions condemning the servant for not putting the money in a bank to gain interest (gaining the fruits of another's labors) and acting harshly by throwing him out (Matt 25:27-30).

The harshness and violence of the master's action is further underlined when we understand what exactly he is praising in the other two slaves. The other two slaves *double* their wealth. The primary means of doing so in the ancient world would have been to engage in predatory lending, seeking to make loans to people who would put up their land as collateral.[22] As we have repeatedly touched upon, this issue of debt was a perennial problem. The danger implicit in lending is captured in the Hebrew root word for "interest," which can also designate the "bite of a serpent."[23] This biting character intensified during the time of Jesus as the elite in Jerusalem had created a work around for the laws of Sabbath release called the *prosbul*—which allowed the debt to be transferred to a court that would collect the debt and technically allow the debtor to not be guilty of breaking the laws of forgiveness.[24] In the First Jewish Revolt, a few decades after the death of Jesus, one of the first acts of the militants was to burn the debt records.[25]

Rather than praising the machinations of wealth accumulation, the parable serves to peel back the glamor of the rich and famous to show their

22. Herzog, *Parables as Subversive Speech*, 161–162.

23. Adams, *Social and Economic Life*, 106.

24. Fiensy, *Social History*, 6.

25. Adams, *Social and Economic Life*, 113.

malice. Unlike the unjust judge, who must at least pretend to observe the demands of the law, the slavemaster in the parable is quite clear about what he views as good. The stewards who foreclose on ancestral lands and gain more wealth for his household are welcomed into "the joy of their master" (Matt 25:21, 23). That is, they are welcomed to the festive joy of his banquet table. They have honored what he values. The third servant, who refuses to exploit others and who sees the monstrous nature of his master, by contrast, is explicitly viewed as worthless in the unjust order of the elite. His honesty, in the space of the parable, unveils the misery and violence that is behind the conspicuous consumption of the wealthy.[26] Rather than commending the ways of profit-seeking and wrapping up entrepreneurial gumption in faithful robes, the parable strips such actions of their pretense and gives its hearers a glimpse behind the curtain.

The antithesis being drawn is underlined and circled in the Gospel of Matthew in that this section is immediately followed by the scene of divine judgment in which the Human One will gather "all the nations" and separate those who have followed God's ways from those who have not (Matt 25:31–33). The invitation into the banquet of God's kingdom is issued on the basis of whether or not one fed, gave drink to, welcomed, clothed, cared for, or visited Christ. To which the just will ask: "Lord, when was it that we saw you hungry and gave you food, or thirsty and gave you something to drink? And when was it that we saw you a stranger and welcomed you, or naked and gave you clothing? And when was it that we saw you sick or in prison and visited you?" (Matt 25:37–39). To which the ruler of the kingdom of God will answer, "Truly I tell you, just as you did it to one of the least of these who are members of my family, you did it to me" (Matt 25:40).

While the parable asks us to compare this situation of the slavemaster to the kingdom of God, this comparison is not one of similarity, but of profound difference (Matt 25:1, 14). These little stories serve to point toward structures of power that organize the material world of their hearers and shape their hearts. The peasants too have been shaped by the culture that paints the poor as lazy or slothful (one of the slavemaster's words) and the elite as just and honorable. Jesus names the cruelty of this order *and* shows how it can be unveiled by marginal figures who resist or whistle blow. In so doing his hearers may come to see the ways of Empire that are too often invisible because they are taken as normal and natural, and they can begin to see how the world and their ways of life could be different.

---

26. Herzog, *Parables as Subversive Speech*, 166.

The Underside of Wealth

Moving in the opposite direction of the narratives in our culture of the plucky boot-strap, self-starting, hard-working, upwardly mobile poor, are stories in Jesus' parables about how systems of wealth exploit the agrarian workers of the ancient world. By following this thread, we can come to see a more detailed picture of the injustice of the Empire, and through contrast, get a clearer vision of what the kingdom, or commonwealth, of God looks like. This contrast is especially stark in a few parables that reveal the downward spiral into poverty that the economy of empire produced for so many (and for the land that they worked). Jesus speaks of those who have moved from sustainable peasant communities, to becoming *tenants* on the land, to displaced *day laborers*, to diseased and dying *beggars*. While this world is profoundly distant from our own, the mode of the parable presents us with thick stories that we inhabit, and which can in turn interpret us and transfigure our ordinary lives.

The parable often referred to as "the Wicked Tenants" might better be called the parable of "the Cycle of Violence." The parable tells of a man who planted a vineyard and leased it out to tenants and went to another country (Mark 12:1). While this initial framing may seem innocent enough, by now we should hear in the background the familiar tale of debt and foreclosure. To be *starting* a vineyard would likely mean that the rich man had seized new land and was converting it to growing something more profitable. A vineyard requires years before it bears the fruit that can yield wine, so starting one is a speculative business venture that requires a good deal of wealth.[27] The owner's wealth is underlined by his capacity to retain several tenants.[28] From the beginning the parable stages a conflict between the loss of subsistence community and elite extraction.

This is compounded by the resonance of the traditional image of Israel as a vineyard (somewhat like the United State's association with a melting pot). The prophet Isaiah paints an idyllic pastoral image of God planting the vineyard of Israel on "a fertile hill" (Isa 5:1). Yet, the elite of Israel corrupt this covenantal and agrarian scene through their unjust ways. Isaiah laments that the Lord "expected justice but saw bloodshed; righteousness, but heard a cry! Ah, you who join house to house, who add field to field, until there is room for no one but you, and you are left to live alone in the midst of the land!" (Isa 5:7–8). This prophetic condemnation is directed toward the elite of Jerusalem in the parable of the Tenants, as Jesus tells it

---

27. Herzog, *Parables as Subversive Speech*, 102.

28. Herzog, *Parables as Subversive Speech*, 103.

during his final week of direct action and protest (Mark 12:12). The rich man, then, should not be read as God, but the rich man acts in ways that are diametrically opposed to God's covenant, which minimizes debt so as to maintain sustainable community and care for the land.[29]

The opening lines of the parable evoke cycles of economic predation and violence. As the saying goes on, these chickens come home to roost. The vineyard owner sends a series of slaves to collect their share of the produce, and they are beaten, insulted, and killed by the tenants (Mark 12:2–5). The vineyard owner eventually sends his own son, who they also kill (Mark 12:6–8).

Jesus does not see this retaliatory violence as a solution or the realization of justice but asks, "What then will the owner of the vineyard do? He will come and destroy the tenants and give the vineyard to others" (Mark 12:9). Christ is highlighting the weakness of violent rebellion.[30] Instead, he points toward the nonviolent path of his messianic mission (Ps 118:22–23/ Mark 12:10–11). Through the parable the structures of tenancy that are taken for granted are shown to be violent. The initial violence perpetrated by the structural violence of predatory debt, commodity farming, and exploited labor.[31] Christ, who will in turn be executed by this spiral of violence, gestures toward an alternative nonviolent way, and incarnates it through the path of the cross.

In another parable, which also takes place in a vineyard, Jesus tells of the plight of day laborers. Whereas tenants still live on the land, day laborers were an extremely vulnerable class that were regarded, in some ways, as lower than slaves. Ancient Roman manuals advised landowners to use day laborers for backbreaking work in place of slaves to avoid damaging one's own property (the body of the slave). At best, our image of day laborers could be as the fathers of families, in which every member is working desperately to scrape by.[32] At worst, the day laborers were a part of the "expendable" class—people who had fallen outside of the bonds of familial relationship through lost land or perhaps as the younger children of a subsistence family that could only pass on the inheritance to the oldest child. Skeletal remains from the period show the pressures of this work. The remains of an older man who had found refuge in the Qumran community bear the marks of this oppressive labor, as endless hours of carrying heavy

---

29. Schottroff, *Parables of Jesus*, 17.

30. Herzog, *Parables as Subversive Speech*, 113.

31. Moe-Lobeda, *Resisting Structural Evil*.

32. Schottroff, *Parables of Jesus*, 211–13.

weights on his shoulders had permanently deformed his bone structure.[33] The precarity and exploitation of the Empire meant that people were always drifting into this class, making up somewhere between 5 percent and 15 percent of the population.[34] Their abundance in first-century Palestine is illustrated by Jesus' reference in the parable to a seemingly endless supply of workers who are waiting in the marketplace through the entire day to get whatever work they can.

In the parable, Jesus compares the kingdom of God with a landowner who went out in the morning to hire laborers to work in his vineyard. He returned at noon, at three, and five o'clock to hire more workers (Matt 20:1–6). At the end of the day he directed the manager to line the workers up and pay "beginning with the last and then going to the first" (Matt 20:8). Having seen those who were hired last receiving the wage of one denarius, the laborers who had worked the whole day expected to be paid more, but they were paid the same. When they grumbled against the landowner about this, he replied that he was giving them the wage that they had agreed upon, and that it was his decision to do with his wealth as he desired (Matt 20:9–15). He asked, "Are you envious because I am generous?" (Matt 20:15).

Sometimes the landowner is read as God, and his acts are seen as manifestations of God's equality and generosity. Yet, while the landowner calls himself generous, his actions are closer to what we would call charitable. That is, he does nothing to make people whole or change structures; rather he does slightly more than is demanded of him by the unjust economy. Similar to a great deal of the actions of the philanthropist, the main function of the "gift" is to make the wealthy person appear and feel generous.[35] Even in his generosity the landowner structures the payment to provoke an antagonism among the workers. He devalues the work of those who had labored all day by making it replaceable and appear as a matter of his charity rather than their effort.[36] While the owner pays the workers who came later a full day's wage, he is careful not to hire any more workers than he needs, only returning to the marketplace when it is clear that he needs more to get the job done (harvesting is, after all, time sensitive). Far from being generous, the land owner is paying as few people as possible a below living wage, and he is making a show of it.

It demands a good deal of reflection if it feels natural to read the land owner as a metaphor for God. On this reading the final line of the parable

33. Fiensy, *Social History*, 86.

34. Herzog, *Parables as Subversive Speech*, 88–89.

35. Schottroff, *Parables of Jesus*, 211.

36. Herzog, *Parables as Subversive Speech*, 91.

seems to be stating its moral or thesis. Jesus declares, "So the last will be first, and the first will be last" (Matt 20:16). Do we really think that the kingdom of God is realized in the widespread distribution of a single day's below living wage to those who did not work a full day? Has our experience with the acts of mercy pursued by churches where we feed the poor on Styrofoam plates the fruit of the industrial food system trained us into thinking that such acts are the extent of Christ's vision of new life? Might the vision of the kingdom of God instead call into question the order and empire that creates a situation where people are forced off their land, where communities have their resources extracted, where subsistence is replaced with desperation and people are forced to work for the elite, who imagine themselves to be the owners of God's creation to do with as they please?

The final line of the parable does not serve as an abstract principle that underlies the story. Rather the declaration that the last shall be first is the antithesis of the story. It reveals the hollow generosity that lines people up so as to maintain the asymmetrical power of the rich giving scraps from their abundance to the poor, and which fosters antagonisms between those who should find solidarity. The final line of the parable turns its hearer around so that they might imagine their role in this system and to set their heart on a world that is ordered differently.

This stark contrast between the ways of the empire of wealth and the commonwealth of God, which is good news to the poor, appears in starkest relief in the parable that portrays the bleakest poverty—the parable of Lazarus and the Rich Man. Jesus begins the parable with a short sketch of two figures that brings together two sides of a system that seldom interact (and therefore it has a cartoonish quality that is more true than ordinary experience). Jesus says, "There was a rich man who was dressed in purple and fine linen and who feasted sumptuously every day. And at his gate lay a poor man named Lazarus, covered with sores, who longed to satisfy his hunger with what fell from the rich man's table; even the dogs would come and lick his sores" (Luke 16:19–21).

The rich man's clothing and consumption speaks to his profound privilege. The bread that Lazarus longs for is likely a kind of bread that was used for napkins—a pile of pita loaves employed to wipe one's hands at meals. It was a form of conspicuous consumption that highlighted the status of the rich, and which the presence of the starving Lazarus shows in a different light.[37]

Not only does the poor man at the gate covered in sores and near death show their lack of compassion in that instance, but it also connects the dots between the source of the rich man's excess and the cause of Lazarus's

---

37. Herzog, *Parables as Subversive Speech*, 117–18.

poverty. Most of the people who ended up in Lazarus's desperate position were born as peasants and slid down the social ladder through the loss of family lands, the exploitation of workers, and the crumbling of physical health and social supports.[38] After entering into this expendable class they would likely start as a day laborer and live an average of five to seven years.[39] Finding a lack of work or simply meeting the limits of exploitation and malnutrition, Lazarus has succumbed to disease and is nearing death. Therefore, there is little that the rich man can do for Lazarus at this point, though there were doubtless many other bids for work and assistance from the wealthy that marked Lazarus's downward spiral.[40]

The parable takes a radical turn as the place of these two men is reversed when they both die. Lazarus is now at the messianic banquet in the bosom of father Abraham. The dispossessed and landless beggar now dwells with Abraham, the father of the promise of covenant and land (Gen 15:18). He is given comfort, that which is given to the people after exile (Isa 40:1).[41] The formerly landed rich man is in Hades "being tormented" (Luke 16:22–23). Hades, in the first-century religious imaginary, is not the same as the eternal Hell that we might think of today. It is better understood of as a waiting room after death.[42]

The emphasis in this story is not on the vengeful punishment that the rich man receives, but on his lack of repentance. He calls out to Abraham for mercy. He asks him first to send *Lazarus* "to dip the tip of his finger in water and cool my tongue; for I am in agony in these flames" (Luke 16:24). Later he begs Abraham to send *Lazarus* to his house to warn his brothers that their opulent lives will lead to their torment (Luke 16:27–28). In so doing he continues to appeal to his position of privilege and fails to see Lazarus as a fellow creature. In fact, he betrays that he was aware enough of the poor, starving, sore-covered man outside of his gate to know his name, but he did nothing to help him.[43] Furthermore, even after seeing Lazarus at the messianic banquet he still views him as a servant, asking Abraham to send him to bring him water or to send a message to his brothers. The rich man's concern is still limited to those who are rich. His understanding of the faith is like that of the wealthy and the scribes who only see the purity

---

38. Herzog, *Parables as Subversive Speech*, 119.

39. Herzog, *Parables as Subversive Speech*, 66.

40. Herzog, *Parables as Subversive Speech*, 120.

41. Brueggemann, *Land*, 162.

42. Herzog, *Parables as Subversive Speech*, 122.

43. Herzog, *Parables as Subversive Speech*, 123.

of the elite and have no regard for the other children of God.[44] Abraham highlights this as he rejects the rich man's request to send Lazarus as a ghost to frighten his brothers into repentance. True repentance does not come from privileged dispensations but from the promise of the law and the prophets (Luke 16:30–31).[45]

Jesus' parables bring to light the poor figures who are blamed for their plight. Furthermore, he connects these overlooked people with the structures of debt, wealth, the commodification of land, and the exploitation or workers. These structures, and the gentlemen and middle managers who operate them, resonate with the order that is leading to ecological catastrophe and profound exploitation and poverty today.

We are unlikely to see these marginalized figures or to view these systems as problems because of other stories that populate our culture. The rags to riches stories that haunt the American past through the tales of Horatio Alger and Benjamin Franklin continue to pollute the American moral imaginary through narratives of self-made business men, athletes who escaped their past, and more quotidian accounts of upward mobility championed in college brochures. The only challenge typically directed toward such narratives concerns the degree to which they are true, the degree to which it is possible to actualize the American dream. Jesus' parables are the antithesis of these stories. They do not extol the virtues of the rich and a fair playing field where everyone has a chance to be on top. They call into question the structure of this pyramidal hierarchy and bring to light the underside of all the people who must be bent over and broken for some to move on up.

Transforming Narratives and Practices

The civilizing light of our distantly held facts and our posture as experts often makes it difficult to see our role in the underside of unjust order. The statistics on local poverty do not require a systemic interpretation. They might, instead, inspire a reactive response where we only seek to charitably share from our abundance.

We are shaped by assessments and advertisements that happen behind our back. We have been shaped to look for market-based solutions as the only means of practical engagement. We have been taught that the vision of the good life, into which we should invite others, is the self-sufficient suburban world of super-consumption. Jesus' pedagogy of the parables serves to

44. Herzog, *Parables as Subversive Speech*, 124.

45. Herzog, *Parables as Subversive Speech*, 125.

turn things over and to turn us around—and shows us subtle ways in which our world might be transformed.

The twisted understanding of the difference between the haves and the have-nots in our time and in the dominant interpretations of the parables seems to have a complicated relationship with our vision of God. What effect does it have on our understanding of the Creator, creation, and creatures, when we repeatedly hear stories that portray the divine as a vengeful slave owner, a profit-seeking businessman, a condescending rich man, a petty and murderous king, or a capriciously forgiving ruler? Alternatively, what vision of God and creation leads us to read a story of terrible violence and exploitation and assume that the perpetrator is a metaphor for the divine? And yet, this is how the parables are too often still read.

This perverse use of the parables and of the little stories we are told in our culture performs a subtle pedagogy that is not unlike that of Jesus' parables in form, but which is diametrically opposed to their content. The genius of advertising is that it does not simply present us with the facts, but it appeals to our hearts through tiny narratives and culturally charged images. We inhabit these stories and allow them to interpret us as they shape our everyday action.[46] Will we secure blessings for ourselves and our families by trusting that investment firm? Will we participate in the joyful banquet with our friends over that bucket of chicken? Will we gain a new and redeemed life with those stainless-steel appliances and open floor plans? Will we be wonderfully and beautifully remade with that exercise equipment? The glossy and thick image of the advertisement draws us in and asks us to compare ourselves to its ideals and demands change from us when we are found wanting.

These narratives that divinize the powerful and wealthy, that align success with virtue, and that blame the dark ignorant other and the poor are some of the primary obstacles to our seeing the unjust order that haunts us and the ways that we could transform it. These are the narratives that form suburbanites who are informed about the pain caused by their actions but who persist in their ways of life—who poison their lawns and public health for the public good of appearance and property values.

The parables serve as a counter-pedagogy, telling little stories that reframe the ordinary. They point us to a vision of the divine that does not give more to those seeking profit, but they hint at a Creator who loves all of creation and lavishes it with an abundance that must be shared in simplicity. These stories call us to inhabit a scene that resembles our everyday lives, where we can see that the cause of violence is unjust order and that the way

46. Myers, *Who Will Roll*, 58–64.

to God's kingdom follows nonviolence. The reversals of a God who brings good news to the poor, heals the lame, and frees the prisoners call upon us to do greater works than to share the scraps from our table or line up the poor so that they may see our generosity.

The aspect of the pedagogy of the parables that I take as most central is their engagement with the everyday and the habits and relationships that we often take for granted. This is why, in this book, I have not focused on spectacular narratives of exotic locations and world-historical change. I have focused on vignettes taken from my life that are not newsworthy. I have narrowed in on little moments of joy and failure from my small, sub-urban, mainline, privileged, middle-class, over-educated, un-noteworthy life because I think that these are the spaces where both the power of the dominant order and the promise of its transformation are hiding.

The narrative structure of our over-mediatized culture points us away from these spaces. Both in terms of the stories that it tells, that are excep-tional, fast, flashy, terrifying, or glamorous *and* because our consumption of this media turns our gaze away from the places where we are. (With the proliferation of smart phones, it has literally done this, as we fail to attend to the world in front of us because we are looking through the window to the world of elsewhere.)

In this fast and flashy world problems are solved by powerful indi-viduals, cartoonishly drawn as superheroes. Bruce Wayne, the benevolent billionaire, fights dark chaotic, irrational criminals in narrative arcs with pyrotechnic climaxes. But what if instead of becoming Batman, he became Boardman—the bratty billionaire attempting to harness the power of his priv-ilege for economic and social justice? Perhaps the fighter of the unjust order could be pictured as someone entrenched in trying to transform his family company—constrained by laws, structures, power players, existing brick and mortar assets, and supply chains. Rather than tired tales about crime fighters who must fight their own chaotic and malicious heart within, we could tell stories of privileged people who are at war with themselves, striving for justice and solidarity in contexts that have trained them to be successful, on top, out front, at the least christened for their generosity. Even more importantly, we will need to follow the lead of Jesus and listen to the stories of those who have been rendered marginalized, if not invisible.

Following the reversals of the kingdom, the pedagogy of the parable need not happen up front, on stage, on television, or in the papers. It might happen in smaller, more ordinary places—through the transformation of the classroom, the Sunday school class, or small group. As such, it will likely follow less the format of the expert lecturer than the shared con-versation. In formal classroom contexts it might mean shifting emphasis from just writing research papers (which hold knowledge at a distance) to fostering and encouraging wider forms of writing that bring insights closer to life or which creatively transfigure the ordinary—writing stories, journals, letters, liturgies, poems, and even parables. In less formal situations this might mean reframing the demands of the test, highlighting forms of mutual accountability and effort required when a teacher is no longer watching to provide a grade.

A pedagogy capable of transformation might demand moving analysis elsewhere, bringing a critical eye to familiar spaces and places, like churches, homes, neighborhoods, parks, cafeterias, supermarkets, and offices. Or in theological disciplines to consider more media than just texts, considering popular, artistic, social, news, and liturgical media, and not just creative works but also habits, relationships, and ecosystems.

Such a pedagogy will need to open avenues to action by more fully integrating that which is thought of as intellectual with what is regarded as practical. In addition to knowledge we need to engage in crafts—like cooking and gardening. Formal and informal learning environments could turn their attention to community-based projects. This work would need to engage in the fostering of long-term relationships (lasting more than the semester or the service event). They should topple asymmetrical relationships, in which white saviors reach out to dark others, seeking instead mutuality if not more humbly showing up to simply learn and be transformed.

These are all pedagogies that resonate with those deployed by the great teacher, the Rabbi Jesus Christ. He was a storyteller, a questioner, an organizer, a counselor, a healer, and an interpreter. Through these teachings he did not just present a set of facts or even a worldview, but he enacted exercises that shaped a revolutionary way of life.

The Kingdom of God is Like

The pedagogy of parables also serves to inspire the imagination. Just as important as this critical work of the parables is their painting a picture of how life should be. This picture calls attention to an aspect of the ordinary and transfigures it. Here our daily labor, friendships, meals, and gatherings are bathed in a divine light.

In one parable, Jesus declares that the kingdom of God is like "yeast that a woman took and mixed in with three measures of flour until all of it was leavened" (Matt 13:33). The kingdom can be seen in the ordinary acts of care whereby the fruits of creation are pressed and kneaded to form food that is sustaining and delightful.[47] The amount of flour here is enough to feed several families. The kingdom, then, is realized through the acts of love that bring people together and that nurture their bodies.

Even more there are two details here that are discordant with the imaginary of empire. First of all, women would not usually be thought of as the agents of empire who are bringing about change. They are marginal and subjected in its order. But here those hands that are usually invisible are paralleled with the hands of God.[48] Secondly, leaven is often viewed as an agent of impurity (Exod 12:15–20).[49] Jesus says by contrast that in God's kingdom those who are marginalized and that which is considered impure will serve as forces for care and growth.

In the kingdom we are all invited to participate in the small and ordinary acts that will transform communities, institutions, and the land. In a sense all of Jesus' acts in the Gospels are practices and parables of the kingdom that foster a new creation. His healing, teaching, organizing, feeding, mobilizing, and praying all have cascading effects driving toward the new creation.[50] We in turn are invited to participate in these efforts. As with the woman kneading the flour, we are just participants. God's grace blesses our creation with grain, that others help to nurture. The microbes of the yeast and the processes of nature conspire with us in our kneading to bring growth. With God, in relationships with other creatures, we subvert and sustain—this is what the kingdom of God is like.[51]

Jesus illuminates what life in God's kingdom looks like by pointing toward covenantal community. In the parable of the Friend at Midnight, Christ tells a story of relationships and villages pulled apart by the extraction of the Empire that has not left enough bounty for generosity, mutuality, hospitality, and sustenance. Jesus begins the parable by asking one to suppose you have a friend, "and you go to him at midnight and say to him, 'Friend, lend me three loaves of bread; for a friend of mine has arrived, and I have nothing to set before him'" (Luke 11:5). In our private well-compartmentalized lives, this question sounds rude. But in the context of village life property was not seen as quite so private and families were not so nuclear. Sharing was at the heart of sustaining. The presumption in *you* asking for *my* bread is not so stark. Instead, the assumption would be that we all share

---

47. Schottroff, *Parables of Jesus*, 206.

48. Schottroff, *Lydia's Impatient Sisters*, 85.

49. Scott, *Re-Imagine the World*, 34.

50. Bauckham, *Living with Other Creatures*, 73–74.

51. Keller, *On the Mystery*, 148.

in the demand of hospitality.[52] Furthermore, the timing of midnight would not denote the irresponsible socializing of neighbors who just won't turn down the music and go to bed but would heighten the need of the person who is seeking shelter, sustenance, and possibly, sanctuary.

The hinge of the story is the friend's reply, "Do not bother me; the door has already been locked, and my children are with me in bed; I cannot get up and give you anything" (Luke 11:6). This is the action that goes against the covenantal community of the peasant village. The morality of village life was built around an understanding of *limited good*.[53] That is, there are limits to the gifts that sustain us. The land will only yield so much if we intend to care for generations. We must live *under* its carrying capacity. We can only grow so much of one thing if we are to maintain the soil's fertility. Instead, we must diversify. We must observe the contours of the land, its needs and blessings and use it optimally. We must bear one another's burdens and take care of our neighbors so they will, in turn, take care of us.[54] Given these limits no person or family should use too much or hoard for themselves. Success is not shown through one person having more than others—through so conspicuously consuming food that they use bread as napkins—but success is shown through a healthy, joyful community exemplified in the shared harvest at the banquet. To deny a friend's request then would be to go against this order.

Read alongside the other parables, this story tells of the institution of hospitality that is crumbling under the weight of the demands of the Empire in village life. The friend's reply reflects the morality of the elite, in which one does with one's wealth as one pleases (the vineyard owner) and thinks only of their family (the rich man). But in this instance, the friend's reply is likely not motivated by the family's wealth but their vulnerability.[55] Living off of one-fifth to one-thirteenth of the harvest has left the cupboard bare. Families now live on the razor's edge of debt, foreclosure, tenancy, day labor, and destitution. As a result, the collective powers of sharing, community, solidarity, and sustainability have also dissolved, and people are isolated, rendered individuals standing against an entire empire.

Jesus contrasts the ways of this empire with the kingdom of God. He encourages his hearers, telling them that all they need to do is ask God, and it will be given, to "knock, and the door will be opened" (Luke 11:9). Decontextualized, this might seem like a proof text of the prosperity gospel,

52. Herzog, *Parables as Subversive Speech*, 201.

53. Herzog, *Parables as Subversive Speech*, 204.

54. Boer and Petterson, *Time of Troubles*, 72–73.

55. Herzog, *Parables as Subversive Speech*, 206–7.

but what God gives is "the Holy Spirit" (Luke 11:13). God promises to give the power that enables those who are on the path of the anointed to heal the sick, to spread the good news, and to have courage in the face of empire (Luke 4:1, 18–19).[56] What is given is, in part, the restoration of the communities of care, mutuality, hospitality, generosity, and joy that make these alternative forms of power possible.

Like other parables, this teaching does not render an abstract principle that the reader mines out. One inhabits the ordinary but thick scene of the parable, seeing themselves in everyday village life. They see themselves knocking on the door, asking but not receiving. They see themselves hearing the knock but turning the friend away for fear there will not be enough for their family. They see themselves asking of God, and they are told that what they receive is the power to be able to respond to the knocking of others.

This pedagogical practice does not put all of the pressure back on us to do the work of the kingdom ourselves, to become masters. Rather, it asks us to take the position of creatures in a bountiful creation. In that collection of botanical parables that we started with back in chapter 2, Christ says that "The kingdom of God is as if someone would scatter seed on the ground, and would sleep and rise night and day, and the seed would sprout and grow, he does not know how. The earth produces of itself, first the stalk, then the head, then the full grain in the head" (Mark 4:26–28). This is a vision of a creature working with the mysterious and wonderful rhythms of the Creator that lead to the fullness and joy of life. Here *adam* serves and observes *adamah*.

The empire wants us to behold a field and see wealth that can be extracted—wealth that is meant to be lavishly displayed in fine garments, conspicuously consumed in sumptuous banquets, and constantly grown through predatory lending. From the imperial perspective the land cannot possibly be felt and known as God's blessing, with limits to be observed and wisdom of its own. The empire does not want to see the man spreading the seed and working with God, but it wants the worker giving his land over to become a tenant, or even better to give his time over and become a day laborer, and if he must, to give his life over and become one more discarded body on the trash heap. The empire expects that we see its ability to make wealth grow day and night, and that we will call it just and generous.

The parable seeks to show us our place in the community of creatures. This is a pedagogy that transforms the habits, relationships, stories, and values that have formed us, and it calls upon us creatively, critically, imaginatively, and practically to live differently.

---

56. Schottroff, *Parables of Jesus*, 189.

Furthermore, it presses us to be interpreted by these visions. We are left to wonder what path we are on and what order is guiding our lives. Jesus ends the parable saying that "when the grain is ripe, at once he goes in with his sickle because the harvest has come" (Mark 4:29). This image reminds us not only of the hard work of harvest time and the joyous festivals that come with it, but in the Scriptures this is a figure for God's coming judgement. For those who would like to see the empire rule eternally this judgement is a terrifying scene. But for those who value the restoration of covenantal life, the judgment is a promise of renewal and new creation.[57] The coming of God's kingdom will mean losing one way of life, but it will mean gaining another.

> *Exhausted from work, the middle manager considered skipping the meeting. What would it matter if he was there at all? Regardless, he remembered his friend's invitation and left the comfort of his home for an evening in another neighborhood. While the opening of the gathering was marked by the standard awkwardness, something shifted when they were placed in circles and given a chance to listen to one another's stories. At, first the manager was irritated that this group was no committee. He was annoyed that they would not be accomplishing anything tonight. But as people began to share their pain and encourage each other to hope, he felt something in him move. It was all connected: his work, his privilege, their pain. But they too were all connected and together, facing each other in a circle. They could change. It could all be transformed.*

---

57. Schottroff, *Parables of Jesus*, 121.

5

Healing Physical and Social Bodies

ONE OF THE MOST difficult things I have ever done is leave my job without a clear path to another one in sight. There were all kinds of particular and personal reasons for this—some concerning my love for the community I served and others regarding my hope for what the work could become. But I think that the greatest difficulty was that such an act was heretical to the American Gospel of Work.

Leaving this job would mark several losses. I would lose a certain degree of financial security. Given my class position and networks of support, the risk of sliding into poverty was very, very small. This decision also meant the unthinkable reality (given my social location) of taking a step back on the ladder of wealth and success. I had spent a tremendous amount of time in school amassing a pile of degrees. The job I was leaving had, at first, seemed to be a marriage of my training to be both pastor and professor in a field with very few positions that paid a living wage. To give up my foothold would not just mean the slight risk of tumbling to the bottom, but the great likelihood that I had reached a certain kind of professional ceiling. This latter reality was compounded as I also risked a certain kind of social death. When asked the defining opening question of American privileged society: "And what do you do?" I would no longer have an answer. While my past answer was not something that inspired looks of admiration or even further conversation, it at least was an answer that seemed to come with the mild, if disinterested, recognition of personhood.

If this sounds too melodramatic, I want you to pause for a moment to reflect on how venerable and central employment is for the social and moral fabric of the United States. In the great fragmentation of our times, the primary agreed-upon value seems to be wage-earning work. Politicians in both dominating parties are focused on creating jobs. The only poor that can be mentioned are the working poor, who have several different jobs and hope to climb the ladder themselves. I once served on the board for a nonprofit with a multi-million-dollar budget that was founded more than half a century ago to *empower* poor *communities*. Yet, in one of my first meetings the executive director outlined a vision in which he said that the only way that he knew to lift people out of poverty was to get an individual a job (a vision that was applauded by the board). This individualistic approach limits the scope of collective action to the *business community*.

Jobs are at the center of the American Gospel of Work. This Gospel is focused not so much on a wide creation, but sees the world as a great market. In this narrative, the market, so long as it is not fettered by regulation, is both natural and rational. It rewards the merit (or talent) and hard work of individuals. This simple story explains our reality of winners (the worthy, talented, industrious success stories) and losers (the unworthy, damaged, lazy poor).

This Gospel of Work, despite the ways it is dressed up in Christendom, is the opposite of the Good News of Jesus Christ. Christ's eyes are set on God's creation that is animated by grace, the outpouring of God's *unmerited* love. Creatures do not prove their worth through works or find their reward through wealth. Rather, these conceits are at the root of sin and they lead to the impoverishment of others and the desecration of creation. Christ's good news is for the poor precisely because it promises to topple the structures of domination, exploitation, extraction, and wealth.

Because I have been shaped by and continue to live in a world that trumpets the American Gospel of Work, it felt like madness—like the loss of civilizing reason—to leave my job. But I felt called to leave for two reasons. One was personal. The workplace had become toxic. My physical and emotional health and my relationships had started to suffer. More systemically, I no longer felt like my work was making a difference. I felt my labor shifting into being a chaplain of empire rather than being an agent of God's kingdom. I felt that I was on the road to ruin. Yet, even with such pitfalls clearly in sight, I was still hesitant to step off that path because it meant going against the conventional wisdom that organizes the world in which I live, which tells us that we are defined by our jobs and the only networks that we can trust are those sealed with monetary exchange.

This tangled knot of problems is an enormous impediment for any collective action in beginning to bring about healing and wholeness in the web of life. How we think about work and our shared life together is one of the most central but overlooked aspects of how we care for creation. This is the place where the vast economic systems and the rule of the household intersect.[1] A false story animates our lives, and it causes us to misrecog-

---

1. Berry, *Art of the Commonplace*, 309.

nize the true source of danger, threat, and harm. This myth of the virtue of work in a supposedly benevolent market keeps us laboring in alienating environments and broken communities. Our primary efforts and greatest energies end up being directed toward maintaining the structures and machinery that are poisoning us and that obscure and defer deeper problems. We sacrifice our first (and second and third) fruits at its altar in the form of our work week, our homes, and our investments, only volunteering on the side for something else. We are too exhausted to build alternatives because we are so busily running the races of empire—competing in its gladiatorial games that end in our death.

I confess that I continue to feel possessed by the Gospel of Work. I find myself answering to its calls and striving after its markers of status and success. My energies are too often stolen by the folly of seeing myself an entrepreneur championing the brand "Wilson Dickinson." While this is an internal struggle that is inherent to authors who both want to make a contribution *and* a name for themselves, this mentality is not limited to creative types. Rather, the structures that we live in are directed toward individuating us so that we all imagine that we are little businesses who are responsible for our own suffering or success. Such training serves to promote a certain kind of individualism, if not narcissism, in which I see the world as a stage for the true story, which is about *me*. It also serves to make us feel as though we are responsible for everything that befalls us.

The response to such isolation and alienation is not simply to change our minds (an individualistic effort that again places all the power and responsibility back in our own hands). We need to find ways to enter different kinds of lives. Some of this might happen by leaving behind certain broken communities, by walking out the door. Yet, this is often an option reserved for people of privilege, that seems still too centered on the quasi-heroic action of an individual. The true hope is found in alternative relationships, animated by different rituals and incarnating different stories. These problems cannot be solved individually but must be approached socially. No small part of the healing is to be found in the restoration of healthy communities and relationships.

Perhaps we can find release and healing by being touched by the body of Christ. This healing addresses social ills and mends lives with therapeutic and whole communities. Jesus' acts of healing hold the promise of ridding us of the names placed on us by empire. Named as a child of Christ, we can live into a different identity. Christ will first need to exorcise the elements of empire that possess us by revealing their cruel and malicious underside. After we have learned the cruel names of empire, we can begin to live into the alternative vision of living in a community guided by Christ. This is a community in which power does not so much flow down the hierarchy, as it conducts through relationships and practices of compassion, solidarity, justice, and joy. These practices of healing rid us of the names of consumer or entrepreneur and restore us to being creatures caring for and nurtured by creation.

Illness and Therapy–The Power of Naming

The social and political significance of the healing stories of Jesus are often lost because we look at the stories through unhelpful categories. For example, they are often treated as *miracles* through which God intervenes in the natural order to prove divine power. Instead, as we will see, these stories are better understood as instances of the renewal of the wholeness of creation that has been damaged by human sin. In these cases, it is the power of empire that has broken bodies rather than the act of Jesus that goes *against* creation. God's power is not expressed by the overcoming of fallen matter, but through the restoration of creatures in their bodies in this life.

Furthermore, these stories are often understood through the lens of contemporary biomedicine, which is focused on the *disease* found in an individual. In these cases, Jesus appears to be a doctor who is employing magic rather than modern medicine. As medical anthropologists have helped us see, given the cultural context of first-century Palestine, we would be better served thinking in terms of *illness*. Whereas diseases are located in individual bodies and call for cures, illness is located in wider networks and calls for healing and therapy (the Greek word often translated as "cure" in the Gospels is *therapeia*). An illness is located in processes of emotion and language, is rooted in relationships, and can be the result of historical, political, and economic forces.[2] The injuries from trauma, for example, are better thought of as illnesses. They certainly manifest in individuals, but often at the level of emotion (in feelings of numbness or a loss of hope) and language (in the complete loss of words in the face of triggers). Traumas are rooted in past experiences that are brought on by the political conflict of war, the desperation of poverty, or even intergenerational oppression. Furthermore, traumas are not just experienced by individuals, but an entire town or nation can be traumatized by an event.[3]

John the Baptist sends his disciples to ask if Jesus was the Messiah, the Christ, to which Jesus responds with the prophetic formula to tell him: "the blind receive sight, the lame walk, the lepers are cleansed, the deaf hear,

---

2. Myers, *Binding the Strong Man*, 145–46; Horsley, *Jesus and the Powers*, 113.

3. Jones, *Trauma and Grace*, 12–18.

the dead are raised, and the poor have good news brought to them" (Matt 11:5). The message here is not so much that individuals encountered magic, as slaves have been set free from empire. In the ancient world slaves were often blinded to prevent their escape from monotonous work. Slaves were maimed and mutilated to cause psychological damage. The healing, then, does not necessarily refer to bodies being transformed but to sociopolitical orders being overcome.[4]

To look at these matters in terms of illness is not to erase the centrality of embodied suffering in the name of spiritual maladies, but it highlights the interrelation of poverty and illness, of bodies and social forces. Jesus heals bodies that have been maimed, beaten, blinded, and paralyzed, some no doubt by the violent rule of empire. He touches people who have been declared unclean and exiled from social life. While one may see diseases manifest in poor bodies, one can also come to understand the ways that their social and economic context has contributed to these hardships (like poor Lazarus in the parable). In extended family groups that directly depend upon one another, broken bodies that keep one member from working have cascading economic and political consequences for the whole group. Furthermore, oppression and trauma leave bodily marks and have ripple effects throughout communities.[5]

This shift in thinking helps us see the *social* stakes in, for example, Jesus' healing of a leper. The condition described in the Gospels is not necessarily what biomedicine would call "Hansen's Disease" (which was rare and possibly nonexistent in first-century Palestine).[6] Rather, the condition described in Leviticus refers to something quite different and much less threatening, likely covering an array of different skin conditions (including conditions that biomedicine would call eczema or psoriasis). At the heart of this condition was the religious and social status of being rendered unclean.

The story, then, does not center on the ability to identify and cure a pathogen, but on the power that comes with naming and setting social boundaries. Priests exercised the power to identify the condition and to pronounce someone unclean (Lev 13:3–11). The person who was named as such was instructed to "wear torn clothes, and let the hair of the head be disheveled" and to cover one's "lips and cry out, 'Unclean, unclean.'" As long as a person had this condition, they were to dwell outside the community (Lev 13:45–46). When the condition passed, they could return to the priest and engage in costly rituals of cleansing and sacrifice (Lev 14:5–12, 21).

---

4. Betcher, *Spirit of Disablement*, 127–31.

5. Carter, *Matthew and the Margins*, 124.

6. Carter, *Matthew and the Margins*, 199.

When the leper approaches Jesus, he appeals to the power of naming that will restore his social standing, asking Jesus to "declare me clean" (Mark 1:40).[7] The man wants Jesus to reverse the diagnosis and label of the priests. Jesus reaches out and touches the man. Jesus reverses the purity order, as rather than being made unclean by touching the man, the "leper" is declared clean. He touches the socially marginalized man and in so doing, and through his alternative authority, names him as once again a part of the social body.

The ways that the man had been named and categorized by the elite placed him apart. Jesus responds to this, as Mark tells us, by being "moved with anger" (some manuscript traditions render this "pity") (Mark 1:41). Further Jesus "sternly" warns the man, or "snorting with indignation" sends him back to the priests as a form of protest and challenge to their authority (Mark 1:43).[8] Jesus' outrage and indignation show that something deeper is at stake than the presence of a disease.[9] The illness displayed in the "leper" is a manifestation of networks of power that do not simply exclude, but which blame the poor for their conditions, which in turn damage the social body. The callous, unjust naming power of the priests has driven this man into a place of suffering and desperation, and Jesus restores him into loving community.

The social aspect of illness means that symbolic and social matters are not ephemeral or illusory in relation to concrete bodies, but that symbol and life are interrelated. The symbolic proclamation of a man as a "leper" marks him as an outcast and materially changes his life. The word impresses upon his body in the form of disheveled hair and clothing and the cries of "unclean" that keep people at a distance. In a similar manner the healing stories are symbolic in that they show these bodies within wider networks of power. They hold together the aching and desperate need of the ill person and the broken community in which their illness exists.

The dominant reading of these healing stories renders them distant and supernatural. Understanding the healing of the man with leprosy as a miracle cure sets Jesus against our understanding of nature rather than against empire. But as an account of the power of the elite to misrepresent, blame, and exclude we might hear resonances with our own time. In our time entire communities have been named in ways in which their being is criminalized under the auspice of protecting a clean and pure (white)

---

7. This is often obscured as it is translated: to "make me clean." Myers, *Binding the Strong Man*, 153.

8. Myers, *Binding the Strong Man*, 153.

9. Hendricks, *Politics of Jesus*, 163.

society, oppressing people and their families with the designation of terrorist, thug, or illegal.

This power of naming functions clandestinely in forms that we think grant us freedom. In being named an "autonomous individual," the "entrepreneur" in charge of our own venture, or the "free consumer" we are supposed to be the ones in control. But in being named such we are actually separated off—severed from community, abstracted from systems. When things go wrong we are the ones to blame. The irresponsible millennial is at fault, not the system that saddled her with debt, the gig economy that fails to offer a living wage, or the bleak future that undermines hope. It is the individual worker who did not take advantage of opportunities or who had a difficult personality that led to failure, not the institutional decisions that created an impossible work load by piling responsibilities that were previously accomplished by multiple people onto one person and a toxic work environment that pitted workers against each other.

The name of "autonomous individual" and "entrepreneur" places the responsibility upon each of us. This turns us against ourselves through self-blame. It makes each problem seem like an isolated case, which each person is left to bear on their own. Because we are so focused on our own action the collective power wielded by businesses and institutions remains hidden. We are left to blame ourselves for not exercising self-care, rather than seeing how the institutional requirements and pressures of work hours and a context of serial crises has led to our burn out. Since we have accepted the name of sovereign consumer, we hold ourselves responsible for the exploitation of workers through each small purchase, but we fail to see the long-standing forms of policy, infrastructure, and organization bought by corporate interest that makes alternatives profoundly difficult. Most importantly, these names have obscured the forms of community and solidarity that should bring us closer together. Instead, we are left to deal with our failures alone and unclean.

Jesus' form of healing and therapy shows us another way. As Jesus relieves the man of the name of "leper," we can also come to see ourselves in a new light. We are not separated off and alone, but are members of the body. We can once again be defined by our belonging to a place and a people. This healing brings us back to the place where we see ourselves as creatures, brought into wholeness through God's creation.

Bringing Wholeness to the People of the Land

The shift to illness (and away from disease) brings into view the social environment. It highlights the ways that relationships, values, communities, and institutions contribute to or undermine health. In the story immediately following the restoration of the "leper" in the Gospel of Mark, a paralyzed man is placed within two wider social contexts—that of the poor and the elite. First, we are told that Jesus returned to his base of operations, Capernaum. When word spread that he was home, the house was inundated by a "*crowd.*" This is the first occurrence of this important term in Mark, *crowd*, in Greek *ocholos*, which refers to the poor. It is not the standard word for the poor used in the Greek version of the Old Testament. Rather, the antecedent for "crowd" in the Hebrew bible—'*am ha'aretz*, "the people of the land"—initially designated Jewish landowners, but after the time of the exile, it came to refer to the poor, uneducated, and dispossessed.[10] Jesus' ministry is often directed toward this crowd, this people of the land, with whom God had originally made a covenant but who, because of the violence of empire and the purity regulations of the elite, have become alienated.

This crowd is so numerous and in such need that they press in on Jesus. The reader of the Gospel should not lose sight of them as mere window dressing, but should see, smell, and hear them crowd this scene. The people of the land are so tightly packed in that when a paralyzed man is brought to be healed by Jesus his helpers cannot even enter the door. Those who have brought the man dig through the earthen roof and lower him down on a mat. Both of these images serve to underline the simplicity and poverty of the setting, as Jesus is in the house of a peasant, and the man's thin mat is the bed of a poor man (Mark 2:2–4).[11]

Mark narrates that "when Jesus saw their faith, he said to the paralytic, 'Son, your sins are forgiven'" (Mark 2:5). Notice that Jesus does not see the internal belief of an individual. Rather he sees *their* faith, their trust and loyalty. He sees the paralyzed man within the context of the people of the land and in the specific relationships of those who care for him, who would not let their way be blocked. Jesus replies by verbally bringing the man to his bosom. He calls him "my Son" or "my child." In the context of first-century Palestine, it would likely have been assumed that the man's condition was due to some transgression or impurity that he had committed or that was committed by his parents.[12] This would have meant he would have been

---

10. Myers, *Binding the Strong Man*, 156.

11. Myers, *Binding the Strong Man*, 154.

12. Myers, *Binding the Strong Man*, 155.

ostracized by the community. Jesus, instead, brings the man in close and declares that "your sins are forgiven." He brings him back into the community and relieves him of blame.

The story shifts to the scribes who were present. Jesus detects their ire, as they think he has blasphemed in declaring that the man's sins are forgiven. They think, "Who can forgive sins but God alone?" (Mark 2:7). Yet, what they are really protesting is the undermining of their own authority. It is the elites who are supposed to be able to confer forgiveness and to restore people through their system. Jesus, however, through his healing and therapy is showing an alternative way. For the man who could not walk, who had his path to Jesus blocked, Jesus goes further and says, "Stand up, take your mat and go to your home" (Mark 2:11). Under the gaze of the elite and living in one order, the man is unable to move. In the order opened by Jesus, the man is animated to follow a different path and his way to his home—his place, his community, the land—is restored.[13]

At the heart of the story are broken bodies, but also opposing orders. The paralyzed man is kept down by one order, but he is also a figure for the rising of a whole crowd. The people of the land have been blamed for their condition.[14] Jesus comes to restore them to wholeness, and to overturn the violent and internally oppressive orders of empire that have rendered them excluded.

The elite support a system where the paralytic is singled out and blamed for his malady. The faith that allows him to find forgiveness comes through *their* faith—the shared faith of the man and those who love him. The man finds forgiveness and is otherwise named through solidarity. This trust transforms an illness that rendered the man disabled to one where the man can move and act.

The shift to the social perspective makes the resonances of the story pressing today as it transforms our approach to those who are called disabled. As contemporary disability activists and theologians argue, the challenge of disability need not be confined to an individual. Persons who are otherwise-abled often object that there is nothing broken about them. They are simply different, and they live in a society that does not empower them to function wholly as they are. They are dis-abled by an environment that makes it difficult for them to simply enter buildings, and, as in the story, to move through doorways. What is needed is a healing transformation of the environment that accommodates their needs. By adding ramps, providing sign language interpreters, or audio recordings, those who are

13. Brueggemann, *Land*, 163.

14. Hendricks, *Politics of Jesus*, 71–73.

otherwise-abled can begin to be given access to a world that fails to address their needs and abilities. The therapy, in this case, is social as it takes our collective faith, trust, and loyalty to live in solidarity and to more fully share the world with others. This allows us to transform the implicit message written above every doorway that the disabled person has done something wrong or is someone in need of forgiveness and repair. We must, instead, begin to transform the structures of our lives, to dig out roofs and to challenge the elite, so that we understand that we are all children of God.

The order of empire has left many of us injured and feeling incapable. As I noted in the previous section, its names for us—autonomous individual or entrepreneur—claim to make us powerful but end up rendering us motionless as we are made responsible for the inevitable outcomes of a rigged game. The best way to escape these names is to take on alternative names—like being named a child of Christ. As in the story, we can communally be brought into the embrace of Christ and told that our supposed sins are forgiven by being addressed as Christ's child. This is not unlike the therapeutic power of a workaholic forcing himself to spend time with family and friends, or to engage in a hobby. So long as he is persistent in his commitment of time, the workaholic can begin to see himself again not as supervisor Michael or as Dr. Smith, but as someone's brother, son, or college roommate. Through these relationships, parts of himself that had become dormant or atrophied are once again animated.

Even more important, in becoming a member of the family of Christ, the values, bonds, and rituals are necessarily different from those of the prevailing work culture. The culture of entrepreneurship trains us to look up, to strive after the status and spoils of those who are a level above us in the hierarchy. This fosters competition, coveting, and contempt as we constantly see what we lack. But to be a child of Christ is to begin to look around and see the suffering that surrounds us. It is to see the crowd—the people of the land—and to find solidarity. This shift in identity and relationships frees us from petty grievances. It is a shift I struggled to make when I worked at a college, to stop resenting the fact that I did not have tenure or higher pay, and, instead, to see the staff who were paid less and the students amassing debt. The cycle of coveting what is above and blaming oneself for not having it is alienating. It is like running at a full sprint and getting nowhere. The self-interested gaze is also an obstacle to asking deeper questions beyond an increase in one's own pay or title, to thinking about a living wage for all or the subtle ways institutional power is being exercised to change the nature and values of the community. By looking around, instead of up, we can come into different relationships of trust, solidarity, and love that help us find wholeness *together*.

Neoliberalism and the Broken Web of Life

Our world is ill. Our society is tottering toward ecological catastrophe, and yet we cannot act. A healthy, sustainable society is often said to rest on three pillars: the environmental, the economic, and the social. In our context the environmental pillar is crumbling under the stress of ecosystems devastated through extraction (of minerals, forests, and topsoil), pollution, and the change of climatic conditions through carbon emissions. All of this extraction and fuel has served to build up an economic pillar—a physical and cultural architecture—that is premised on its unending growth. Pressures from environmental collapse and economic inequality have in turn led to the profound erosion of the social pillar, as all forms of community and collective action—other than that of the profit-seeking institutions—have been actively undermined. If you will allow me to switch metaphors, it is as though we are in a car with the accelerator stuck to the floor (the economy) racing toward a bridge that has collapsed (the environment) without any means of changing course (the social).

These pillars have been crumbling for centuries. Some trace it back to colonialism and the slave trade, others to the industrial revolution, others to the mid-twentieth century growth of consumer culture. All of these narratives are both true and useful. We should not lose sight of longer arcs of time and cultural formations in diagnosing the problem, as we must see the role that racism, sexism, classism, the objectification of the natural world, mechanization, urbanization, suburbanization, and the pursuit of wealth play in our current predicament. This is part of the premise of this book, which is drawing a strong analogy to millennia-old formations of empire and current orders. But, I think given the systemic problems that are menacing us, specifically around what is called the social pillar, it is helpful to look a little closer to home.

The erosion of the three pillars of sustainability was greatly intensified in the political, economic, and cultural movement known as neoliberalism, that came into power in the 1980s. Given the dominant categories that are often used to characterize political life in the United States, this term is a bit misleading. Most of those who are called liberals *and* conservatives in the USA are a part of the neoliberal movement. Neoliberalism refers to the ideology that freedom is realized through an unfettered market—liberty is achieved by economic means. It is linked with the political project of privatization (so that utilities, schools, prisons, or even the water is governed by private corporations), the deregulation of markets (only "market forces" dictate the use of land, humans, water, and air), and the lowering of taxes (no "property" is collectively held or reserved for the common good). Neoliberalism is manifest in the social realities of the loss of public spaces, dividing the world into the private property where one lives, works, shops, or pays for entertainment. The proliferation of programs at public libraries is an illustration that they are one of the last bastions of public space centered on the common good. Everywhere else has been privatized and protected with a pay wall.

Neoliberalism is most powerfully and clandestinely manifest in the ways that all aspects of life are understood through the calculus of the market—reducing humans to human capital.[15] Here one invests in their children's future, working to give them opportunities and earning potential.[16] The logic of the market is applied to analyzing and judging marriage, education, or criminality—understanding them in terms of the optimal application and management of scarce resources.[17] One views one's self as a business—managing time, energy, relationships, and risk exposure accordingly.[18]

Neoliberalism has become the dominant force on the earth for the last several decades. Hence, while conservatives in the United States are often its most fierce advocates, even liberals typically tout market-based solutions. Even when a left-of-center politician makes an argument for a program concerned with the common good it is for the purpose of growing the economy: We need to educate our children, *so that* we can compete in the global economy. We need to provide health care, *because* it will ultimately save us money. We need to switch to a green economy *because* it will provide new, good-paying jobs.[19] This limited form of thinking and acting includes the environmental movement, which has focused on changes in consumer behavior, partnerships with private corporations, or market-driven solutions like new markets created by technologies (solar power) and forms of economically incentivized restraint (carbon offsets).

The hegemony of neoliberalism intensifies the problems connected to climate change. Not only is unfettered economic growth at the heart of the problem, the destruction of all alternative forms of collective action make it difficult to change course.[20] There is no way to separate out these injuries and crises. Ecological devastation, economic exploitation, and social alienation are inextricably linked.

15. Brown, *Undoing the Demos*, 31.
16. Foucault, *Birth of Biopolitics*, 229.
17. Foucault, *Birth of Biopolitics*, 268–69.
18. Brown, *Undoing the Demos*, 34–37.
19. Brown, *Undoing the Demos*, 26.
20. Klein, *This Changes Everything*, 19–21.

The response to this tangle of problems means that we need to repair bodies and habitats, to work for justice and equity, *and* to mend and build up community. We need to transform the pillars of sustainability—the environmental, the economic, *and* the social. Social issues are often neglected in the work of the care of creation. This is in part because social change is not easily measured. The committee of the concerned does not want to pause to connect and consider how to change their everyday lives. They want to get on with the *real* business of achievable and measurable tasks.

Perhaps the greatest obstacle is that social issues are undeniably matters of value. Unlike the supposedly value-free measurables of emissions or improved efficiencies, issues of social repair call into question the individualized, inequitable, consumptive, wealth-centered values and ways that animate our lives. Furthermore, we avoid this work of social repair because the apparatuses, assessments, and architecture of neoliberalism have created single-serving, individually achieving, and privacy-protecting lives in which our capacity for collaboration has been profoundly diminished.[21] We are out of practice with being and working together. The structures and institutions that serve to hold us in relationship and to channel our energies have been worn down from the onslaught of privatization, deregulation, and cost-benefit assessment (with the notable exception of the floundering hold-outs of the family and the church).[22] Our ecological context and social bodies are suffering from illness and in need of healing and therapy.

If we are to begin to respond adequately to the crises of climate disruption and profound injustice, we will need to build up forms of practice and communities that foster sustainable life and which have the power to resist and transform the structures of neoliberalism and empire. Some of our central tasks will be to heal the broken bodies, spirits, and communities that have been left in the wake of the great economic machine.

We are called to heal people and institutions. First by naming and casting out the invasive and debilitating power, spirituality, and narratives of empire, and then by inviting people into an alternative kingdom. The most vital work will not be done by committee but in community.

Possessed by Empire

Earlier I noted that I sometimes feel *possessed* by the American Gospel of Work. Despite what I say I value, I find myself drawn into forms of desire and action that place me at odds with myself. Part of me sees the cascading

21. Darot and Laval, *New Way*, 306.
22. Rogers-Vaughn, *Caring for Souls*, 72.

consequences of my striving after success or even security. Part of me wants to be defined by gentleness, humility, compassion, and wisdom. But often my days are driven by fears of being judged a failure by the criteria of empire (Rom 7:15–20). Sometimes I feel like I am living in someone else's dream, like the American dream alters the reality around me. I am not confessing to insanity, but I am trying to name a tension that marks our lives. This play of cultural forces reinforced by institutional pressures, advertising, and everyday relationships are not far from what is meant by the power of spirits and demons in the Scriptures. What they called Satan and demons are what we today name oppressive power structures.[23] Jesus' acts of exorcism, then, are the unveiling and overcoming of these powers.

The language of demon possession is often used by colonialized communities, in which an invading, brutal, and oppressive occupying power has changed indigenous ways of life. Colonial and imperial forces will often simply eradicate any direct opposition with violence and death. Therefore, it is safer if the dissonance, injury, and rage is internalized.[24] Colonized people often speak of invading spirits as a form of self-preservation.[25] Subjected peoples can name the problems they currently face, without confronting the oppressor who would execute them. But for some the pressures and traumas become so great that they break under the weight.

Galilee and Judea were subject to these kinds of Roman domination and violence.[26] These dynamics are perhaps most pronounced in the story of Jesus' exorcism of the Gerasene demoniac. Mark opens the story, writing, "they came to the other side of the sea, to the country of the Gerasenes. And when [Jesus] had stepped out of the boat, immediately a man out of the tombs with an unclean spirit met him" (Mark 5:1). There are a couple of aspects of the staging of this scene that draw our attention to the oppressive presence of empire. Though Mark draws our attention to Gerasa, that city is about thirty miles southeast of the seaside where Jesus gets out of the boat and confronts the man. Gerasa is invoked because it was a place of revolt against and slaughter by the Romans. In terms of geography Jesus' seaside landing in the story is closer to Tiberias, the second imperial city constructed by Herod Antipas. A city that was built on a graveyard.[27]

Mark goes into uncharacteristic detail in this scene, providing markers that point toward its political significance. We are told that the man

---

23. Fiorenza, *In Memory of Her*, 123.

24. Horsley, *Jesus and the Powers*, 117.

25. Horsley, *Jesus and the Powers*, 122–23.

26. Horsley, *Jesus and the Powers*, 122.

27. Myers, *Binding the Strong Man*, 190–91.

could not be restrained even by chains, and that he spent night and day in the tombs "always howling and bruising himself with stones" (Mark 5:3–5). When he sees Jesus, he recognizes him as "Son of the Most High God" (Mark 5:6). It is typical of the demonic powers that they know the identity of Jesus and correctly identify his power and opposition, even when others cannot. Jesus demands that the demon tell him its name. It replies, "my name is Legion; for we are many" (Mark 5:9). *Legion* is a Latin word with one meaning in this context: it names a group of Roman soldiers. We are presented with something like a political cartoon. At the site of a known revolt and slaughter, in the shadow of an unnamed imperial city, Jesus meets a man possessed by the violence of the Roman military who has turned his rage on himself.

The story takes an even more cartoonish turn as the spirit begs him to be sent into a nearby herd of swine (Mark 5:10–12). Whereas kosher eating practices prohibited Jews from eating swine, Roman soldiers often raised pigs for food and trade. Jews often referred to Romans as pigs.[28] Jesus grants this wish, and Mark describes the scene with military terminology (often lost in translation), as the "herd" (a Greek term used for a group of military recruits but not pigs) is *ordered* to *charge* into the sea.[29] Jesus' power of exorcism here echoes the exodus led by Moses that marks safe passage into new life while the oppressive forces are drowned in the sea.

In this scene of exorcism Christ comes upon a man imploding under the violence of empire.[30] Jesus first displays his power by demanding that the demon give its name. Here the power of naming that excludes the leper is employed in a different way to make clear the identity of the invader. The name is "Legion," the force that claims to provide peace, abundance, and security. But in this man, it reveals itself to be demonic. Jesus proceeds to open a path for a new exodus outside of the bonds of subjection. He does so with a different and greater kind of power.

The story ends not with Jesus being congratulated, but with being asked to leave. The swine herders run off and tell people what they had seen. When they saw the demoniac acting differently, they begged Jesus to leave (Mark 5:14–17). They were familiar with the kind of power the Romans wielded and knew what direct opposition would bring.[31]

---

28. Carter, *Matthew and the Margins*, 212–13.

29. Myers, *Binding the Strong Man*, 191.

30. Brock, *Journeys by Heart*, 80.

31. Hollenbach, "Jesus," 583.

Healing What the Empire Cannot

The agents of the empire are not simply demonized in the Gospels. There is hope that they might be changed and transformed. Even those with power and privilege are, in their own ways, trapped and possessed. In the story of the rich man who Jesus tells to sell his estates that he gained from exploiting others (which we explored in chapter 3), Jesus attempts to call him into discipleship. The verbiage in the story, Jesus' initial command for the man to get up, echoes healing stories (Mark 10:21).[32] Jesus attempts to heal the man of the sickness of excess or to exorcise him from his possession by wealth. In this account the man fails to follow the ways of Christ (it is difficult for the rich to enter the kingdom of God).

In an encounter with a centurion Jesus was a bit more hopeful. This commander of one hundred Roman soldiers approached Jesus and said to him, "Lord, my servant is lying at home paralyzed, in terrible distress" (Matt 8:6). Calling Jesus "Lord" is seditious. This is a title for Caesar. Yet, here a retainer for the Empire, a man who wields power but who himself is also subject to orders, approaches a Jewish teacher and healer and recognizes his authority. Furthermore, he does so for the sake of a servant who is in terrible pain.

Jesus responds that he will come and heal him. The centurion replies that he does not measure up to Jesus and he cannot have Christ under his roof. The centurion asks him to "only speak the word" so that the servant may be healed (Matt 8:7–8). The centurion is still shaped by the form of power and order that rules the Empire. This order is all about hierarchy and subjection. In acknowledging Jesus' authority, he seems to imagine that it is somewhat like the power he wields as centurion but greater. The centurion says, "for I also am a man under authority, with soldiers under me; and I say to one, 'Go,' and he goes, and to another, 'Come,' and he comes, and to my slave, 'Do this,' and the slave does it" (Matt 8:9).

As the story illustrates, Jesus' power operates in a different way. His is not the force exercised over those who are lower, but it is a power that lifts up the poor, oppressed, and broken. His authority does not leave those below him paralyzed, but animates them for action and wholeness.

Nonetheless, Jesus is "amazed" by what the centurion says. Christ extols his faith (Matt 8:10). The term *faith* (*pistis* in Greek) in the Gospels means something close to our words "trust" or "loyalty"—present in our use of the word "faithful." Reducing faith to belief—as an individualized mental assent to an assertion for which we do not have accurate proof—is misleading.

---

32. Myers, *Binding the Strong Man*, 273.

Rather "faith" in the Empire (or *fides* in Latin) referred to the loyalty of relationships of patronage. One shows their faith through loyal service to someone above them in the hierarchy.[33] In the Empire, one shows their faith, or loyalty, by paying their debts or honoring their oaths, by paying their taxes and providing soldiers.[34] We show what we trust every day by giving of our time, our labor, and our children. This shapes what we think is possible in the world. The faith that heals is the power that comes from trusting that God is good. This trust overcomes fatalism, and is not a paternalistic power, but the empowering spirit of the kingdom that animates those who are suffering.[35] This power does not move unilaterally, but it breaks through old power structures and is conducted through the participation and animation of new relationships and communities.[36]

The centurion showed his faith in another form of power. Even though the soldier had been trained by the order of empire, he was able to recognize something different and greater in Jesus. He did not turn to the Lord of his imperial superiors and their power and wealth. He sought to find healing for what the Empire could not heal, and for the injuries that the Empire had wrought. He stepped outside of the world he had been taught to trust and obey, and he humbled himself before Christ for the sake of a servant.

Jesus restored the servant to health, but he made clear that he was no chaplain of empire. His ministry is not to keep slaves functioning and productive.[37] Nor is he the military champion of Israel that will turn the Romans into its slaves. Rather, he speaks of the coming messianic banquet and the kingdom of God that will topple the present order. He declares, "many will come from east and west and will eat with Abraham and Isaac and Jacob in the kingdom of heaven" (Matt 8:11). The image and gathering of the banquet, which will be the focus of chapter 6, points to a restored creation in which everyone joyfully feasts together with the Creator. In painting this image Jesus includes gentiles. He even has hope for this soldier who has begun to trust in a different kind of power—one that lifts up the poor, that heals the broken, and that transforms the world.

33. Carter, *John and Empire*, 266.

34. Carter, *John and Empire*, 267.

35. Sobrino, *Jesus the Liberator*, 92–93.

36. Brock, *Journeys by Heart*, 87.

37. Carter, *Matthew and the Margins*, 200.

Transforming Middle Managers

Christ points toward the nearness of the kingdom of God through the shifting loyalties and faith of a Gentile retainer of the Empire. The centurion wields a certain kind of power. He exercises force, subjection, and coercion. But as a middle manager he is also subject to these forces. Though he has not left this world, he has come to see that there is a different kind of power. He knows that this other authority cannot be brought under the rule of his house as presently ordered, *but* it can come to transform and heal the suffering of his house.

Power moves and is conducted by certain relays and circuits, as displayed in this healing story. In our houses the power of electricity pulses through wires hidden in our walls. It is conducted by ubiquitous apparatuses, power lines and substations, that we have come to look past and ignore. The operations and architecture of the power of the empire similarly surround us and hide in plain sight.

Neoliberalism—the culture and systems that force everything to conform to market mechanisms—works through specific large formations. Work is abstracted from home and from a sense of place by a road system that allows a long commute and forms of reasoning that reduce realities to monetized calculations. The suburban home in the neighborhood without sidewalks or common space separates people. Its ownership also demands debt. This debt and the culture of conspicuous consumption, in turn, puts greater emphasis on work and income. In this geography many relationships are defined by market forces. Furthermore, the pressures on time— from the commute and the demands of a frantic workplace—mean that non-market driven relationships become increasingly tenuous. And so, it becomes normal and seemingly natural, to look at all of life in terms of neoliberal values and calculations.

But neoliberalism also works through more ephemeral and less obvious spiritualities and forms of power. As Margaret Thatcher, one of the great champions of neoliberalism, quipped, "Economics are the method. *The object is to change the soul.*"[38] The centurion's life is structured by relationships of patronage and a world of commands and subjection. The middle managers and functionaries of neoliberalism lead lives structured by assessment and self-monitoring. Whereas contemporary regimes of management were established in the 1990s under the pretense of being anti-bureaucratic, what formed is simply a different, more individualized, and competitive mode of bureaucracy. The shift to flexible and creative networks of management

38. Darot and Laval, *New Way*, 292.

has served to move the surveillance and supervision from a centralized and regularized space onto the individual worker.[39] The seemingly neutral grids and mechanisms of assessment that the worker constantly applies to her own action produces a kind of enterprising subject. The worker polices herself in constantly seeking to be more efficient, and increasingly colonizes her time in relation to work.[40] Power, in this neoliberal spirituality, works by getting the subject to adopt the game of striving after success in all aspects of life.[41]

Shifting attention onto seemingly neutral modes of assessment that are self-driven serves to make actual institutional forms of power invisible. This means that not only is it difficult to name or understand the forces that oppress one's life, but it privatizes suffering. Now one owns their own suffering, as it is one's individual failure that appears to be the cause. Furthermore, many modes of therapy serve to place the onus of change on the individual. The increasing emphasis in the world of psychological healing is to make people *adapt to* the system that causes them pain. Here the individual is isolated from her social and political context and is directed to focus on the symptoms of social illness as it is expressed in her stress, depression, or anxiety, and is in turn counseled to take responsibility and to personally manage her pain.[42]

This power can be transformed so long as it is identified and named—if we can make the possessing force confess its name as "Legion" and uncover the violent and exploitative ways in which it operates. There is hope for further change if we can begin to see a liberating path through a new exodus or through alternative forms of power that heal. Likewise, by coming to further understand the mechanisms of neoliberalism we can begin to oppose them. So long as we do not see an alternative, we are left with the negative task of resistance. Which is why it is so vital to oppose the order of alienated placeless individuals with life-giving, place-based communities.

There is hope for the middle managers of empire if they will begin to heal their social networks. There is also hope for the kingdom if the middle managers use their points of access to institutions of power to begin to transform them. This will mean doing *the opposite* of what is currently done. In the neoliberal age, well-meaning middle managers import the strategies and mechanisms of the market-driven world everywhere. Churches discern their mission and organize their work through corporate processes of strategic planning. Communities imagine how they might work together and help

39. Darot and Laval, *New Way*, 291.

40. Darot and Laval, *New Way*, 292.

41. Darot and Laval, *New Way*, 312.

42. Rogers-Vaughn, *Caring for Souls*, 100.

their members grow through secular personality assessments and personal coaching that take the values of efficiency, productivity, upward mobility, and wealth accumulation for granted. Nonprofit boards and churches organize their time around budgets and measurable outcomes. In these contexts, the middle managers continue to exercise the power and spiritualities of empire in the last bastions of hope for transformation.

Instead, we should be seeking conversion. Those who are midstream between the few elite and the mass of poor should be finding communities of solidarity and transformation that help them to understand how the world could be different. And then they must undertake the difficult work of taking these subversive and healing alternatives into the belly of the beast.

A Community of Healing in a Sick Society

The Gospel of Matthew closely links Jesus healing with his acts of teaching and organizing. The work of his followers to renew covenantal communities and restore the relationships between God, neighbor, and the land is part of the act of casting out the imperial powers and healing broken bodies. Directly preceding the Sermon on the Mount, Jesus' first teaching discourse in Matthew, Christ's ministry is described: "Jesus went throughout Galilee, teaching in their synagogues and proclaiming the good news of the kingdom and curing every disease and every sickness among the people" (Matt 4:23). The sermon is immediately followed by the healing stories explored in this chapter—the leper, the centurion's servant, the demoniac, the paralytic. Both teaching and healing are centered on the ushering in of a new social structure or a new family with God as a Father. This ministry fosters wholeness. As Christ declares in the sermon, "You shall therefore be whole [*teleioi*], as your heavenly Father is whole" (Matt 5:48).[43] We can see in Christ's teaching portraits and practices that help to shape communities that can heal a sick society and earth.

At the heart of this healing ministry is the rejection of the imperial way of living that is centered upon greed, consumption, hoarding, exploitation, and violence. As Christ puts it, "No one can serve two masters . . . You cannot serve God and wealth" (Matt 6:24). Followers of Christ are advised not to hoard and store up wealth in the economy of the empire, but to place their treasures in God's abode—the heavens (Matt 6:19–21). This is the order in which abundance actually lasts and sustains, and therefore, at stake is the pursuit of justice against wealth rather than making a deposit in the

43. Translation from Davis, *Biblical Prophecy*, 217.

bank of the afterlife.[44] The prayer of Jesus is that God's will be done *on earth* as it is in the heavens (Matt 6:10).

In contrast to the ways of empire, the sermon extols the just and sustainable communities of covenant renewal. The sermon echoes some of the reversals of the kingdom at the heart of Luke's Sermon on the Plain, which we treated in chapter 3. In Matthew, Jesus declares similar beatitudes: blessing the poor in spirit, those who mourn, those who are hungry, and those who are persecuted (Matt 5:3–4, 6, 11). Likewise, he underlines the generosity and forgiveness that will be necessary for community to be restored and nurtured (Matt 5:38–48; 7:1–5, 12, 15–20). This opening also echoes the Jubilee declarations of Isaiah, the passage Jesus reads at his first sermon at Nazareth in Luke, in which he declares that he is anointed to bring good news to the poor. Both the messianic passage from Isaiah and the opening passage of the Sermon on the Mount bring good news to the oppressed, the brokenhearted, the captives, and those who mourn (Isa 61:1–3).[45]

This declaration of Jubilee—of the Sabbath restoration of equity among people and justice for the land—is most directly captured in a beatitude only found in Matthew, which is a quotation from Psalm thirty-seven: "the meek shall inherit the earth/soil/land" (Matt 5:5/Ps 37:11). The word *meek* is used only two other times in the Gospel and both refer to Jesus and designate his humble submission to the ways of God (Matt 11:29; 21:5). Psalm 37 provides a portrait of this meekness by contrast with the wicked who seek power and wealth through violence and exploitation. This is the perennial tension between the agrarian context of faithful living and imperial extraction.[46] The Psalm calls upon its hearers to take delight in the Lord and to trust God (Ps 37:4–5). They are to wait patiently and not to fret (Ps 37:7). The Psalter acknowledges that, by contrast, the wicked plot, "they draw their sword and bend their bows to bring down the poor and needy and kill those who walk uprightly" (Ps 37:12, 14). While the wicked borrow and do not pay back, the just "are generous and keep giving, for those blessed by the LORD shall inherit the land" (Ps 37:21–22). The vision outlined in the Sermon seeks to fulfill the justice of the prophets and the covenant with God and the land in the face of a sick culture of ruthless exploitation and wicked profiteering (Matt 5:17–19).[47]

The sermon is not extolling the acts of individual piety but the kinds of practices and values that make a community of blessing and compassion

---

44. Kinsler and Kinsler, *Biblical Jubilee*, 101.

45. Davis, *Biblical Prophecy*, 210–20.

46. Davis, *Biblical Prophecy*, 226.

47. Crosby, *House of Disciples*, 180.

flourish. The counsels are about shared life and a way of dwelling together. Christ proposes the metaphor of those who hear his words and act are like "a wise man who built his house on rock" (Matt 7:24). Even when rains and floods come, the house stands (Matt 7:25). But for those who do not act, their house—and presumably their household, the social structure in which they live—is washed away (Matt 7:34–35).[48]

These acts are concerned with the character of community. Hence one should not trumpet when they give alms because doing so reinforces the economy that made almsgiving necessary in the first place (Matt 6:2). The public giving of alms lifts up the privileged and lowers the poor. It also obscures that the source of the bounty comes from creation, not from our own action. Therefore, Christ counsels, "when you give alms, do not let your left hand know what your right hand is doing" (Matt 6:3). We must remove the calculations of the imperial economy from our act, *and* the pretense that the work of our hands provided the gift in the first place. The true reward comes from God, here named as "Father" (6:4). That is, the true reward comes from living in God's household here and now in which abundance is shared and there is always enough.[49]

Likewise, Jesus outlines acts of mercy, peacemaking, and forgiveness within the community that make a certain kind of social life possible.[50] For example, he advises that one should avoid being angry with a member of their community and should place reconciliation above religious rituals and outside of dominant structures of power (Matt 5:21–24). Living a spiteful and litigious life has the consequence of being in a social environment where one will be thrown into prison or stripped of every last penny (Matt 5:25–26).

In the Sermon Christ directs us to shape our way of life around joyful and simple creatures—lilies and birds—rather than kings. In everyday matters like food and dress we are told not to worry (Matt 6:25). Jesus advises, "Consider the lilies of the field, how they grow, they neither toil nor spin, yet I tell you, even Solomon in all his glory was not clothed like one of these" (Matt 6:28–29). Solomon is introduced here not just as an exemplar of fine dress, but as a negative example of opulence and excess.[51] This excess has a seductive function in empire as it grips our hearts. Clothing can, in the blink of an eye, communicate our place in pyramidal structures. The game of dress and display directs our cares and worries to the hierarchy

48. Crosby, *House of Disciples*, 195.

49. Malina and Rohrbaugh, *Social Science Commentary*, 58–59.

50. Malina and Rohrbaugh, *Social Science Commentary*, 52–53.

51. Carter, *Matthew and the Margins*, 178.

of status. Turning our attention to the ways of creation strips us of this pretense. It points us toward ways of being and creatures that are beautiful as they are. The verbs used here, to look and observe the lilies and the birds, carry the connotation of really taking time to attend to and learn from creation.[52] This spiritual practice takes off the names and fine robes of empire and renames us as creatures of God.

The call to not worry about food and clothing is centered on fostering the kind of life that comes from trusting in God rather than one's own industriousness or the bounty of empire. There is no denial here of the need for food and clothing or the effort required to procure it. Rather, Jesus directs us to "Look at the birds of the air; they neither sow nor reap nor gather into barns, and yet your heavenly father feeds them" (Matt 6:26). Jesus is not ignorant of the fact that birds do forage and look for food throughout the day. Rather, he is highlighting that they do not engage in specific kinds of agricultural work that place some distance between the blessings of creation and what nurtures us.[53] As we gather into barns, we might imagine that we are feeding ourselves. But an orientation toward the world as God's creation make every loaf, even those baked by us, bread from heaven. The soil, the sunshine, the rain, the growth always comes from God. The kind of work the birds undertake makes that blessing more obvious. They labor for daily bread and "do not worry about tomorrow" (Matt 6:34).

We are shaped by the ways that we eat, dress, and understand our work. The empire grips our heart in these everyday and seemingly invisible spaces, but so can God. In transforming these practices and relationships we can begin to heal our sick social systems. Jesus calls upon us to "strive first for the kingdom of God and his justice, and all these things will be given to you as well" (Matt 6:33, translation slightly altered).

Healed to Serve

The social illness that plagues us undermines our efforts to change course and to bring about wholeness. We need social healing and therapies. Like the leper we need to come to see the ways that we are mis-named, blamed, and exploited. Like the paralytic, we need to find forms of faith, trust, and solidarity that allow us to take on new names. We are not autonomous individuals, success-seeking entrepreneurs, or free consumers. These names obscure the ways that institutional and corporate power keep us oppressed

52. Bauckham, *Living with Other Creatures*, 138.

53. Bauckham, *Living with Other Creatures*, 140.

and paralyzed. We are, instead, members of places and communities. We can be children of the anointed one of God.

These societal maladies appear more clearly if we, like the Gerasene demoniac, are able to speak their cruel name. We are possessed by the violent forces of empire, the occupying legions. For some communities, these forces take the shape of actual brutal police. But for everyone in empire, there is an internal form of policing that moves along relays of discipline and assessment, and through specific architectures and lifestyles.[54] Seeing these forms of power, like the centurion, might allow us to see that alternatives are possible. Knowing the violent ways of neoliberalism may mean that the middle managers of our empire can begin to learn in solidarity with others and intervene in their points of access to power.

In all of this, healing comes through alternative relationships and communities. These communities move against the Gospel of Work that extols wealth, status, competition, and an opulent vision of the good life. The community of covenantal renewal sees the blessing of the meek. The meek who inherit the earth are not passive, but they are courageously and nonviolently devoted to God in the face of wickedness. They live in trust, solidarity, and generosity. This generosity is based on a sense of blessing. As everything comes from the goodness of creation, our job is not about extracting and accumulating, but sharing and repairing. The reward that one gets from giving with one hand without the other knowing is to live in a healthier and more loving creaturely community. This community is driven by peacemaking and mercy. The exemplars of this joyful life are humble creatures, not kings. The lilies and birds point us toward different forms of everyday conduct that shape our hearts to be less centered upon status and autonomy. Learning from creation, we are trained to enter into a more egalitarian and simple way of living.

We often miss these social aspects of the healing stories, in part, because we reduce them to being miracles or matters of supernatural proof. In my presentation of the healing stories I hope I have not robbed them of their enchantment, of the mysterious and mystical improbability that the marginalized can find new life and become agents for a different kingdom. For example, in the first healing story in Mark, Jesus enters Peter's house and finds his mother-in-law in bed with a fever (Mark 1:29–30). Jesus "took her by the hand and lifted her up. Then the fever left her, and she began to serve them" (Mark 1:31). Something odd and beyond our normal modes of understanding is at work here. Not the least of which is

---

54. Foucault, *Discipline and Punish*.

the enchanting possibility that a poor woman might be able to find new life outside the powers of the Empire.[55]

This story illustrates two important aspects of discipleship. First, just a few verses after we are told that Peter and Andrew are called to leave their current occupations we are shown that Peter still has a home *and a wife.* The disciples are simply trying to transform communal relationships so that they can live in the kingdom of God rather than in the kingdom of Caesar. Second, the task that Peter's mother-in-law is said to take up, serving, is a central term in Christianity. It could be translated: she "began to minister" or "deacon them." While Peter's mother-in-law is not the first called disciple, she is perhaps the first to understand what it really means to follow Jesus. This is not because Peter's mother-in-law is undertaking some complicated task that is different from the commonsense understanding of what this term means—typically to serve *food.* But rather, the community of the children of Christ are often formed around a table of shared food and service. We now turn to the everyday and enchanting act of sharing a meal that challenges what is commonly taken as "the real world."

---

55. Betcher, *Spirit of Disablement*, xi.

6

Sharing Meals

WHEN MY FATHER DIED, the loss initially felt twofold—as we had lost both his life and the memory of elements of his identity. For about a decade he had suffered from dementia. This long process of saying goodbye meant that we had slowly and informally been mourning the death of parts of him. While his ability to teach physics was the first layer to be peeled away, over the following years we would unconsciously bid farewell to different aspects of his personality. As our roles flipped from children to caregivers, *our* memory of his fatherly presence began to fade.

A simple meal began a process that would restore many of these memories. After holding a night time vigil by my father's death bed, my brothers and sister gathered in my mother's home. Friends started bringing over food. One family, the McLeans, who had served as the co-pastors of our church during my childhood, lingered and shared a meal with us. They had not been strangers to my dad during his illness, but their memories of him were much more pronounced around who he had been. They recalled a church elder and physicist talking about the spirit of God in terms of the forces of electromagnetism. They remembered the kind-hearted, even-keeled, and introverted father of four. As we sat around the table, we shared a meal that nourished our exhausted bodies and stories that comforted our aching spirits.

As we broke bread with our dear friends and shared stories about my father, I found that my own memories of who he had been were beginning to be restored. This not only diminished my sense of loss, but it also strengthened my feeling of connection to the communities of which I am a part. We, each of us, are parts of a larger body. When one of us dies we do not simply feel an internal loss of our own experiences and possibilities. Rather, the loss of a member is the loss of an essential part of a body that I am a part of, which means part of who we are is missing. Mourning is a healing process of finding the way that we will all move forward, injured and hobbled, but still living and loving. Together, we feel and see the connections that still exist.

Yet, this sense of community feels like it is fading too. At my father's funeral I felt a sense of community that is often lacking in my life. The church sanctuary that is sparsely populated on typical Sundays was packed. Family and friends who we used to see on a regular basis were in the same place. These social bodies do not simply feel distant because of the passing of previous generations, but like the gradual process of dementia, there seem to be cultural forces that have slowly peeled away some of these layers of togetherness. The pressures of employment and the seductions of success have intensified what is often spoken of as the freedom of mobility. Though I now live in my hometown, many of the people who I was closest to in my youth live elsewhere. Even for those with whom I live in proximity, because of the complexity of schedules, the foreclosing of common space and the expansion of our private worlds, the demands of work, the diminished capacity for attention, and the fraying of social structures that hold us together around shared values, it is difficult to connect. Slowly and unconsciously people of privilege (and I suspect most everyone shaped by neoliberal structures) have been engaged in saying the long goodbye to community, as members are severed from social bodies.

The shared meal is one of the few common spaces remaining where we can still easily, and almost intuitively, find community and a sense of health. At its best, this meal can be the enfleshment of shared life—as the fruits of our labors of caring for the land are prepared so that our bodies might be nourished, and our spirits delighted. In this way, the meal is not a break from our way of living, but it can be its fullest expression. Our fragmented schedules, alienated labor, compartmentalized dwelling places, and broken food systems mean that meals that embody that kind of integrated living are likely rare experiences, but glimmers of them exist throughout our lives. Dramatic events, like the death of a loved one or a wedding, might make the potency and promise of the meal palpable. On a much more regular basis, we all experience the gift of good food and companionship. And so, we know the ways that meals can restore and heal our lives.

The shared meal is a place where we can come to know—to bodily witness, to habitually shape, and to communally learn—a way of life that restores a sustainable and joyful rhythm. Gathered around a table, we can begin to remember the types of community that we have forgotten. Through the shared, sustainably sourced seasonal dish we can start to heal our relationships with the land. Through honest and faithful conversation whereby we share burdens and echo praises, we can deepen relationships with neighbors. By seeing the sacramental character of food and fellowship, we can be invigorated by the spirit of God that pulsates throughout creation. By breaking bread from house to house we can gain a vision of how beautiful community can be and build solidarity for collective action.

Stories about similarly transformative meals abound in the Gospels, and in them are cultural visions and practical strategies to transform community. Through banquets and wedding feasts Christ gave people a foretaste of a more joyful life. These joyful meals enlivened imaginations to envision what could be. These meals served to help people remember the covenantal ways that had been lost and the paths to liberation that could be opened. Through engaging in social experiments in the low-risk space of someone's home, Jesus subverted hierarchies, boundaries, and etiquette to foster a different way of life. Through joyful meals Jesus sought to heal and restore those who had been injured by empire—both those who had been weighed down by its injustice *and* those who had lost themselves in their pursuit of success and their service to the structures of extraction.

Banquets on the Path of God's Anointed

In the Gospel of John, Jesus begins his ministry in Galilee at a party. The first sign of his glory is to keep the celebration going. Jesus, his mother, and his disciples are at a wedding banquet. Just as the wine runs out, Jesus' mother calls on him to do something about it. He instructs the servants to fill up "six stone water jars for the Jewish rites of purification" with water. When they filled them up with water, they drew some out and took it to the chief steward, who was amazed that it was good wine, which had been kept for the end no less. While the servants knew the source, the chief steward had not seen (John 2:1–11).

Like many other signs and wonders, this is a story about healing and restoration. In this story, what is being healed is the social body. Here traditions of purity typically kept in stone jars are transformed into the gift of the joy of good wine and the celebration of abiding love. At this party, the servants understand what their boss does not. The Empire often named itself as the source of abundance. It declared the "good news" that Caesar had conquered the world and ushered in a golden age where banquets abounded, and wine flowed. Jesus, instead, performs a sign that that there is another source of blessing.[1] Here a wonderworker from Galilee procures somewhere between 120 and 180 gallons of good wine. This moment of delight in community inspires Jesus' followers to trust in him and his alternative way of spirit and light against the darkness (John 2:11).

1. Carter, *John and Empire*, 224.

John places this simple celebration on a cosmic stage. He introduces the story by telling us that "on the third day there was a wedding in Cana of Galilee" (John 2:1). Following the sequence of days already mentioned in the Gospel, this is the seventh day—the Sabbath day. As the Gospel begins with placing Christ at creation and as the wisdom that shapes creation, this story is staged as the opening of a new creation.[2] Understanding a banquet as the manifestation of an idealized or utopian order was not uncommon in the late ancient world. Banquets and symposiums were often thought to be glimpses of the world as it should be governed.

This wedding banquet is both an embodiment *and* a symbol of what the glory of Christ can do in the world. In the Hebrew Scriptures, when the prophets speak of what a restored relationship with God, neighbor, and the land looks like, they speak of weddings and wine.[3] At the beginning of his ministry and with his first s.ign, Jesus gives the disciples and the people of Galilee a taste of the goodness of the fruit of the vine and the bounty of a new creation.

It is important to start with this scene of joy and delight, because the meal scenes, as with so many elements of the Gospels, are steeped in controversy and judgement. This ostensible negativity is at the forefront because the good news of Jesus is gloom and doom for those invested in the ways of empire. At its heart, Jesus' vision is an affirmation of creation and community.

For those familiar with the prophetic tradition, this positive vision serves as the background for each of these banquet scenes. The ideal of the banquet is a culturally charged image that communicates volumes in an instant. Like the association of the house with the white picket fence with the American dream, the messianic banquet captures a whole set of values and assumptions about how a well-ordered life and community should look. Because we are likely not familiar with this vision, it is worth fleshing out this implied ideal. The messianic banquet marks the restoration and realization of a new covenant. As Isaiah imagines, when God has overcome the

---

2. Howard-Brook, *Becoming Children*, 77.

3. Isaiah envisions the restoration of the people of Israel after the exile by singing, "You shall no more be termed Forsaken, and your land shall no more be termed Desolate; but you shall be called My Delight Is in Her, and your land Married; for the LORD delights in you" (Isa 62:4). Living rightly on God's good earth means the joy of harvest time when there is enough for all. As Amos promises, "The time is surely coming, says the LORD, when the one who plows shall overtake the one who reaps, and the treader of grapes the one who sows the seed; the mountains shall drip sweet wine, and all the hills shall flow with it. I will restore the fortunes of my people Israel, and they shall rebuild the ruined cities and inhabit them; they shall plant vineyards and drink their wine, and they shall make gardens and eat their fruit" (Amos 9:13–14).

death-dealing ways of empire, in the kingdom of God, "the LORD of hosts will make for all peoples *a feast* of rich food, *a feast* of well-aged wines" (Isa 25:6-8).[4] At this messianic banquet God will wipe away all tears, and people shall say that this is the Lord for whom we have waited. They will declare in praise, "Let us be glad and rejoice in his salvation" (Isa 25:8-9).

The messianic banquet fulfills the reversals of the kingdom, where the relationships of the covenant are restored (Isa 55). The image of the banquet is animated by joy and justice for a new creation.[5] This ideal meal plays upon experiences of loving communion, where people celebrate the bounty of the harvest with food, wine, song, and conversation. This imagined banquet also incarnates the promise of the Messiah, where all are not simply fed for one meal, but the food system is healed, so that all are sustained (Luke 6:21; 12:37; 14:15; 22:16, 29-30). When Christ speaks of the kingdom, he speaks of a time when "people will come from east and west, from north and south, and will eat in the kingdom of God. Indeed some are last who will be first, and some are first who will be last" (Luke 13:29-30).

The reversals of the messianic banquet undermine the glamor of wealth and success, and they show that the banquets of the elite are not refined, but they are excessive, and they require the suffering of others and the degradation of the land. As Mark draws in stark contrast, the banquet of Herod, eaten on the backs of slaves and with the main course being the severed head of the prophet John the Baptist on a platter, is profoundly different from Jesus and his disciples organizing a banquet for five thousand in the wilderness, in which everyone was filled, and food was still left over (Mark 6:14-44).

Yet, because people were trained to see from the perspective of empire, the positive vision was often lost. The elite named themselves virtuous and pointed to the corruption of tax collectors and the impurity (in our terms, laziness) of the poor as the root of social problems. As Luke tells us, the "children sitting in the marketplace" see that "the Son of Man has come eating and drinking," and say: "Look, a glutton and a drunkard, a friend of tax collectors and sinners" (Luke 7:32, 34).

The positive valence of Jesus' banquets are also often lost, because they are *not* centered on the opulence and excess of empire, but on the subtle ways of *joy*. In the Gospel of Luke, joy is associated with the restoration of what had been lost, with a present condition of solidarity and love, and the hope of a future fullness and peace. When asked about his practice of eating with sinners, Jesus responds with parables about the joy that is felt when

4. Brueggemann, *Isaiah 1-39*, 199.
5. McFague, *Body of God*, 139.

a shepherd finds a lost sheep and when a woman finds a lost coin (Luke 15:4–5, 8–9). This is the joy of God over the repentance, or change of life, of one who will follow the path of Christ to covenantal renewal (Luke 15:7, 10). This joy is like a father whose prodigal son returns home and greets him with a great banquet (Luke 15:11–32). It is the joy of the seventy, who Christ sent out to engage in his work of countering the powers of the Empire through the practices of hospitality, solidarity, and the healing of people, who return and *rejoice* at the transformation they have seen (Luke 10:17–20). This is the joy of the promise and hope felt by John the Baptist's father, Zechariah, when he heard of his son's birth and prophetic calling (Luke 1:14). Likewise, the joy of the banquet is felt in the restoration of the ties of the covenant, the present realization of solidarity and love, and the hope that this combination of sustenance and shalom can be sustained.

This vision of joy is, perhaps, most profoundly obscured by the stumbling block of the cross that is placed on the path to the messianic banquet. Empires meet prophetic radicalism with resistance and violence, not with open arms. And so, Jesus warns in the parable of the Sower that those who initially receive the word with joy but "have no root" will fall away "in a time of testing" (Luke 8:13). This is realized in the joy of the crowd gathered at the Mount of Olives, who rejoice upon seeing the messianic Jesus approach Jerusalem in hopes of a militaristic revolution and who soon abandon Christ's cause (Luke 19:37). This is why Jesus calls those who are excluded, reviled, and defamed on his account "blessed." They should "leap for joy" when this happens, not because Christ is a masochist, but because they know that their provocations are unsettling the unjust powers of empire (Luke 6:22).

The Gospel of Mark lifts up as the exemplar of discipleship an unnamed woman who anoints Jesus for his messianic task. She understands that Christ's path leads both to judgement and a banquet. As they are sitting at a table in the house of Simon the Leper in Bethany, "a woman came with an alabaster jar of very costly ointment of nard, and she broke open the jar and poured the ointment on his head" (Mark 14:3). As Jesus describes it, "She has done what she could; she has anointed my body beforehand for its burial. Truly I tell you, wherever the good news is proclaimed in the whole world, what she has done will be told in remembrance of her" (Mark 14:8–9). Unlike the disciple who betrays him (Judas), the one who denies him (Peter), or those who imagine that following them will give them status (James and John), this follower understands that the Messiah will suffer and be crucified.[6]

---

6. Fiorenza, *In Memory of Her*, xiv.

She knows that the path to the messianic banquet, by way of the cross, comes with great cost and the promise of profound change. Her act is to anoint Jesus with a material that is lavish and beautiful, capturing the joy of the banquet, while also preparing him for conflict with the Empire. Therefore, when some scold the woman because the ointment could have been sold and the money given to the poor Jesus responds, "Let her alone; why do you trouble her? She has performed a good service for me. For you always have the poor with you, and you can show kindness to them whenever you wish; but you will not always have me" (Mark 14:4–7). In this instance, those who scold the woman look toward charity, toward giving people fish for a day, whereas Jesus' task is to restore the health of the lake and the bonds of a community who will know how to fish and share generously. They see a commodity that could be used within a system; she sees the long, joyful, and suffering path of the anointed that could bring about systemic change.

This contrast between treating symptoms and treating causes is often lost because readers of the passage misunderstand Jesus' reference to the poor. Jesus' declaration that "you will always have the poor with you" is a riff on the realistic acknowledgment from Deuteronomy that "there will never cease to be some in need on the earth" (Deut 15:11).[7] Far from confirming the inevitability of poverty, this passage about the economic relationships of the covenant is critical of the structures that produce poverty and calls for systemic change. The declaration that the poor are always with you is completed: "I therefore command you, 'Open your hand to the poor and needy neighbor in your land'" (Deut 15:11).[8] The contrast that Jesus draws is between the small kindness of alms and the transformative potential of the way of the one anointed by God for reordering social and economic life writ large. The emphasis is placed, then, on the lavish anointing of the Messiah and the backdrop of the banquet, which can bring about transformation.

As we think of the transformative potential of the meals of Christ, we should not lose sight of the wedding feast that promises to restore our place as God's beloved and the land as married to the Lord. We must look for the ways that these scenes measure up to or differ from the messianic banquet in which all are included, and the hierarchies of empire are toppled. We should understand the purpose of banquets is to incarnate the joy that comes from

---

7. Brueggemann, *Money and Possessions*, 197.

8. This passage is a commentary on the cultural and human tendency to make a mess of things. It begins by noting that *if only* people would keep the covenant there would be no one in need (Deut 15:4). To address these issues, then, it calls for the *structural* changes of the sabbath forgiveness of debt, open-handed lending to those in need, a mentality of generosity, and honoring reparations owed to former slaves (Deut 15:1, 6, 8, 10, 14).

the restoration of the lost, and the love, solidarity, and hope of covenantal life. Yet, because the ways of empire still hold sway, the path of the anointed will lead to conflict, and as his followers, so will ours.

Dinner Church, or the Political Power of a Meal

The prophetic woman who anointed Jesus understood the path of discipleship—the cost, the suffering, and the beauty required to walk it. This path moves through trials, but it is oriented and sustained by the joyful banquet. We often miss the positive vision of the banquet because we are shaped by the norms and values of the empire, and this extends toward our effort to work for justice.

Efforts to bring about structural change in liberal and even progressive circles in the United States often limit their focus to the type of power exercised by civic institutions. While these institutions must change, and doing so will take a great deal of organization, circumscribing political action to simply voting, protesting, or demonstrating misses out on alternative forms of power. For example, following the civil rights movement, Student Nonviolent Coordinating Committee leader John Lewis turned his attention to organizing cooperatives, credit unions, and community development groups, which served to take care of the needs of people, build just community and economic institutions, and cultivate collective power that could be used in direct action.[9] Followers of Jesus are not simply called to resist or to change minds, but to build joyful community and to change communal life. The work of justice should be concerned with fullness—the realization of goodness, love, and peace among people, God, and the land. This sets our eyes on working *for* transformation and not just *against* empire.

Part of this work is to build structures and practices that actively shape relationships and values. This way we are not simply trying to debate with others, but we can invite them into a different, better way of life. Social practices, like transformative meals, incarnate alternatives and create a sense that another way is not just possible but *viable*. If we are to sustain the long work of social change, we must come to know—viscerally and communally—the viability of a different path.[10]

The contemporary movement of dinner churches holds the promise of fostering one kind of transformative space into which we can invite

9. Nembhard, *Collective Courage*, 214–20. Along similar lines, but in a different cultural context, see Elizondo, *Galilean Journey*, 117–19.

10. Schade, *Creation Crisis Preaching*, 52.

people. Though the term *dinner church* points toward a wide variety of communal practices, what holds them together is the simple desire to combine worship, fellowship, and nourishment. These gatherings often feel fresh and inventive, yet they are deeply rooted in the ways that early Christian communities gathered—as described in Paul's letters, the Acts of the Apostles, and, of course, the Gospels. Some communities combine the gathering of a meal with a formal liturgy and a teaching led by ordained clergy. Others eat together around a table and share a simple worship service in a separate space. There are dinner churches that have transformed their structure to accommodate intergenerational participation, adapting a version of Godly Play to tell the stories of Scripture and to cultivate wonder. Some dinner churches are a part of an established congregation, others exist as their own community and their membership often cuts across traditional lines of religious identity.

The Green Christians community, which my wife and I began, is animated by a flat leadership structure and a loose liturgy. We gather around a meal, which is prepared with attention both to the dietary needs of the group and with a concern for the land from which it came. While we begin the meal with a blessing, the entire meal is a form of prayer, as we share joys and concerns as we eat. During this time, we learn to pray with our eyes open—our laughter and lament mingles with our reaching for God. Here that which is personal and religious is integrated with the everyday and the public. After everyone has shared both food and faith, we chew on a piece of Scripture together through a modified version of *lectio divina*. We read and discuss a passage of Scripture three times—the first time we try to listen to it on its own, the second we listen for how it connects to our lives and communities, and the third we listen for what the Scriptures are calling us to do in the coming weeks. Through this practice the words of tradition come to frame our lives in ways that are sobering and invigorating. We conclude by sharing communion—re*membering* Christ's liberatory meal.

This dinner church meets in our house. While this location was initially chosen out of necessity—so that both my wife and I could participate within earshot of our infant son—it has been a blessing to bring these practices and relationships into our domestic space. The compartmentalizing of church to a singular building and to a special time allows for all kinds of values to be held at a distance. The mortgage, the new television, the home improvement project, and the all-consuming job come to feel like a part of a different world that plays by its own rules. The idealism of the gospel seems to be a force that is exceptional. But by meeting in our home, in the space of everyday practice and mundane decisions, the path of discipleship seems closer. Here a deeper form of integration becomes possible, as we begin to practically understand the roots of the term *economics*—the rule of the household.

This sense of integrity is further facilitated by the meal. The worshipful spirit that hovers over the dinner serves to transform the food from simply being fuel, to sacrament. This food is a sign of the love of the Creator, and the holiness of the life of creatures. Such spiritual eating heightens a sense of care and attention to the source of the meal, whether it is a blessing that cares for creation or a bounty that feels like it was robbed from the land. The materiality of food, in turn, brings the divine closer. Here the sacred is not ephemeral but embodied. The demands of faith flow out into the practical space of daily life.

Though I am ostensibly the leader of this group, I do not come with a well-ordered plan. I come on my knees. Many weeks I greet everyone with a thin veneer of calm hiding my exhaustion and struggles with despair. The simple structure of the meal, worship, and study allow for openness and vulnerability, because it is the practices that provide the hands that hold us together and that guide our actions. Here the words of tradition—of prayer, Scripture, and sacrament—are taken up and used in our conversation. They color how we understand what is happening in our world and our lives. They point us toward understanding problems not as private, but as part of long spiritual and political struggles. They direct us to look toward values and forms of power that heal through service, that teach through loving witness, and that see the Creator pulsing through all parts of creation.

I always leave our gatherings emboldened with hope—not because the worries I brought to the group have been solved, but because I have been built up by the moral courage of those with whom I have broken bread. The gathering reverses my everyday experience in which the structures of empire speak loudly with moral authority, but everyday interactions hum along at the level of small talk. Normally, the advertisement tells me what happiness and success look like and mechanisms of assessment force me to fill out their forms and describe my days in their terms. Etiquette demands that when I speak to coworkers and neighbors I not share too much of my struggles and requires that I avoid giving voice to deep frustrations with the priorities of our bosses, our complicity in economic exploitation, or call into question our games of status. In the intimacy and honesty of our dinner conversation, by contrast, we can give voice to these pains and reach for alternative hopes. The values of Christian tradition frame our lives in terms of justice and love, rather than productivity or success. The gathering repeatedly reinforces this. We cannot learn these lessons once, just as we cannot shower once and for all, because we are constantly soiled by the filth of empire. The dinner church provides a consistent, loving, communal space where I begin to see the viability and beauty of another, shared way of life.

Our dinner church typically begins in the evening and concludes after dusk. As our conversation progresses, and we have spoken of the blessings in our lives and the profound pain and folly that surrounds us, the light streaming in through the windows diminishes. As we meditatively pore over the words of Scripture, the darkness settles in outside. All that is left by the end is the yellow electrical light illuminating our dining room, which makes the space feel smaller. It is at this time, when we are huddled together, more awake to the empire outside our door and more committed to pursuing the way of love to transform it, that we turn to the Lord's Supper. In this context Jesus' transformation of the Passover—the celebration of liberation from Egypt—does not feel so abstract. The fearful empire that found it necessary to arrest and execute Christ seems less ancient and strange. Even more importantly, in the closeness of community, the gift of bread and wine taste sweeter. As we serve one another the Eucharist—following the ways of our Lord who followed the servant's path—the promise of a new start and a new covenant feel less otherworldly and more incarnational.

In the social space of this meal norms are transformed, relationships are altered and deepened. Aspects of our lives that are normally separated, are integrated. Gathered around a table, feasting on word and sacrament, tradition improvisationally shapes our community and makes a new world possible.

The Last Supper of the New Exodus

While it is important not to lose sight of the images of the messianic banquet, in which our shared lives are bathed in the light of God's goodness, sometimes an attention to darkness can make the light seem brighter. For example, the chiaroscuro of art—the use of a pervading darkness in relief with a bright light—brings forth the boldness of a figure. In Caravaggio's *Supper at Emmaus*, which portrays the appearance of the risen Christ to two disciples, the foreboding blacks and browns of the background make the rays of light cast upon Jesus' and the disciples' faces even more striking—focusing the viewer on the moment of epiphany (Luke 24:30–31). I find that attending to the darkness of the conflict with empire that underscores the Gospels' telling of the Last Supper serves to bring to the forefront the promise of liberation that this meal offers. The darkness that looms outside of the upper room where Jesus gathers with his disciples, his new family, draws our eye to the light that surrounds their table fellowship. Here the ordinary acts of sharing bread and wine serve to enflesh a new household, which holds the power of liberation and transformation.

Set against the backdrop of the observance of Passover, the Last Supper is illuminated by the memory of the liberation of the people of Israel from bondage in Egypt (Exod 12:14–17; Deut 16:1). The darkness of the empire absorbs any background light at the meal. The conflict with imperial occupation and the memory of liberation meant that the annual observance of Passover in Jerusalem, when pilgrims would flood into the city, often boiled over into acts of rebellion against the Romans and the elite.[11] This foreboding backdrop heightens the significance of what happens at the table. Here Christ transforms the Passover into a new exodus—a liberation from empire that moves through trials in the wilderness, but which inaugurates a new covenant.

The Gospel narrative dramatizes the looming darkness, as the Last Supper takes place after Jesus has occupied the Temple. Christ has made his opposition to the Empire and its collaborators known and they now sought to arrest and execute him (Luke 22:2). The Synoptic Gospels record the detailed directions he gives to his disciples to set up the meal. This serves to highlight that Jesus has inspired the ire of the elite and must now move through the city clandestinely. He directs the disciples to look for "a man carrying a jar of water"—a task usually carried out by a woman, making it just strange enough for them to notice, but not so odd as to draw the attention of his imperial adversaries (Luke 22:10–12).[12]

With the Romans and their collaborators (the new Egyptians) hot on his trail, Jesus looks forward to the coming kingdom, to the messianic banquet where people will be freed from the Empire.[13] He opens the meal, saying to them, "I have eagerly desired to eat this Passover with you before I suffer; for I tell you, I will not eat it until it is fulfilled in the kingdom of God" (Luke 22:15). Through sharing and remembering, this meal inspires people who live under oppression to hope for a different world.[14]

The darkness looming in the background makes the light of God that is close to us in everyday practices much more striking. Christ draws attention to the simple elements that make up their meal: bread and wine. In addition to having a religious and political backdrop, Passover and the Day of the Unleavened Bread have an ecological and economic context—they are

11. Horsley, *Jesus and the Powers*, 168–69.

12. Myers, *Binding the Strong Man*, 360–61.

13. Street, *Subversive Meals*, 180.

14. Bieler and Schottroff, *Eucharist*, 19–23, 53.

part of the harvest festival of barley.[15] Barley is coarser than wheat but can be grown in worse soils and is harvested earlier. Unlike the whiter breads, which were reserved for the rich, barley bread was the poor person's food.[16] During the harvest festival of the bread of the poor, Jesus "took a loaf of bread, and when he had given thanks, he broke it and gave it to them" (Luke 22:19). The actions here are the same that animated the sign and wonder of covenantal organization and sharing that fed five thousand in the wilderness. Now, sitting with his friends at the table, the barley bread from the wilderness—which echoes the blessing of the manna from heaven that requires restraint, sufficiency, and thanksgiving—is shown to be at the heart of the household. This staple of life is revealed as a blessing, not a commodity, which must be honored and shared.

By enacting this sharing of the bread, Christ is echoing the typical blessing of the *paterfamilias*, the head of the household, who would say a prayer and hand the bread to each member.[17] This ritual passing of the bread from the father of the household to his wife, children, extended family, and possibly servants bonded them together. The small piece of sustenance was a sign of a greater commitment to inclusion and care.

When Jesus takes the loaf of bread and breaks, blesses, and shares, he is instituting a new household, which will subvert the ways of empire. This aspect is made clearer if we understand that a wider group than twelve men are present at this meal. In our mind's eye we should see a collection of disciples that included women, and the symbolic presence of the twelve that represent the tribes of Israel.[18] Christ transforms who is included, how the household is governed, and how the world (*oikoumene*) is organized. By claiming this mantle, Christ redraws lines of kinship and care. By giving the gathered followers this bread, they are given a new set of brothers and sisters to care for and rely upon (Luke 8:19–21; 22:32). The intimacy and reciprocity of this new household is extended much more widely, an extension that, with God or Christ at the head, moves to the ends of the earth.[19] This extension undermines the extractive economy of the Empire with a household rule of mutuality and generosity.[20] Placing Christ at the center serves not only to seemingly infinitely expand the circumference of who and what are included, but it also serves to topple and reorder how things work within. Christ's way

15. King and Stager, *Life in Biblical Israel*, 86.

16. King and Stager, *Life in Biblical Israel*, 95.

17. Myers, *Binding the Strong Man*, 262.

18. Bieler and Schottroff, *The Eucharist*, 53–54.

19. Elliott, "Temple versus Household," 105.

20. Elliott, "Temple versus Household," 114.

of leading by service transforms the hierarchical, unilateral, and patriarchal structures of the normal household.[21] As, for starters, no male could claim to be *the* father but was now always a brother and son.

Having given them the bread, Christ shifts the event that the Passover commemorates from the exodus out of Egypt to the exodus of his life, death, and resurrection.[22] Jesus says to them, "This is my body, which is given for you. Do this in remembrance of me" (Luke 22:19). It is the liberation that *Christ* enacts that we are to now remember at this meal. The new exodus from empire follows the path of teaching, healing, and organizing, which results in persecution but ultimately leads to new life. This remembrance is enacted in this meal and in the form of table fellowship he has practiced throughout the Gospel and which will serve to shape the communities that follow him.[23]

The mixture of joy and sacrifice that marks Christ's path is highlighted as, after the meal, Jesus takes the cup, and says: "This cup that is poured out for you is the new covenant in my blood" (Luke 22:20).[24] Through this meal the disciples are given a taste of a restored covenant with God, neighbor, and the land. In this upper room the darkness of the Empire is overcome by the light of liberation. The fruit of the barley festival, the poor man's bread, is shown to be a sacramental blessing that should be shared. In sharing it with them, and calling upon them to share, Christ has begun to topple the hierarchies of the elite and the Empire. Jesus does not see this meal as a single event. Rather, he passes it on to them as a ritual and a celebration to be remembered. In their observance of this meal the disciples can continue the work of remembering covenantal community and enacting liberation.

---

21. Copeland, *Enfleshing Freedom*, 63–64.

22. Street, *Subversive Meals*, 185.

23. Karris, *Eating Your Way*, 89.

24. The invocation of blood points to the Jewish tradition of martyrdom. The courage of the martyrs shows that resistance is possible. Life under the empire can lead to the living death of a fatalistic acceptance of oppression. The sacrifice of a martyr who holds on to their faith and hope in the face of the worst that the empire has to offer, counterintuitively, shows that there is an alternative. Their shed blood bears witness to the hope of returning to living in God's covenant under any circumstances, that not even death can rob us of this. Bieler and Schottroff, *Eucharist*, 61. The Gospel of Matthew adds at the end of this declaration, that this has been done, "for the forgiveness of sins" (Matt 26:28). The word for forgiveness here (*aphesis*), could also be translated as "release." This is a word used repeatedly to designate the year of Jubilee, the remission of debts, the release of captives, and release for imperial taxes (Lev 25; Deut 15:1–31; Isa 61:1; 1 Macc 13:34). The implication here is that the new covenant of Christ enacts a Jubilee release that is cosmic, political, and personal. Carter, *Matthew and the Margins*, 507.

The Last Supper of the Servants–Turning over the Tables of Empire

As is the case with most lessons and revolutions, the disciples do not immediately realize this promise of the new household. A dispute breaks out among them "as to which one of them was to be regarded as the greatest" (Luke 22:24). In this moment they give voice to the orders of empire that still live within them—that cultivate a desire for status within their hearts, and places them apart from and above others.

Jesus unveils the structures behind this urge to be "the greatest." He says, "The kings of the Gentiles lord it over them; and those in authority over them are called benefactors" (Luke 22:25). In the Empire, the kings and the elite lord their power over people by demanding not just their compliance but also their gratitude and admiration. In this world "benefactors" are the elite who give not necessarily what is needed, but who contribute their time and money based on their whims. As such, their supposed generosity often perpetuates neediness and merely cultivates feelings of indebtedness. Christ is not describing here the immoral abuse of neutral systems of power, but the way that this entire moral order is structured.[25]

This hierarchical structure is most clearly staged through banquets that reinforce status.[26] There is a power that comes with being the host. Whether one is the benefactor of an elite party or a soup kitchen line, there remains the dynamic in which those who receive whatever the host chooses to share are supposed to feel indebted.

Christ's advice to the disciples is to not seek the place of the benefactor at the banquet, upon whom all feel compelled to heap praise, but to play the role of the servant. He tells them that they are different from those shaped by the Empire: "rather the greatest among you must become like the youngest, and the leader like one who serves. For who is greater, the one who is at the table or the one who serves? Is it not the one at the table? But I am among you as one who serves" (Luke 22:26–27). Their hearts should not be set on status but on the needs of others.[27] Yet, to observe this in everyday life would be to subvert the very social logic of empire, and in turn, to lose whatever status one might have.[28] In their world, as in ours, not playing the games of status means losing status.

25. Green, *Gospel of Luke*, 767–68.
26. Street, *Subversive Meals*, 193.
27. Green, *Gospel of Luke*, 769.
28. Street, *Subversive Meals*, 193.

Christ is calling for the reordering of households around relationships and structures of mutual service and cooperative love. At stake, then, is not simply the reversal of hierarchies, where those on the bottom are now on top, nor is it just resistance to the dominant structure. Rather, he is pointing toward the processes that will bring about healing and health. It is a bit like toppling the hierarchical order of our inequitable international economy with the formation of local cooperatives. This would mean redistributing the power and wealth centralized into of the hands of a few elite owners and corporations, into cooperative communities of shared governance, responsibility, and sufficiency.[29] Through this way of organizing, households are animated by shared service and sufficiency, rather than resources being extracted from the many and shipped off to the few.

In the Gospel of John this new order of servanthood is incarnated at the Last Supper through Jesus' act of washing his disciples' feet. This is an act of hospitality typically performed by slaves after a long journey.[30] In taking off his outer robe, pouring a basin of water, and wiping the disciples' feet, Jesus engages in a subversive act that inspires Peter's objection. Peter cannot conceive of how he could be worthy to have Christ wash his feet, but Jesus makes clear that his path requires both the reception and the performance of loving service (John 13:1–8). Christ is not seeking to normalize the imperial hierarchy of master and slave or to reverse it, but he is enacting a new practice and order of mutual service.[31] Christ instructs them, "So if I, your Lord and Teacher, have washed your feet, you also ought to wash one another's feet. For I have set you an example, that you also should do as I have done to you" (John 13:14–15).

Through this bodily, communal practice we move down a path to new life. By breaking bread and sharing we can institute a new household order and see the shape of a different economy. Through the shared cup we can understand the connection between joy and sacrifice. By taking on the role of servant we can begin to repent of the ways that the empire has shaped our hearts and relationships.

Transformative Meals for the Oppressed and Oppressors

Jesus and the movement that followed him were not alone in using meals as social laboratories. In the ancient world the private space of the meal

29. Eberhart, *Rooted and Grounded*, 129–50.

30. O'Day and Hylen, *John*, 137.

31. Carter, *John and Empire*, 275.

in the home allowed for a somewhat safer domain to challenge and transform the hierarchies that ruled public life.[32] Groups and associations used meals as spaces to resist the Empire, to find ways to play with and subvert hierarchies, to claim different loyalties, and to flirt with alternative forms of power.[33] Throughout the Gospels, but especially in Luke, meals are a site of repentance and transformation. Meals serve as experimental spaces that allow for radical change to emerge. Here people find forgiveness and new life through an alternative, joyful form of gathering.

The dynamics of this social and personal change play out quite differently between oppressors and those who are oppressed. The oppressed are healed by being embraced by a new covenantal community. Though they have been *called* sinners by the elite, Christ rejects this way of naming them. By contrast, those who are part of systems of oppression are told to repent of their lives, to change their hearts, and to turn things around.[34] We can see this in the tale of two banquets held by tax collectors that bookend Jesus' ministry—that of Levi and Zacchaeus.

Early in his ministry, when he is gathering the initial twelve disciples, Jesus encounters "a tax collector named Levi, sitting in a tax booth" (Luke 5:27). Because he is sitting in the booth, we can assume that Levi is not a rich man. In the Empire, many taxes were collected in the form of tolls, which we might understand as duties collected on traded goods (mentioned in chapter 3 in our discussion of the Galilean fishing industry). People with means could bid on the right to collect these tolls for the Empire. This was profitable because the collector could overcharge and keep the excess for himself. The ubiquity of corruption in this system, in addition to the act of collaborating with the Empire, meant that people in this business were reviled. The person who bid on the right to collect these taxes was not, however, the same person who would sit at the booth and collect the tolls. Rather, these toll booth employees were poor, often desperate, people with few options. The stench of both poverty and their loathed profession radiated from them.[35]

Jesus sees Levi and, like the revolutionary fishermen, he calls out to him: "follow me" (Luke 5:27). In this forsaken figure, Jesus sees a leader for his movement. Levi's response is dramatic and decisive. Luke tells us, "he got up, left everything, and followed him" (Luke 5:28). Yet, leaving everything does not mean that Levi now lives in a kind of possessionless wandering

32. Taussig, *In the Beginning*, 35.

33. Taussig, *In the Beginning*, 122–25

34. Sobrino, *Jesus the Liberator*, 96–99.

35. Schottroff and Stegemann, *Hope of the Poor*, 8,9.

state. Rather, it means his life becomes completely reoriented around the path of following Jesus.[36] This is illustrated by Levi's next act, which is to give "a great banquet for [Jesus] in his house." This radical change for Levi demands a joyful response, in which Levi seeks to transform his social world and his economic life. He brings together the people that he knows to show them this new path, as "a large crowd of tax collectors and others" sit at the table with them (Luke 5:29).

Where the agents of the kingdom see the beginning of the messianic banquet, those shaped by empire see problems. The elite in the area, "the Pharisees and their scribes," see this fellowship and complain to the disciples, saying "Why do you eat and drink with tax collectors and sinners?" (Luke 5:30). It is important to underline here that it is the elite who have called Levi and his friends "sinners."[37] On their interpretation of the law it is the poor and the disenfranchised who do not observe the purity laws and pay the Temple tax that have led to social decay.[38] By calling them "sinners," they have sought to deny them a place within the community of covenant.[39]

This little experiment of the banquet upsets the social boundaries that the elite want to police. To offer someone hospitality and to engage in table fellowship in this culture is to offer them a place in a community, to make them a member of the body.[40] Jesus, however, frames this act as primarily healing rather than subversive. He replies to them saying, "Those who are well have no need of a physician, but those who are sick" (Luke 5:31). Through these meals, Jesus continues his ministry of healing those who have been broken by empire. The excluded and scapegoated are invited into a new kind of community where they are no longer called to bear the burdens of the Empire, or the heavy loads of purity called for by the elite. These social pressures, like the material conditions of poverty and exploitation perpetrated by the Empire, weigh down on them. They oppress them.

Jesus calls for a different social logic and set of relationships. He declares, "I have come to call not the righteous but sinners to repentance" (Luke 5:32). We might imagine Jesus using his fingers to put scare quotes around "the righteous" as he speaks. What the elite consider to be righteous and just is what is being contested and transformed by this banquet. Matthew makes this clear in his account as he adds the prophetic citation, "Go and learn what this means, 'It's mercy I desire instead of sacrifice'" (Matt

36. Green, *Gospel of Luke*, 246.

37. Green, *Gospel of Luke*, 247.

38. Street, *Subversive Meals*, 136.

39. Carter, *Matthew and the Margins*, 219.

40. Smith, *From Symposium to Eucharist*, 245.

9:13/Hos 6:6). Here Jesus echoes the prophets' critique of the false self-righteousness of the elite, who focus on the purity codes of the Temple *to the exclusion* of the work of justice, release, and sabbath (Isa 58:3–9). Through this meal Jesus calls those who have been excluded to repentance (*metanoia*), meaning a change of life. They are healed of their past oppression—forgiven what the elite called their sins—partially through their embrace by this new community incarnated through the banquet.[41]

As he nears Jerusalem toward the end of his life, Jesus encounters another tax collector: Zacchaeus. In contrast to the toll booth worker Levi, Zacchaeus was a "chief tax collector and was rich" (Luke 19:1–2). Whereas the oppressed find acceptance and affirmation in the new community, those who have power in structures of oppression are first called to transform their lives so that they too may enter into the new covenant. Unlike the rich young ruler who, in the previous chapter of Luke, Jesus has called to sell off his plantations and give reparations to the poor, Zacchaeus is able to hear Christ's call (Luke 18:18–30).

While the chief tax collector takes some initiative in seeking out Jesus, it is the practice of hospitality that does its work on him. Zacchaeus is so desiring to see Jesus that he climbs into a sycamore tree to get a glimpse. Jesus calls him by name and tells him, "I must stay at your house today" (Luke 19:3–5). Zacchaeus responds to this call with *joy*, welcoming him (Luke 19:6). Hospitality does the same work here as it does in the mission of the twelve and the seventy, who carry out the work of renewing covenantal community both by their own gifts of teaching and healing, and in their reliance on the hospitality and generosity of others (examined in chapter 3). Zacchaeus finds himself changed by opening up his household. He says to Jesus, "Look, half of my possession, Lord, I will give to the poor; and if I have defrauded anyone of anything, I will pay back four times as much" (Luke 19:8). Through the fellowship of the meal the rich Zacchaeus, whose job it is to render a share of the fruits of the earth unto Caesar, comes to know Christ as his Lord. Doing so means that he must materially transform his life and redistribute his wealth.

41. The righteousness and conversion found at the banquet is different from the personal piety that focuses on denial. The Pharisees articulate their skepticism about the faithfulness of the power of the joyful banquet as they say to Jesus, "John's disciples, like the disciples of the Pharisees, frequently fast and pray, but your disciples eat and drink" (Luke 5:33). The Pharisees seem to think that the serious work of repairing and strengthening one's relationship with God involves withdrawing from the world and the gifts of creation. Jesus, however, holds up the ideal of the renewed covenant realized in the image of the wedding feast (Luke 5:34). Yet, he also acknowledges that in the face of empire, suffering will come, and fasting has its place along the path of the cross (Luke 5:35). Street, *Subversive Meals*, 137–38.

Are we able to hear the joy that animates all of this story? The scene of climbing a tree and being called out by name by the great teacher might awaken within us a sense of childish wonder. Here we might come to know the joy of being lost to the pursuits of imperial success, only to be invited to a fresh start. Can we feel the same joy in imagining hosting these strange figures in our house and finding a sense of love and solidarity for which we have been longing? Or perhaps most challenging of all, do we know the joy of giving away that for which we have clawed and clung, but which ultimately imprisons us? Zacchaeus, on this fortuitous day, came to know in his household the truth that it is only by losing his life that he can save it.

Significantly, Christ speaks here precisely in the terms of salvation. Yet, he does not say that Zacchaeus will be saved in the sweet by and by. Rather, after hearing of the chief tax collector's transformation of his economic life he says to him, "*Today* salvation has come to this house, because he too is a son of Abraham. For the Son of Man came to seek out and to save the lost" (Luke 19:10–11). By returning to the covenantal life of justice, equity, and generosity, Zacchaeus is affirmed as the son of Abraham, the son of the one with whom the covenant of land was made.[42]

In both of these stories the meal cultivates an alternative community. This is made possible by the transformation of oppressive social and economic structures. Jesus offers something more profound than simple inclusion or acceptance. He initiates and shapes social practices that empower people—the oppressed and oppressors—to walk in solidarity and joy. Levi is no longer spit on as sinner and forced to do the dirty work of empire, but he is called as an agent who will renew the covenant. Zacchaeus no longer hoards the scraps of the Empire's plunder, but his household is restored to the ways of the covenant. If the path of Christ were to wind by our house, what kind of meals might his call to discipleship demand?

Sustaining Justice—On Not Being the Host

In seeking to incarnate these transformative meals it is important to be careful about who we imagine the host to be. Levi hosts a banquet, but this is after he has left behind his former life, and Jesus seems to be the person holding sway. Zacchaeus welcomes Jesus, but this is initiated by Christ and it leads to the complete reordering of his household. In our efforts to work for realizing the messianic banquet we must follow similar patterns whereby we challenge the structures of empire. At the banquet, we are not the benefactors but the servants. This transformation of conventional forms

42. Brueggemann, *Land*, 165.

of relationship means the structures of benefaction are challenged *so as to create* different kinds of mutuality and solidarity.

We should be careful not to imagine ourselves the messianic host of these meals. The temptation to play the role of white savior is more subtle than many of us would like to imagine. I have slowly and falteringly recognized this tendency in myself. While some of this can be chalked up to being a character flaw, more often what is at stake is not *about me* but is about long practiced hierarchies.

For example, I recently attempted to create a community of clergy and community-based nonprofit leaders who were committed to sustainability and social justice (named the Sustaining Justice Project). I wanted to bring them together as a community of mutual support. The idea was that through shared study, prayer, and relationship we could sustain one another in the long, hard work of social change, and from this space of solidarity and love, create a concrete network for collaboration and future action.

I worked with a couple of friends to put together some visioning documents and a list of friends and acquaintances working in a shared geography to invite. We decided to start the process by gathering a dozen leaders from churches and organizations whose work was centered on downtown Lexington, Kentucky (an area with a large African American population that has long struggled with poverty, but was now also wrestling with gentrification). We planned to host a lunch where we could present the idea, have an open conversation, and figure out how to expand the circle and move forward.

At this initial gathering, I was surprised to be welcomed by skepticism, hostility, and distrust. I had anticipated that people would pat me on the back and say: "I like the idea, but I don't have time" (and this was the response of about a third of the group). Another third, however, were brutally honest about how unwelcome the idea was.

While there were a lot of obstacles toward forming this community, I think that one of the central problems was that I imagined myself to be the host. This meant that the spirit of collaboration that I wanted to animate the group did not drive the process of planning and presentation. The three of us who had been involved from the beginning were all white clergy, two of us were men, and the meal took place in a church. I initially defended myself thinking that we were just presenting the *idea* and were hoping to open the entire project to others at this point. Furthermore, I had not invited strangers, but people who, over the course of the previous year, I had conversations with that suggested to me they longed for such a group. Yet, at the heart of the problem was not simply an issue of representation on the planning committee, but the pretense that I knew what other people needed and that I could serve as the host.

After the sting of feeling misunderstood wore off, I felt like this un-messianic meal was instructive in a couple of ways. First, it was a reminder that people of power and privilege should be very careful about playing host to others. This is not to say that people of different social classes should keep to their own, but that those of us identified with power should be more inclined to listen for invitations, to show up, to learn, and to stand in solidarity. Rather than starting a new initiative driven by our vision, we would be better served by joining with existing initiatives already being led by others. When we are looking to start something new (and we must, for so much of what already exists has been coopted by empire) we will need to be guided by processes and structures that challenge and flip normal power relations.[43]

This meal also impressed upon me that much of the work of someone in my position is to go home and change the communities and structures of which I am a part. Just as the issue of race is not confined to people of color and issues of gender are not limited to women, the problems of empire are not confined to low-income communities. Rather, many of the problems that menace those communities begin upstream, from the decisions made in board rooms and the consumption of the living rooms of the rich and their middle managers. As in these previous cases, white communities and men are not called to simply help others, they are called to engage in the work of repentance and transformation.[44] This is part of the promise of liberation and joy, not a matter of guilt or shame.

Meals can serve as the space where some of the work of rooting and revitalizing places like the suburbs can happen. Seated around a table, we can find forms of recognition that are built on mutuality. Here I do not need to be up front leading, displaying my status, nor am I relegated below someone else, but we can be united in communion. Through a simple meal we can find an alternative to the destructive consumption that ravages the earth and enslaves the poor. By coming together, we can begin to be cured of our isolation and emptiness. This will mean dismantling the traps of self-aggrandizement, excessive consumption, and profound alienation that plague the lives of people in the suburbs. Curing these people of their isolation will mean the joy of redirecting their resources to the poor and learning what it means to live in covenant with God, neighbor, and the land in their household.

The task is not to get the middle managers of empire to just volunteer a few hours on their weekends or to be benefactors of the poor. It does nothing for the poor if Zacchaeus tithes to the Temple, just as it likely does little for the poor if one just tithes to a suburban church. True transformation

---

43. Salvatierra and Heltzel, *Faith-Rooted Organizing*, 38–39.

44. Harvey, *Dear White Christians*, 169.

begins when we ask difficult questions at work about what is truly valued. Repentance is realized when we examine the real cost of our consumption for the poor, ecosystems, and future generations. Righteousness is enacted when we find a way contribute to alternative food economies, when we transform lawns fed by poisonous chemicals to vegetable gardens, when we build community that does not promote empty consumption but that shows us the way to sabbath delight.

We cannot wait for such efforts to be completed before we seek to stand in solidarity with others. But so long as we do not allow the work of repentance and hospitality to transform our own households, we will continue to imagine that we are the hosts at the messianic banquet, which means that we will attempt to take the place of Christ and miss the path of the servant.

Transformative Meals for the Privileged

Christ offers us concrete instruction as to how we might find transformation if we are more often at the banquets of empire rather than the banquets of the kingdom, if we tend to see ourselves as benefactors rather than servants. This is especially pronounced in his interaction with Pharisees. Though his dealings with these affluent figures in village life is often characterized by conflict (especially when they are in the company of even more elite figures closely associated with the Temple, like scribes and lawyers), Jesus still seems to be hopeful that they can change. For example, Simon the Pharisee invites Jesus to his house, calls Jesus "Teacher," and Jesus attempts to instruct him, presumably still hoping he can be transformed (Luke 7:36–50). The Gospel moves on without telling us if Simon found repentance.[45] In these meal scenes we find counsel for how the privileged might navigate the intransigent world of status to find solidarity, justice, and love.

In a later scene in Luke, Jesus is invited by a Pharisee to dine with him. At this meal Jesus speaks truth to power by unveiling the way that etiquette can conceal injustice. Christ draws this distinction in response to the Pharisee's objection that Jesus did not wash before dinner (Luke 11:38). Jesus responds by connecting this ritual of purity to another similar convention of the Pharisees: to "tithe mint and rue and herbs" (which they view as a kind of prophylactic or protection against accidentally eating impure foods).[46] Jesus objects that they are careful to observe these details religiously but they "neglect justice and the love of God" (Luke 11:42). While Jesus does not entirely dismiss their rituals of purity, he states in the strongest terms that justice and

45. Gonzalez, *Story Luke Tells*, 84.
46. Green, *Gospel of Luke*, 472.

the love of God must be the driving force in all action. He warns of God's judgement for those who do not observe this, saying: "Woe" to those who observe minor rites but do not keep the heart of the covenant.

I compare ritual washing and preventative tithing to etiquette because they are like the observance of manners and politeness in refined society in our time. There is a certain association of virtue with wealth and power. To dress up in a black tie, to use the flatware in the proper order, and to make pleasant conversation is to be found agreeable and good. The observance of these rituals allows us to continue to labor under the illusion that our benefactors are righteous and our observant participation in their banquets is the path to goodness. But what this gilding covers up are the chains that bind together the whole affair. It would be rude to question the host's ill-gotten gains, if say they made a fortune off of fossil fuel or student loans. It would be impolite to talk about all of our complicity in these systems—that our dinners are soaked in the same oil, that our institutions feed off the same economy, and that our retirement accounts are built on the same injustice. Or, as in the case of Jesus, it would be more objectionable to simply not wash one's hands than it would be to make a *killing* in the market and pretend like everything is acceptable. Jesus highlights that this petty politeness serves to cover over cruelty and injustice, as he warns them: "Now you Pharisees clean the outside of the cup and of the dish, but inside you are full of greed and wickedness" (Luke 11:39).

Jesus does not paint a picture of their wickedness as though it were driven by hate. Rather he highlights that what is at stake is that which they love and that to which they give attention. After telling them that they neglect justice and the love of God, he warns them: "Woe to you Pharisees! For you *love* to have the seat of honor in the synagogues and to be greeted with respect in the marketplaces" (Luke 11:43).[47] They love and turn their attention to respect, success, acknowledgment, and the hierarchy that makes this possible. And too often—in the way that we spend our time, in the acts that we habitually and religiously engage in, in the company we keep—so do we.

As an antidote to the ritualistically ingested poison of status, Christ suggests that they "give for alms those things that are within; and see, everything will be clean for you" (Luke 11:41). By this Christ is not referring to the charity of benefactors, the giving of meager resources that comes with no risk, but almsgiving in this context closes the distance between the wealthy and the poor as an act of social solidarity. Through this act of giving, it is as if the other is now a part of one's kinship group.[48]

---

47. Green, *Gospel of Luke*, 473.

48. Green, *Gospel of Luke*, 471.

In response to this reprimand directed at the Pharisees, an expert on the Law (a person of even more elite status) objects to Jesus, saying, "Teacher, when you say these things, you insult us too" (Luke 11:45). This objection is important. The lawyer does not speak up for how their lives are actually centered on justice, the care of the poor, or the love of God. Rather, he notes that Jesus has been impolite. This is a bit like the contemporary appeal to civility in response to the powerful taking away health care from children, redistributing resources to the rich, justifying violence against communities of color, deepening mass incarceration, compounding carbon emissions, pushing down wages, undermining the power of labor, and expanding the war industry. If the response to the charge of greed and wickedness is: "We don't talk that way in polite society," then there is something fundamentally wrong with that society.

Jesus responds to this objection by hurling more judgement. He declares, "Woe also to you lawyers! For you load people with burdens hard to bear, and you yourselves do not lift a finger to ease them." (Luke 11:46). He goes further, tying their violence to long-standing systems of injustice, noting that it was their type that murdered the prophets, going back to "the foundation of the world" (Luke 11:47–51). For those of us who belong to this generation and to these structures of power, the example being set to guide our action is less likely the prophetic position of Jesus, who speaks boldly. Rather, if we are still dining at the banquets of the empire, then we are the ones *addressed* by Jesus. The gift he offers us is the counsel to give alms and act in solidarity with others and to turn our attention, our habitual action, our sacrifices, and desire onto justice and the love of God.

A few chapters later in Luke, Jesus offers more practical advice on how to address the impulses of insatiable consumption and greed. At this meal, Jesus is eating in "the house of a leader of the Pharisees" on the Sabbath (Luke 14:1). A man with "dropsy" appears—a potentially fatal condition in which someone's body is retaining water but they suffer from an unquenchable thirst. It is a case where one can literally consume themselves to death, and in the ancient world it was often used as a figure of destructive consumption.[49] The man with dropsy is presented in the Gospel almost as an apparition that materializes out of thin air. Luke writes, "Just then, in front of him, there was a man who had dropsy" (Luke 14:2). The man with dropsy is a figure for the entire gathering of elite banqueters, who are engaged in destructive consumption. The scene portrays how the condition of a twisted heart centered on greed and wickedness can be healed.

---

49. Karris, *Eating Your Way*, 47.

The Gospel points toward the larger patterns of Sabbath release. This story is another instance of the contrast between a focus on Sabbath observance as purifying rest and the Sabbath laws that restore right relationship between God, neighbors, and land (which we explored in chapter 3). Jesus, once again, raises this tension about the sabbath and then he heals the man. The New Revised Standard Version renders the final phrase in the scene that Jesus "sent him away," but the verb here means release. This is an act of Jubilee.[50]

Christ goes on to propose how one can behave differently at banquets so as to challenge two central structures of empire: hierarchy and patriarchal charity.[51] Regarding hierarchical division, Christ points toward its everyday manifestation at meals. In the cultural tradition of the Greco-Roman banquet, there was a seating arrangement that established an order of honor among guests—next to the host was the seat that held the greatest glory. Jesus advises people to not sit as high as they can in the hierarchy, but to sit at the lowest place (Luke 14:7–10). While his advice on this point resembles that given by Roman gentlemen to help people shrewdly navigate the etiquette of the banquet, Christ inserts an important value here that is completely foreign to the world of the elite: humility.[52] Humility is the recognition of God's greatness (not a wallowing in our lowliness). It is the recognition that all blessings and glory come from the Creator, and that we are creatures in a beautiful creation.[53] The tendency when sitting at the head of the table is to set oneself apart and to attempt to possess glory. Christ's advice is to intentionally distance oneself from this position.

To consciously place oneself at the bottom of the hierarchy at a banquet can serve as therapy for our spiritual dropsy. At the dinner party we should not try to rub elbows with the people who can help our career or elevate our status. Instead, we should seek out those who might be uncomfortable, those who are on the bottom rung, or those who are overlooked as "the help." This act is not a magical way whereby we will be seen as virtuous and made into the honored guest, but it is instead a way in which we can be released from these concerns and come to know the simpler joy of the blessings and glory of being among God's creatures. At the head of the table, God's creation is regarded as an object to be consumed, not a blessing to be honored, and the creatureliness that places us on equal footing is shrouded with the glitz of status. Distancing ourselves from this way of being at the banquet means that the night does not end with our grasping

---

50. Green, *Gospel of Luke*, 548.

51. Street, *Subversive Meals*, 154.

52. Smith, *From Symposium to Eucharist*, 255.

53. Trainor, *About Earth's Child*, 206.

after a professional contact, deal, or alliance, but with a sense of gratitude that comes from being in fellowship. "Those who humble themselves will be exalted," because they will be entering into a kingdom with a different set of social relationships (Luke 14:11).[54]

Christ goes on to undermine the rule of benefactors and the feelings of indebtedness that accompany the supposed generosity of the elite. These mechanisms of quid pro quo kept the hierarchies of the Empire gelled together, just as today when the sales representative pays for the meal or golf game, or the charity gala solidifies bonds in wealthy networks. Christ proposes that instead of organizing these kind of events that, "when you give a luncheon or a dinner, do not invite your friends or your brothers or your relatives or rich neighbors, in case they may invite you in return, and you would be repaid. But when you give a banquet, invite the poor, the crippled, the lame, and the blind. And you will be blessed, because they cannot repay you, for you will be repaid at the resurrection of the righteous" (Luke 14:12–14).

The people we are instructed to invite are not now included in the social structures as they are, but they are the representatives of the change of that very structure. "The poor, the crippled, the lame, and the blind" parallel the Jubilee declaration that Christ made at his first sermon in Nazareth, when he read from the scroll of Isaiah.[55] The point is not to make the outcast the prom queen, but to undermine the entire structure of the prom that puts wealth on display. This would demand undermining the time of the celebration where everyone stops their dancing and is made to honor and admire the crowning of those on top of the social hierarchy. With the Jubilee, the land is recognized as a blessing of God and it is equitably distributed. The age of kings and queens should come to an end, as should the rituals of benefaction. To follow Jesus' advice to change both the members and structure of our gathering is, for a certain world, social suicide.[56] But, in practical terms, it also means the undermining of the social boundaries and bonding that help keep the empire in power.[57]

When people of power and privilege attempt to enact the messianic banquet, however, they often fail to challenge these organizing structures of status, hierarchy, and benefaction. This leads them to pursue the false ideal of simply *including* those who have been excluded without challenging structures of oppression. White affluent churches, for example, will not be realizing

---

54. Street, *Subversive Meals*, 154–55.

55. Ringe, *Jesus, Liberation*, 58.

56. Street, *Subversive Meals*, 155–56.

57. Green, *Gospel of Luke*, 553.

the kingdom of God if they simply invite oppressed peoples into their fellowship hall for a meal. We must be careful in our desire to play the host. In such gatherings attention must be paid to the signs of social status and division—displayed in the clothes we wear, whose space is occupied, who speaks, and who serves whom. The privileged should find transformation through the messianic banquet for the rest of their lives through the meal (rather than playing host to a sideshow that is in tension with the rest of their lives).

Jesus is laying out a certain exit strategy for the Pharisees—showing them a way to sneak out the back door of the imperial banquet. He is seeking to topple hierarchies and to change structures. Christ, in no uncertain terms, pronounces judgements and woe upon those who will not change their ways. But at the heart of all of this is a vision of joy and blessing. Even in the meal at the leader of the Pharisee's house, after Christ gives the advice to sit at the lowest position and to organize meals for the people of the Jubilee, a member of the gathering is able to see that it carries the hope of a new life and world. One of the dinner guests pronounces a beatitude, "Blessed is anyone who will eat bread in the kingdom of God" (Luke 14:15)! To be released from the games of status and competition is to be restored into joy, solidarity, justice, love, and hope.

Knowing Christ in the Breaking of the Bread

Meals can be spaces where we find healing—both for our aching hearts and for our struggling communities. The disciples discovered this when they were grieving the loss of Jesus. Luke tells us that on the same day that the risen Christ appeared to Mary, Joanna, the other female disciples, Peter, and two of the other disciples were traveling from Jerusalem to Emmaus. They were moving from the center of power, back to the space of village life. On their journey they came upon Jesus, only they did not recognize him. To these disciples Jesus appeared to be a stranger (Luke 24:13–16). They only saw him as Christ *after* they extended him hospitality and broke bread with each other.

Like the Last Supper, this scene has a dark backdrop. As the disciples travel with the stranger, they talk about how the mighty prophet Jesus of Nazareth was crucified by the elite. They had hoped he would be the one to redeem, release, and liberate Israel. They struggled with the possibility that the Empire had won, but were also perplexed about reports that Jesus had risen (Luke 24:17–24).

With their eyes fixed on the surrounding imperial darkness, the disciples cannot see Jesus. They do not see the light of the kingdom that was kindled through table fellowship and the renewal of covenantal communities. Perhaps they expected the kingdom of God to look like the Roman Empire, only with Christ sitting on the throne. Jesus corrects their foolish and slow hearts by pointing them to the prophets. He declares that on this account the Christ, the Messiah, is supposed to suffer. Luke tells us that "beginning with Moses and all the prophets" Jesus interprets "to them the things about himself in all the scriptures" (Luke 24:25–27). Yet, even having heard the lesson of the master teacher, the disciples still do not recognize him.

As they near the village, they invite the stranger to stay with them. Unlike the parable of the Friend at Midnight, where the fraying of covenantal community is illustrated by a friend who refuses hospitality to another, the disciples urged the apparent stranger "strongly, saying 'Stay with us, because it is almost evening and the day is now nearly over'" (Luke 24:29). Here they incarnate the teachings of Jesus as they extend the care of the household beyond the boundaries of their family. In this moment, they stoke the spark of the new covenant against empire.

As they sat at the table, something interesting happened. The disciples who extended the invitation are not playing host. They are not benefactors to the stranger. But rather, when "he was at the table with them, he took bread, blessed and broke it, and gave it to them" (Luke 24:30). Christ is now the host, and the suffering servant is introducing a different order. In this everyday space, the formulation breaking, blessing, and giving followed in the organizing of the wilderness (where farmers from the bread basket are placed into small communities of mutual care) and the Last Supper (where the new exodus is announced) is repeated. In the space of the meal, the transformative power of the kingdom of God takes hold as the light of alternative community bursts forth.[58] In the breaking of the bread, "their eyes were opened, and they recognized him; and he vanished from their sight" (Luke 24:31).

This meal brings them joy. The disciples describe the feeling of their hearts burning when he previously spoke to them (Luke 24:32). What was lost, the memory and presence of their teacher, has been restored. The darkness of the Empire had threatened to take this from them, but in the joyful space of solidarity and love they rediscover Jesus *and* the bonds of community. This joy awakens within them the sense of promise and hope, as they get up that same hour and travel to Jerusalem by night. They cannot wait to be with their companions and to share how Christ "had been made known to them in the breaking of the bread" (Luke 24:32–35).

With the darkness of loss and empire looming around us it can be easy to feel as though we too are left to wander confused and alone. So long as

---

58. Karris, "Luke 24:13–35," 59.

we keep our eyes fixed upon the hierarchies of empire—enraptured by its mechanisms of power and our personal status—we will not see the light of the kingdom. We will not find Christ sitting on the throne. But if we turn our attention and efforts toward covenantal community we can start to perceive glimmers.

While a healing meal does not, on its own, topple the structures of industrial agriculture, neoliberal isolation and evaluation, destructive consumption, or oppression, it gives us a place to start and to sustain our work. The celebration of the wedding banquet can ground our labors in the positive vision of a bountiful creation that nourishes a beloved community. The great thanksgiving of communion can shed some light on the path to a new economy through a community of service and mutuality. The topsy-turvy banquets that move across boundaries, like those of Levi and Zacchaeus, can serve to embrace and affirm the oppressed and to open a path to transformation for oppressors.

Before we can recognize Christ and practice these forms of hospitality and solidarity, we might need to engage in some therapeutic action to heal our broken hearts. Those of us who are accustomed to being honored and in power might need to spend some time challenging our tendencies to think that we are the host and the benefactor. We might be well served by lowering ourselves so that we may learn the humility of creaturehood—where the world is not a collection of possessions and honors, but it is a blessing that demands our reverent care. We would be well served to twist free of the strictures of etiquette and politeness that obscure the injustice of our lives, and to begin to act as if others are a part of our household. This will have consequences for how we spend our money, direct our labor, and share our love.

Through meals that are sustainably, and perhaps locally, sourced we can begin to materially participate with delight in alternative ways of caring for the land, honoring workers, and nourishing our bodies. In communing with one another we can begin to reshape our hearts through different kinds of social relationships. Here our speech and action is not guided by the values of productivity and efficacy, but we are called into relationship through love, peace, faith, and justice. Through engaging in these social experiments we begin to create a collective power that is firmly rooted and outwardly focused. We can come to know Christ—the path of the Messiah and the new covenant—in the breaking of the bread.

CONCLUSION

Practicing Prayer

THE GOOD NEWS OFTEN feels most distant at night. I spend some of my nights sleepless and feeling weighed down by the scope of the challenges we all face. Untethered from tasks and the wakeful presence of others, at night I often feel adrift and isolated. My heart breaks as I think of the future my son faces as climate change intensifies, ecosystems collapse, and political instability and violence grow. In these moments the concerns of the culture that surrounds me—its voracious consumption, thoughtless busyness, and petty competitiveness—inspire my rage. And, as I acknowledge how much these forces possess me, it kindles self-loathing. I struggle with what I have done and left undone with my day and with my life. What have I done in the face of such great need? The scope, the tragedy, the intensity, and the alienation all converge into one voice that tells me to stop swimming against the current and to give up.

In these dark nights of the soul I struggle most with despair, with losing my trust that the world is animated by love and that life is a blessing. The opposite of faith is not doubt, but it is despair.[1] This is the resignation that the ways of the empire have not simply won, but the resignation that the imperial veneration of greed, competition, self-interest, violence, and consumption is in tune with the laws of the universe.

The depth of the suffering and the systemic scale of the ecological crisis often seem to be so massive that we fear that they are a black hole—that if we get too close to them, we will be irreversibly pulled into darkness. But the opposite seems to be the case. If we do not enter into this struggle, which implicates the logic of our lives, then we will have closed ourselves off from creation and the creatures around us. When we attempt to ignore this suffering, we are forced to numb and distract ourselves, which leads to the trap of apathy and cynicism. There is a certain kind of despair that accompanies what

---

1. Kierkegaard, *Sickness unto Death*, 49.

is often characterized as the *hopeful* action steps of addressing climate change and injustice: simply buying new light bulbs and certified organic products. Such visions of hope risk the resignation that systemic and communal change are impossible and that the ways of empire are normal and natural.

In the light of day, despair masquerades under different masks. It does not show itself in existential struggle, but it moves around in forms of denial. Despair distracts itself from the truth, skeptically declaring that climate change is not happening or ridiculously acknowledging problems but denying their implications—hoping that recycling the products of a disposable life will curb the chaos. Despair conceals itself when we numb ourselves out, escaping into empty entertainment, endless tasks, or alcohol or drugs. Perhaps most cleverly, despair hides under the cover of individual coping, whereby we find ways *not* to resist empire, but to expertly navigate the horrors it presents us with careful techniques. Despair often covers over its negativity and resignation by clinging to a separate peace, where we cut ourselves off from the greater webs of life to cling to our off-grid low-impact righteousness.

The green good news gives us a grand vision in which to hope, and simple practices to guide us on this journey. Among these, Jesus teaches his disciples to pray. Jesus models the importance of rest, withdrawal, and retreat (Mark 6:46; Luke 6:12). He shows us that even he is called to give voice to lament (Mark 14:36; 15:34). Jesus prays for our protection, joy, sanctification, and unity (John 17:1–26). In this conclusion I want to focus on the prayer he gives his disciples, and the part of the Gospels Christians know most intimately: the Lord's Prayer.

The Lord's Prayer brings the ways of God and our everyday practice together as dancing partners. The path of this book ends here because it ties together so many of the elements of the green good news. In its opening petitions, which speak of God, our hopes are set on the vision of God's kingdom come to earth. In its second part, our attention is directed toward everyday practices, where daily bread and debt forgiveness restore covenantal life. It is my hope that by knotting together these threads in a prayer that is regularly recited that this can become a polar star of the green gospel. Every time we utter this prayer we can find ourselves reoriented toward the path that God's anointed is calling us to follow.

We are also concluding the journey of this book with prayer, rather than a summation of practical advice or the formulation of a program, because this is the level of change that I see pursued in the Gospels and that seems appropriate for this time. Prayer—like organizing, gardening, teaching in parables, and dinner churches—is a practice embedded in daily life that is attentive to the contours of a place. This is not the change brought about by a heroic individual, or imposed from above, but it is the kind of transformation that emerges in interdependent community.

I am not opposed to programs, structures, or institutions. Part of what we need are recipe books, manuals, blueprints, and models. But I do not think we are there yet. Rather, we need to challenge some of our practically minded tendencies to rush and get things done. In our efforts of efficiency and productivity we often end up appealing to the very structures and practices that are causing the problems in the first place. Prayer can play a central role in our work as it slows us down and challenges our assumptions about who we are and what we must be. It is, at its heart, a practice of listening, and can be a wellspring that will sustain us for the long hard path ahead.

While the Lord's Prayer does not quite give us a map to the kingdom of God, it does set our eyes on the world as it could and should be and it gives us orienting practices that will help us make the path by walking. Such a prayer does not require that we begin with an attitude of peace or even confidence. Rather, in saying the prayer we begin to take a step toward its vision.[2] It is a prayer that is addressed to, among others, those living on the precipice of despair. Its formulations offer us reassurance and point toward simple actions. Right when we think we are supposed to give up, we are told to give it over. What we have to lose are our lives centered on accumulation, hoarding, jealousy, distrust, anxiety, hostility, productivity, and isolation. We are also shown that we must lose the pride and pretense of thinking that it is as individuals—as consumers, voters, activists, ministers—that we can face these enormous systemic problems. The prayer counsels us, first, to give our hopes over to God, and then to turn to the simple, joyful, day-in-day-out work of cultivating covenantal relationships with God, neighbors, and the land.

Our Father in Heaven

Our eyes have been trained to look at individuals. The grand narrative of life in the United States is especially focused on individual freedom and the capacity of a single person to break through barriers and realize dreams. I have received messages my whole life that I am capable of anything, which is in no small part due to my social location as a straight, white, middle-class, highly educated, man. The shadow side of this supposed freedom and empowerment is the weight of expectations that individuals are responsible for what happens to them.

---

2. Gonzalez, *Luke*, 142.

Because of this constant barrage of individualized messages, it can be difficult to face systemic issues and not feel as though something has short-circuited. We simply do not have the categories to wrestle with such large problems. And while, in a way, many of our current challenges might be thought of as massive collections of individual decisions, I wonder if this is at all helpful or even accurate. Much of what we face with climate change are vast systems and mechanisms that were put into motion centuries ago. Some kind of chemical reaction was set off in modern and colonial Europe, a strange stew of peoples tattered from centuries of war, technological advances, perhaps a desperate population from a "little Ice Age," a version of Christianity that was wedded with empire, and a growing exploitative market system. These systems expanded and mutated through the conquering of lands, the intentional and indirect genocide of peoples, the enslavement of others, massive deforestation and ecological destruction, and the explosion of the combustion engine and modes of industrialization. The chronicle of these systems could go on, from the massive consumption of the post-war era to anesthetize a traumatized population and the end game of neoliberalism beginning in the 1980s. Each of us plays a role in the ecological destruction and injustice that plagues our world today, but not as an autonomous agent, but as a member of a massive chorus, singing tunes that have been scripted for us.

The Lord's Prayer takes individuals who have given up on their own agency by the hand and tells them to look up. In the Gospel of Matthew, during the Sermon on the Mount Jesus tells the peasants languishing under the Empire, "Pray then in this way: Our father in heaven" (Matt 6:9). We are to begin our prayer with opening our hearts to the vastness that exceeds us, and to trust in God.

In looking up to the heavens we are not called to passively watch or to see ourselves as insignificant. Rather, Christ counsels us to pray to God as "Our Father." No one can ever utter this prayer as an individual, but one prays as a member. Stated in the first-person plural, "*our* Father," this means that all of us are on equal footing and that we are standing together. Speaking to the divine as a "Father," also denotes a good deal of intimacy. Between us and God it evokes a relationship of care and connection. With our neighbors, it invokes a sense that we are all of one family, and in this family we are all in the vulnerable and dependent position of children.[3]

As we considered in chapter 6, with the passing of the bread at the Last Supper, this beginning of the prayer also characterizes God as the head of the household. Claiming God as our Father institutes a new household.

---

3. Carter, *Matthew and the Margins*, 164.

Viewed in the light of the rest of the good news, this Father does not simply take the place of other fathers within the same patriarchal, hierarchical, and oppressive structures.[4] As with the case of royal language, God as king does not rule in the same way as Caesar, only with a new set of favored elites.[5] Rather, with God as Father, the way the household works—its economy—is subverted and transformed for the flourishing and joy of all.

This sense of a world that is rightly ordered is largely what is meant here by "heaven." God being in heaven does not mean absolute distance. In the Gospel of Matthew, heaven is never referred to as a place apart from the earth where you go when you die.[6] "Heaven," which here could be translated, "the heavens," is the place where the Father dwells and everything is right.[7]

Jesus guides those of us who are living in empire to move beyond ourselves, to look up at the sky and take in its beauty and vastness. We are to remember that we live in an earthly household, which is animated by God. We are not emperors or agents, but we are children and creatures—dependent upon love and connected to one another by blessings. We can call God our Father, and set our hearts on the dwelling place where everything is right.

Hallowed Be Thy Name

Speaking to the gathered disciples and peasants, Jesus continues to teach them to pray, saying to our Father, "hallowed be your name" (Matt 6:9b). In the Empire, only Caesar's name was supposed to be hallowed.[8] Through this prayer, Jesus is placing us at the crossroads of empire and earth. To hallow or sanctify a name is to prove your trust in it through the acts of your life.[9] By observing the ways of the covenant, a community bears witness to the name of God as liberator against empire. As the Lord says to Moses, the people shall keep the commandments: "You shall not profane my holy name, that I may be sanctified among the people of Israel: I am the LORD; I sanctify you, I who brought you out of the land of Egypt to be your God: I am the LORD" (Lev 22:32–33).

For example, we show what we think is valuable, and holy by how we treat the poor. Are they fellow creatures, brothers and sisters that deserve love and justice, objects of our pity and self-aggrandizement, tools of a

4. Cobb, *Jesus' Abba*, 7.

5. Rieger, *Jesus vs. Caesar*, 23–27, 44–52.

6. Clark, *On Earth as in Heaven*, 64.

7. Clark, *On Earth as in Heaven*, 64–69.

8. Hendricks, *The Politics of Jesus*, 104.

9. Rieger, *Jesus vs. Caesar*, 28.

cheap labor force, or even irresponsible drains on God's people? The way in which our lives answer questions like this serves to set apart the name of God or Caesar as the orienting lord and master of the world. In his direct-action campaign in the Jerusalem Temple during the last week of his life, Jesus highlighted this contrast as the holy place had been made into a den of robbers, whereas it should have been a house of prayer for all people. To hallow or sanctify the name of God is to live one's life as if creation is a blessing to be received with joy and handed on in justice.

Though the prayer is addressed to the Lord, this phrase doubles back on the person praying and causes them to reflect on what is made holy in their lives. Like the parables, prayer can serve as an honest unveiling of what is really at work in our everyday actions. If we do not examine the ways that empire has shaped our hearts, desires, and values, we might miss the ways that our well-meaning responses to the needs of the world can actually be harmful. Without challenging the notion that markets and corporations are the source of blessing, we might go about the work of sustainability ultimately seeking to sustain the current structures of wealth and injustice, rather than transforming our communities and contexts. Without shifting our allegiance from the God of wealth to the God of love and justice, we will limit our work to imagining how we can make consumerism operate more efficiently and restrict our efforts of collective action to trying to make Walmart more "green." We will measure our work by the empire's metrics of profits over people, and production over places. We will work tirelessly to feed people with food systems that are contributing to their hunger. We will imagine ourselves to be the benefactors and hosts, rather than find ways that we can lose our imperial lives so that we can contribute to the healing and nurturing of the web of life.

Hallowing God's name is not a simple choice that we can undertake individually in our hearts. Much of our lives are shaped by the contexts in which we live. We indirectly exploit the poor not on the street corner but through our participation in marketplaces. Jesus does not teach us to utter a phrase that describes our situation. It is a supplication.[10] This is a request uttered on our knees as we give our pride over to God, and seek to participate in a movement that is bigger than ourselves. By speaking this prayer together, we can begin to become the sanctifying community that bears witness to the holy work of the Creator.

---

10. Boff, *The Lord's Prayer*, 43.

Thy Kingdom Come, Thy Will Be Done, on Earth as It Is in Heaven

If in the first couple phrases of this prayer Jesus turns our gaze upward, in the next he turns it forward. At first our eyes are trained on the grandeur and beauty of the heavens, and yet, even then, this transcendence is brought closer by naming the divine as parent. Next, as we are still looking upward, the holiness of God is transformed into a mirror, which reveals what orders our lives. As the prayer proceeds, Jesus turns our attention to our world and the ways that it could be transformed by God. He teaches us to pray, "Your kingdom come. Your will be done, on earth as it is in heaven" (Matt 6:10).

Speaking to peasants living in the Roman Empire, God's coming kingdom and reign is drawn in stark contrast with present economic, political, and social structures. Calling out for "Your kingdom" to come creates some breathing room. It not only speaks of a hope for the future, but it opens the imagination to see that this current regime is not permanent. The empire attempts to present itself as eternal. It wants us to think that "the real world" must play by the rules of endless work, crushing debt, fractured communities, and degraded lands, that we live but by the grace of the virtuous job creators, those few elite who ascend the chain of being through merit and hard work. The prayerful petition of a world ordered differently cracks open the prison cells of empire and allows the Holy Spirit, with its power to transform and sustain, to enter into our midst.

Coupled with our cries for the coming kingdom is the request that God's "will be done." As with so much of this verse in the prayer, this phrase serves as a hinge. It calls us to look upward and beyond ourselves. As individuals we cannot topple the empire. We must call upon God to do so. And yet, we are not left to passively wait for God to act. Rather, in the Sermon on the Mount Jesus speaks of the need for us to do God's will to enter into the kingdom (Matt 7:21). Doing God's will is the basis for being included in the new, radical household of God. As Christ counsels later in the Gospel, "whoever does the will of my Father in heaven is my brother and sister and mother" (Matt 12:50). Christ incarnates God's will and shows us the way through his ministry of teaching, healing, and organizing.[11]

As we look toward the future and act in the present, we are instructed to pray that God's will be done "on earth as it is in heaven." Redemption, reconciliation, and restoration are to flow over the earth. The ideal images of Scripture give us glimpses of this beautiful earthly life. We are to keep our eyes trained on the renewal of the garden, where we can fulfill our

---

11. Carter, *Matthew and the Margins*, 165.

initial calling to till and keep, to serve and preserve the land. Mary sees this possibility by the tomb. In God's kingdom we will celebrate the wedding banquet where a right relationship between neighbor and land yields joy and wine. Jesus' mother and the disciples experience this in Cana. The Lord and Creator will care for his creatures as they care for one another, leading them into green pastures and by still waters. Five thousand hungry people find this in the wilderness.

As we recite this prayer we need not keep our eyes shut tightly. Our hope is not limited to escape. This prayer should stoke our revolutionary dreams that the present system can be transformed. It should quicken our hearts and energize us for the part we have to play. This is a prayer written in green ink. The mysterious love of the heavenly Father will come to change our communities and all of creation. Our eyes are directed to the awe-inspiring beauty of the starry heavens, in which we are reminded of our smallness, *and* our attention is drawn to the loving and careful way of small things.

Jesus gives his disciples a prayer with the vertical power to break open our fixation on ourselves as individuals and the hardened-over assumptions we have about the world we live in. But he also gives us a prayer with profound horizontal dimensions. God is not simply the king at the center of power. The divine is not the possession of the elite kept at the Temple. God is a father, whose household is ordered differently. This opens the exhilarating and terrifying possibility that the divine is scurrying around and hiding in your home. In the ways that we eat, dress, and work we can trust or deny the love of God. Preparing a meal is an opportunity to pray with our eyes open. Such a prayer is not so much about what I experience as an individual. This is not a matter of New Age narcissism where I feel alive to the moment. It is more the vitality that is felt when one is living justly and gently in webs of life. Cooking a meal can be a prayer not simply because I am giggling and glad, but because it is an opportunity to care for neighbors and the land. It is a prayer if this food is the fruit of regenerative agricultural practices, if the creatures that labor to cultivate it are flourishing in their work and life, and if the systems of exchange that were used to bring it to us are not exploitative and extractive. Making a meal is a form of prayer if we can act as creatures animated by love for creation.

The horizontal prayer of a heavenly earth holds the promise of a different kind of life. All of our daily acts harbor the possibility of praying ceaselessly. As we begin to renew the covenant, mending the severed bonds with our neighbors and slowly building institutions that transform our collective action, we can begin to do the will of God in our work, gardening, crafts, arts, chores, and celebrations. This is not something that we can do on our own. This is not a call to try and grip the wheel and steer yourself moment by moment on the right, enlightened, self-actualized path. Those white-knuckled efforts are the definition of sin, of self curved in on self.[12] Rather, this is a prayer that calls us beyond ourselves into the blossoming of a new creation and the hope of what may yet come.

Give Us This Day, Our Daily Bread, and Forgive Us Our Debts as We Forgive Our Debtors

Having placed the hopes of a grand vision for a better world on our lips, Jesus evokes the tastes and sustenance of the practices of daily life. He teaches us to pray, "Give us this day our daily bread. And forgive us our debts, as we also have forgiven our debtors" (Matt 6:11–12). These are the prayers of peasants who are struggling to feed their families and fearful of the corrosive character of debt on their communities and the land. They are also the prayers for a renewed covenant, which calls for interdependence, sharing, and release.[13]

Even if we religiously observe a fad diet that keeps bread out of our daily lives, we should not lose sight of actual loaves. The need for bread in the context of empire is real and desperate. Then *and* now multitudes find sustenance and subsistence to be a struggle. The prayer is concerned with bodily hunger, and its source in the kingdom of Caesar where the land is not treated as a blessing but as the means for accumulating wealth. This extractive system produces poverty and degrades the soil. The prayer evokes the injustice of empires, where starving Lazarus is not even given the pita napkins of the rich.

Christ instructs us to pray in such a way that we keep agricultural and political structures at the forefront of our thoughts. We are counseled to remember the plight of the poor.[14] In uttering these words we are called upon to consider land use and economic practice. Furthermore, as *our* daily bread, we are called to make these concerns and struggles our own. This petition calls upon the blessings of God, but it also calls us to stand in solidarity.

Daily bread is also a figure that reminds us that our lives can be ordered differently. It calls to mind the story of the bread in the wilderness, which God provided when the Israelites were liberated from the Egyptian Empire. This is the gift given, along with the Sabbath, that retrained their hearts to

12. Luther, *Lectures on Romans*, 345.
13. Horsley, *Jesus and the Powers*, 103, 104.
14. Hendricks, *Politics of Jesus*, 63.

no longer rely on the Egyptian economy of extraction. Instead, they were instructed through the daily acts of gleaning only what was needed and finding that everyone had enough. We also might remember the bread that Christ takes, blesses, breaks, and gives in the wilderness and around the Passover table at the Last Supper—the bread of a different economy ordered by God. This is the bread that is asked for in the parable of the Friend at Midnight and is given at Emmaus, which is the act of hospitality that re-stores a community of mutuality, trust, and joy.

While our various English versions of the Lord's Prayer may obscure the economic aspects of the next petition, it should not be missed. Our re-frain to "forgive us our debts, as we also have forgiven our debtors," should call to mind the covenant codes and the situations of desperation and fore-closure in first-century Palestine that we have repeatedly highlighted in this book. Saying this prayer without this concrete sense of release is like the Pharisees' observance of the Sabbath—which sees it as a day of rest that is an exception to the rule of the work week, rather than as an orienting center that changes how we work, consume, and lend.

This petition concerning debt forgiveness looks toward the release of Jubilee, where the land is given a rest. This is the Lord's day that Jesus an-nounced at his first sermon in Nazareth where the bonds of servitude are released. The dissolution of debt is one of the ways in which the rule of the Empire is undermined. It is also the basis of a loving and sustainable community. Forgiveness begins the process of lifting chains *and* of return-ing land to an equitable distribution, which in turn alleviates poverty and reinstates regenerative agricultural practices. Forgiveness is part of an ethos of generosity, that weaves people together in bonds of care and interdepen-dence.[15] As we forgive we find not only that our covenant with our neigh-bor and the land is restored, but also that we are able to find forgiveness from the Creator, and to begin to receive the blessings of creation.

Our requests for daily bread can help sustain us in our long work. The enormity of the problems we face with climate change can stop us in our tracks. We will submit to despair if we fold under the questions of: How is it possible that I can turn the rising tides of an entire planet altered by carbon emissions? How can we even begin to push against the weight and momen-tum of earth movers, factories, barges, tanks, and power plants? What hope do I have against mountains of concrete, rivers of asphalt, streams of money, and deserts of need? The petition of daily bread saves us from the trap of trying to deal with these problems all at once and in isolation. On the one hand, it directs us to the small and sustaining work that is in front of us.

15. Horsley, *Jesus and Empire*, 119.

Today we are called to cultivate tenderness in our children, to speak up for God's justice in our workplaces, to tend our patch of earth, to listen to our place, and to find ways that the covenant can be restored in our homes and communities. Oftentimes, throughout the day, I will recite to myself the phrase "daily bread," so as to be reoriented to the life-giving task at hand. But on the other hand, the remembrance that this is *our* daily bread also drives our work outward. We are not alone in this work, in our sense of responsibility, or in our pangs of hunger. This bread of life is ours to share and it is rooted in the land that is a blessing from God. This petition is a balm that causes us to look to the needs of others and to feel the connection that is possible and pressing in this place on this day.

Yet, even in the moment of daily bread the past continues to weigh us down. The present is often foreclosed by debt. Debt is what maintains power in the empire, as it keeps the poor in chains and it allows wealth to grow. International debt keeps poor countries compliant with the business interests of corporations. Payday lending and credit card debt maintain a pool of desperate workers. Student loan debt and mortgages direct the labor of middle mangers to the service of the elite. Bundled debt, cheap loans, credit default swaps, and derivatives allow capital to grow and consolidate power beyond the limits of manufacturing and service realities.[16]

Beyond these recognized systems of debt, those who benefit from this economy are indebted to the lives and life systems from which they have extracted their wealth. The rich have amassed an incalculable debt to the poor. The consumers of this age carry a debt to the species and ecosystems they have already despoiled and the generations that are still to be born. Consciously and unconsciously, I think we all carry around this burden of feeling helpless as our participation in systems continues to compound this suffering.

Christ teaches us to pray that this debt may be forgiven and directs us to find ways in our lives to forgive debts. Jesus' prayer is that the plantations be broken up, that the land be redistributed, and that reparations be given to the former slaves. Our prayer, then, should be that the economy of empire should be transformed. Monetary debts need to be forgiven—as political will should be galvanized to forgive international debt, predatory lending should be stopped, student loans should be eliminated, and financial instruments should be radically regulated and transformed. Christ's prayer also directs us to realize this work in our daily lives. We can embody this prayer when our workweeks are measured by sustenance and joy rather than extraction and accumulation. As we create institutions—like cooperatives, community

16. Tanner, *New Spirit of Capitalism*, 11–19.

supported agriculture, alternative markets, and land trusts—we can find reprieve from structures that necessitate destructive debt.

Even without the broken systems requiring our complicity in these
schemes of extraction and exploitation, forgiveness is necessary. This is one
of the reasons why Christ made it central to the radicalized covenantal communities he was seeking to form (Matt 18:21–22). Unlike simple machines
that might have predicable effects (the widget machine makes widgets),
human action within the complex networks of life has unforeseeable consequences.[17] Even when I act with the best intentions with my son, I am never
quite sure if what I have done is best for him. I can never know fully how
any effort might be received, or what the world that I am trying to prepare
him for will be like. Such uncertainty and mystery requires forgiveness to
allow newness to enter our world. The proliferation of forgiveness serves to
loosen the grip of the past, so that our present and our future may be transformed. This is the condition for the flourishing of life in birth and rebirth,
for the opening of new creation.[18] Each day we must pray for and practice
this forgiveness of debt.

And Lead Us Not into Temptation but Deliver Us from Evil

Having lifted us up to the heights of the heavens and directed our gaze
toward the hopes of a heavenly earth, the version of the prayer recorded in
Matthew returns to the difficulty of the present situation. Christ concludes
his prayer saying, "And do not bring us to the time of trial but rescue us
from the evil one" (Matt 6:13). The prayer acknowledges the seductive
forces of the Empire, which in the biblical imagination is not simply the
work of a few powerful men, but it is part of a greater force that attempts
to possess people and the earth. The fear that is articulated in this prayer
is of the manner in which systems of oppression come to own our hearts
and spirits. The temptation is to succumb to the pressures of conformity
and to give into the despair that the empire of wealth and violence is more
powerful than God.[19] Christ guides us, instead, to hope for deliverance
from the ways of empire.

Jesus addressed these forces through his ministry of healing and exorcism. He makes the demonic forces of violence that traumatize peoples and
communities speak their name as "Legion." He heals people of the names

17. Arendt, *Human Condition*, 236–43.

18. Caputo, *Weakness of God*, 148.

19. Carter, *Matthew and the Margins*, 168.

they have been given, changing them from "leper" to a child of the covenant. He enacts a form of power that does not lord over people, but which lifts them up through loving community.

The gospel of empire speaks so loudly in our culture that we likely do not even recognize the trials of which Jesus speaks. It parades as the gospel of work, that promises us that the imperial economy is the benevolent source of abundance that rewards merit and hard work. Such a narrative serves not simply to justify the destructive consumption of a few and the suffering of many, but it goes so far as to pretend that such obscenity is natural and praiseworthy. The empire covers over its forms of domination with euphemisms and gilding. It seduces us into seeing ourselves as the entrepreneurs who are the stars of our own success story. The empire tempts us to try to claw our way to the seat of honor. If we have been trained in its ways, then we might even seek to play the host or benefactor—the one who is up front, well-dressed, acknowledged, accepted, admired, and set apart.

But lurking underneath this whitewashing is an underside of isolation, competition, and exploitation. The word *boss*, which we take as an innocuous name for the manager at work, is the Dutch word for *master*. In the nineteenth century, European immigrants to the United States who were thought of as lower than citizens of Anglo-Saxon descent sought to distance themselves from even lower-class blacks by rejecting the idea that their managers were "masters." They, instead, tried to take on the mantle of whiteness and privilege by saying they merely had a "boss."[20] This name not only obscures the violence of the role of the master, but it also betrays a sad acceptance of the rules of the empire, as we adopt it's values in our efforts to claim privilege for ourselves. The euphemism of "boss" obscures the great trial we all face as to whether we will serve God or wealth.

The New Testament's use of the word *Lord* seeks to unveil this dynamic. The Greek word translated as Lord typically designated those in power in the Empire, most especially Caesar. Therefore, by calling Christ "Lord," it was clear where one's allegiance stood.[21] To understand the trial of which Christ speaks, we might be well served to substitute the term "boss" for "Lord" when we are praying and reading. Doing so might serve to unveil the tensions that are often hidden in our economic and working lives, which often call us to place profits over people, that exhaust us and use us to the point that it fractures our communities, and that blame the poor for their plight. Would we use our time and energy differently if we

20. Douglas, *Stand Your Ground*, 36.
21. Taylor, *Executed God*, 83.

thought of Jesus as our boss, or conversely saw the ways our workplaces are sometimes slaves to wealth?

The temptations of the empire are not something that we face alone. It is "*our* time of trial." The antidote for it, likewise, is found in community. Christ healed those broken and isolated by empire by renaming them his children and bringing them into covenantal community. To follow the path of Christ, we will need relationships and practices that will consistently and constantly support us. This will help us to find a rhythm for our life that is different from the isolated commute, the individual to-do list, the single serving meal, and the individuated assessment. We need to find spaces of cooperation, collaboration, connection, and communion, and let those discipline us, shape us, and mold us. This might mean moving away from gatherings where there is a seat of honor, to the places where disciples are brought together by hospitality and service. Such a move might, by some indexes, be characterized as downward mobility. But from another perspective simplicity in living and in relationships makes room for us to receive the blessings of God. Our relationships need not be based on expensive entertainment or status symbols, but can be rooted in the domestic arts, gardening, cooking, studying, praying, worshiping, organizing, protesting, and building alternative economies. At the heart of such a vision is not sack-cloth and fasting, but the joys of the wedding banquet, where we celebrate the gift of love with the fruit of the vine.

Through this work the seeds of the kingdom are subversively sewn in the empire's fields and medicinally sewn in local gardens. Such communities hold the promise of change as they create the collective power needed to build coalitions with others, to build new structures, and to mobilize for wider change. Yet, the empire does not simply dwell outside of us. It has colonized and continues to attempt to colonize our hearts and our imaginations. Together, we must pray for deliverance.

New Life along the Way

Luke does not end his story with Christ's death and resurrection. The path of the anointed one continues in Luke's sequel, the Acts of the Apostles. In its early chapters, the description of the communal life of this early gathering harbors many of the central characteristics of the green good news. The community inspires wonder in people, as its leaders enact the signs of healing and teaching that break through the barriers of empire (Acts 2:43). The community lives by the covenantal relationships of generosity and mutuality, giving up the economic practices of debt and accumulation.[22] They were "together and had all things in common; they would sell their possessions and goods and distribute the proceeds to all, as any had need" (Acts 2:44). Living by the order of daily bread, making sure that the gifts of God's creation nourish God's creatures, these early disciples also share in radical table fellowship. On Luke's account, "day by day, as they spent much time together in the temple, they broke bread" from house to house. This action does not just allow them to share resources, but it fosters a spirit within and among them, as they "ate their food with glad and generous hearts," or a more direct translation would be with "extreme joy and simplicity" (Acts 2:46). These actions do not set the gathering off from others, but it fosters "goodwill" or grace with all of the people. This way of living leads to the healing and saving of more and more people as they are brought into the new life of their community (Acts 2:47).

The good news lives on. The path of Christ continues. Can we take a walk with Christ in our places to see the parallels between the wealth in Sepphoris and the poverty in the streets and the desecration in the countryside? Can we see the path to a renewed garden in our neighborhoods and the neighborhoods that we dare not venture into across town? Are we willing to take the long path of transformation out into the wilderness to live into the rules of a different economy? Will we follow a teacher that unveils the violence of extraction and exploitation that permeates our daily life, and who shows us a joyful alternative? Are we ready to walk in the therapeutic ways that will heal us from the Gospel of Work and Wealth, so that we may live in communion and solidarity? Will we exit the banquets of the empire and journey to a seat at the table of a new kind of kingdom? To discern how we are to walk down these paths we might start by listening to the words of the prayer of our Lord. By embarking on this journey, we will lose our lives. But this is the green good news: by losing our lives, we can save them.

---

22. Wright, *God's People*, 112–13.

Guide for Reflection, Discussion, and Spiritual Exercise

How to Use This Guide

THE FOLLOWING QUESTIONS AND exercises can be used in solitude or in group settings. Feel free to use them as they are helpful and to skip around. For each chapter I will highlight a couple of passages of Scripture to look at more closely, two sets of discussion questions, and two to three exercises.

In the sections on Scripture I single out a central biblical passage treated in the chapter and suggest a passage that is not treated in the book, but which is accompanied with some leading questions to guide your reading. We have been taught to read the Scriptures by highlighting different terms, assuming different concepts and contexts, and, sometimes, by breaking it up into tweet-sized fragments. This form of review will help you to test the readings pursued here and to begin to read with green eyes.

Each chapter has two discussion questions, one which is directed toward how the chapter might change our understanding of Jesus and the other asking you to draw analogies with today. Each question is followed by a series of leading questions that can tease out aspects of the main question, in the case that the first question does not serve as the needed spark for the conversation.

The section on exercises accompanying each chapter contains two to three suggested practices that will facilitate spiritual reflection and a deeper understanding of the rhythms of your life, community, and place. For those exercises that are directed toward journaling, I advise you to free write. Let your imagination do the work so that your pen wonders and wanders. The purpose here is not to articulate precise analysis, but to work the ground for future seeds to be planted in the earth that is close or familiar to you.

Chapter 1

SCRIPTURE

Review Mark 12:13–17.

Read John 18:28–40.

John 18:28–32—What impression does this give you of the justice system and the motives behind Jesus' prosecution?

John 18:33–36—Given a background of frequent insurrectionists who claim the mantle of the Messiah and led a revolt during the Passover, where are the fault lines of conflict in this story? Does "this world" (in Greek, *kosmos*, meaning "order") refer to the earth or empire?

John 18:37–38—How do Pilate and Jesus incarnate or reflect different forms of power?

John 18:39–40—The word translated as *bandit* also means "insurrectionist" or "rebel." How does this reflect on the threat Jesus poses and his form of resistance?

DISCUSSION

The Green Christ: *If the cross was an instrument of execution, how does that change how you look at the life and death of Jesus?* How would it change your experience of church if there was a golden electric chair hanging at the front of the sanctuary? If it was Pilate and the elite who sentenced Jesus to death (and not God) does that change how you look at the cross? Is that challenging? Does it make it more understandable?

Following the path today: *If the temple was a combination of a religious place, a bank, and the hub of political administration of the Roman Empire in Judea, where would Jesus set his protest today?* Is there a good contemporary analogy? Are there several? Or would Jesus be called to carry out a different kind of act in this institution?

EXERCISES

Rediscovering a sense of place: Today, it can be rare to have a sense of place. The particularities and histories of the places we live in are often unknown because we have moved so often and the geographies we live in are virtually standardized. We often think of our living spaces as being separate from "nature." In order to appeal to some childish wonder and to gain a longer timeline, picture the place you lived during your childhood. What was the relationship between the built environment and the land? As a child, what kinds of non-human life did you encounter (animals and plants)? How did you encounter them? Did you wonder at the complexity and beauty of a flower, climb a tree, watch birds, etc.? How did your surroundings facilitate or hinder your attention or interaction? Where did you encounter God, see the face of Jesus, or feel the Spirit?

How did this space foster community, privacy, conflict, solitude, or peace between neighbors? Would you consider the community closed off, tight-knit, or fragmented? How was it related to other communities, both nearby and far away? What was on that patch of earth before you were there? How far back can you go? What is there now (look at Google Earth if you must)?

Webs of Creation and Production: Pick an object in your immediate surroundings. Try to figure out what "raw materials" were used to create this object. Where do these come from? (Both in terms of: plastics come from petroleum [material] and petroleum comes from Alberta, Venezuela, Nigeria, etc. [place].) What sorts of effects does the cultivation or extraction of materials have on a place? Politically? Ecologically? Where were these raw materials transformed into this item? How long will this object last? What was the price of this item? What other costs were there in its manufacture? Do you know of any political factors that affect the extraction of the materials, the treatment of labor, or the price of the item? Search the internet for general information (regarding materials, origins, environmental impacts, working conditions of certain industries, real cost). The purpose is not exhaustive knowledge, but just a sense of possible global and ecological connections. (I strongly recommend watching the documentary *Manufactured Landscapes*. It is intense and slow-paced. You might want to watch the opening tracking shot in double time and take a break after the first half hour.)

How do you feel after this exercise? Connected to God's good earth and the communion of all creatures? Empowered as a consumer with choices? Caught up in a web of sin? Somewhat confused about the world around you? Uninterested in a simple "thing"? Fascinated by the complex and mysterious environment in which you live? Some combination of each? Can you think of different objects that might have made you feel another way? What kind of differences exist between objects that are earth-honoring and those that are not? How prevalent are each type in our lives?

Chapter 2

SCRIPTURE

Review John 20:1–18.

Read John 1:1–15.

John 1:1–4—How does this intertwining of Christ and creation, Genesis and the Gospel, inform our understanding of who Jesus is and the significance of his mission in the world?

John 1:5–9—How does this prologue read if the animating tension is between the ways of the darkness/empire and the light/kingdom of God?

John 1:10–13—What might it mean to be children of a God of creation and redemption?

John 1:14–18—If the Word became flesh, what does that mean about God's intentions for creation?

DISCUSSION

The Green Christ: *What does it mean for the church if disciples are called to follow a risen gardener?* Does this lower Jesus? Does it make him more attractive? How does it fit with your faith to see resurrection life in the garden?

Following the path today: *Where do you think you carry out your vocation to serve and preserve?* In gardens? In caring for people? In attending to beauty? In cultivating community? In abiding in love? How could you plant these acts in the good soil of your life so that they could get plenty of sunlight (energy) and attention (time)?

EXERCISES

Life–giving community: Journal on the nature of nourishing and nurturing community. This series of questions is meant to help tease out some component parts. This is not a test. You do not need to answer every question. Let them serve as prompts: Where have you encountered life-giving community? When have you communed with God's creation? Are there times when these two elements have intersected? At a community garden? At a summer camp? On vacation? On retreat? At home? On a work site? At school? With a religious community?

How was time different in this context? Was the schedule focused on different things? Was it less structured? Structured around leisure, worship, and reflection? How was the organization of space different? Was it more rustic or more refined? Were you closer to people or was there more solitude? Are there lessons from these communities and times that you can use in your current life or apply to groups you are a part of?

Visions of Paradise: Journal or make a collage on your associations with the term *paradise*. When you imagine paradise, what does it look like? Is there a lot of green space? Tropical backdrops? Beautiful buildings? What is the implicit vision of the good life at work here? Are there elements of excessive consumption and exclusionary status? Are there aspects of loving community and flourishing creation? Do you have different associations with "heaven" or the "kingdom of God"? Are these more or less earthy and earthly? What do all of these visions say about your view of creation and hopes for the future?

Planting Liturgy: On the first day of planting in the community garden or in your home plot, perform this simple worship service that pairs a scripturally based responsive reading with the acts of preparing the soil, sowing seeds, composting, and watering:

> One: Scripture begins and ends in a garden. The book of Genesis tells us that we are part of the sacred drama of soil, sacrament, and spirit.

> Many: The LORD formed humans from humus, shaped an earthen vessel and filled it with the breath of God and placed us in a garden.

> One: The Scriptures tell us that God was a gardener. The LORD planted a garden and gave humans the sacred task to till and keep.

> Many: We gather today to till and keep, to serve and preserve, to take up our vocation as creatures to care for creation.

One: Let us now prepare the soil.

[make furrows in the vegetable beds]

One: Christ was a peasant, and he cared for and spoke to peasants. Speaking in parables, he would teach them to care for creation and one another.

Many: He told them of a sower, who cast seed on the ground. Some of it fell on rocky ground, some of it fell on a path, some of it fell in thorns, and these did not grow. But some of it fell on good earth, and it grew a harvest that could feed a kingdom.

One: Christ was a peasant, and he cared and spoke to peasants. Speaking in parables he would teach them about care for creation and one another.

Many: We are both the sowers called to care for the land, and we are the soil, which could bear the seeds of new life.

One: Let us sow seeds of hope and health.

[sow seeds in the earth]

One: Christ went to a garden in a time of trial. He gathered with his disciples in the garden at Gethsemane on the night he was arrested. The garden is a place of lament and comfort.

Many: We gather here today knowing that creation is groaning, that your creatures are in pain. We pray for your healing and hope.

One: Christ prayed to God in vulnerability and honesty. May we have the courage to do likewise.

Many: May our tears not be in vain, but may they water the soil.

One: Let us write prayers of lament on strips of paper, roll them up and place them into the soil. This paper will break down, decompose, become compost, and rejoin the soil. These fears and struggles will not choke out the garden, but they will, eventually, nurture it.

[write a prayer for the earth and those suffering under injustice, roll them up, and add them to soil.]

One: Scripture begins and ends in a garden. The book of Revelation tells us that we are a part of the sacred drama of soil, sacrament, and spirit.

Many: In the New Jerusalem the waters of justice will flow out of God's throne, they will rush through the streets, and the tree of life will grow up around it. The garden will be restored.

One: Christ came so that God's will could be done on *earth* as it is in the heavens. Let us water the garden now, and may these waters wash us so that we may be agents of justice in this creation.

[water the newly planted seeds]

Chapter 3

SCRIPTURE

Review Mark 10:17–31.

Read Luke 4:1–13.

Luke 4:1–2—What is the significance of Jesus' journey out into the wilderness for forty days? What story from the Hebrew Scriptures does this parallel; what story following this in the Gospels does it portend?

Luke 4:3–4—Read the passage Jesus quotes in context: Deuteronomy 8:3–4. What contrast in food economies is Jesus appealing to? What does this say about the temptation he faces?

Luke 4:5–8—Read the passage Jesus quotes in context: Deuteronomy 6:10–13. How is the distinction between Egypt and the land of the covenant relevant here? What does this tell us about the demonic forces on the earth?

Luke 4:9–13—Read the passage Jesus quotes in context: Deuteronomy 6:16–19. How might this charge to follow the commandments echo Jesus' tension with the Temple elite, or the prophetic distinction between sacrifice and mercy?

DISCUSSION

The Green Christ: *What do you think of understanding the kingdom of God as a renewal and radicalization of the covenant between God, neighbor, and land?* Does this take the edge off a Jesus that calls us to leave and give everything away? Does this provide a vision that is more inviting or more challenging because it is more communal and concrete?

Following the path today: *What would an economy or rule of the household centered on generosity, reciprocity, and simplicity look like in your place?* Do you agree that poverty is a symptom that is caused by wealth (which is built on extraction and exploitation)? In what ways do our lives participate or benefit from these forms of wealth? How would our ministries both within and outside our community be different if we saw the goal as simple living and not upward mobility?

EXERCISES

Food ways: Journal on the relationship between culture, biography, and food. How would you describe the food culture of your family growing up (Mom was a Cajun cook, we ate TV dinners watching the news, etc.)? What is the geography of your family's food culture? In what ways did this cultivate a sense of place or a connection to another place? If it did not feel connected to any specific locale what kind of places does it evoke for you now? What sort of community, gatherings, or rituals were organized around food (holidays, celebrations, daily rhythms, church events)? How did food help facilitate some life-giving relationships? How does it or might it in your life now? (If you are doing this in a group, perhaps, plan a meal where everyone brings a dish traditionally served in your family growing up and, over the meal share stories about your dish.)

Seeing the food system: Pick an item from your most recent meal and trace it through a food system. (If your food is not local, the lines are likely obscure, so this will take a good deal of guessing.) What plants or animals did it come from? Was it grown industrially or organically? Do you know where it was grown? What conditions might farm workers have labored in? Where was it processed and what was added? What conditions did workers face there? Where was it shipped to be sold? How far has it traveled up to this point? How is the economic pie of the price of the food divided up between farmers, workers, processors, and distributors? How was it prepared? What kind of community or lack thereof does this food assume or facilitate? Where will the food and its packaging end up (compost, landfill, sewer)? What is your place in this food system? If some or most of these questions were impossible to answer, what might that tell you?

Receiving God's Blessing: Have you ever said a regular blessing over a meal? If so, where did it come from? What are your associations with it? When did you say it? When do you say it? In what settings is it appropriate to say these words? What do these words mean? What do these words do? If you have not said a blessing or do not have one that fits your current life, write a short one animated by gratitude for creation and the hope of the renewal of God's covenant.

Chapter 4

SCRIPTURE

Review Matthew 25:14–30.

Read Luke 12:13–21.

Luke 12:13–15—The inheritance at question is likely a piece of land. How does the covenant relationship with the land as God's blessing contrast with Jesus' initial warning about greed and possessions?

Luke 12:15–16—In the parable who or what *produces* abundance? How is this interpreted by the rich man?

Luke 12:18–19—If Jesus is speaking to peasants in the context of imperial extraction and scarcity, how would they respond to the idea of a rich man *tearing down* barns only to make bigger ones and then living in leisure? What consequences does the rich man's consumption have for people like his hearers?

Luke 12:20–21—The word *fool* in the Scriptures is often associated with someone who rebels against God. In what ways is the rich man breaking the covenant? What might it mean to be "rich toward God"?

DISCUSSION

The Green Christ: *What does our reading of the parables tell us about our vision of God?* Who do you find yourself identifying with in the parables? Who do you find yourself identifying God with? How would both our self-understanding and our understanding of God change if we were to switch up the perspective of these little stories?

Following the path today: *What sorts of parables would Jesus tell today? Who is the day laborer or the owner of the vineyard today?* Who are the violent tenants and absentee landlords? If not with purple robes and sumptuous banquets, how would the rich man be described today? What are the acts of kneading bread today that are an incarnation of the kingdom of God?

EXERCISES

Teaching for formation and transformation: Journal on the ways that learning communities shaped you consciously and unconsciously. What lessons did you learn outside of the classroom in high school and/ or college? What did the cafeteria or dorm teach you about community? What did the pep rally, the career counselor, or award ceremony teach you about success or what is valued? How did the practice of taking tests and receiving grades discipline you in your relationship with authority, your own self-worth, or your relationships with others? What books changed how you thought about the world? What types of things do your read today? What lessons, from the classroom or otherwise, do you carry with you today? What does your memory and experience tell you about the values of the communities in which you were shaped *and* the kinds of pedagogy and activities that can shape and change people today?

Unveiling empire through cartoons: Look at some contemporary political cartoons on poverty or the environment (enter some keywords in a search engine). What dynamics of power are they unveiling? Is there an implied or explicit alternative? Can you find any that implicate consumerism in the US? Does this cartoon make you feel outraged, smug, cynical, etc.? What kind of unveiling would help keep the door of hope open?

Write a contemporary parable or draw a contemporary cartoon that might perform this unveiling (feel free to use humor, but it need not be funny).

Reflecting on the News: Go to the home page of the news outlet you most regularly check. What stories are deemed newsworthy? What kinds of people make news? Who are the villains in these stories? Who are the heroes? If you looked at this page what would you think the main problems in our world are? Is poverty or climate change mentioned? Is it unacknowledged in the background of any stories? Are there stories that are supposed to inspire interest, envy, or hope? What are they about? Search for the word *religion* or *faith* in the search engine provided on the page. What sorts of stories come up? What is being sold on this page? (Both in terms of the ads and in terms of the implicit values.)

How often do you check this page? How does it make you feel? How does it affect your outlook on the world?

Chapter 5

SCRIPTURE

Review Mark 5:1–20.

Read Mark 10:46–52.

Mark 10:46—How is Bartimaeus described? Why is he given a name and familial relationship? How might he have entered this state?

Mark 10:47–48—What does Bartimaeus call Jesus? What significance does this messianic title have for Jesus (who is on his way to Jerusalem)? How does the crowd treat Bartimaeus?

Mark 10:49—Why does Jesus first address the crowd? How does this change their response to Bartimaeus?

Mark 10:50–52—What does Bartimaeus own and cast off? What heals him? What life does this make possible? How is this different from the call story of the rich man (Mark 10:17–22)?

DISCUSSION

The Green Christ: *Does the view of Christ as the healer of illness rather than disease inspire wonder or rob these stories of mystery and power for you?* How does this change Christ's relationship to creation? How does this shift Christ's salvation from being solely individual to being social?

Following the path today: *In what ways might we say that the empire of wealth and the gospel of work possess people today?* How does this shape what we love and pay attention to, where we direct our labor and energy, or who we see as virtuous and worthy? What names are given to people who are cast outside of our social and economic circles today? How might these illnesses find healing in community?

EXERCISES

Where does it hurt?: Let these questions guide you in thinking about the suffering in your particular place: What illnesses plague the town you live in? How might the touch of the body of Christ bring healing to these people or institutions? What are the names that cause suffering or that inhibit action in your life or in the lives of marginalized people in your context? How might these names be challenged? How would the name of being a child of Christ be healing or not given this situation? (You might consult this map, which indicates food access in your town: https://www.ers.usda.gov/data-products/food-access-research-atlas/go-to-the-atlas/ or this tool that indicates environmental justice issues in your region: https://ejatlas.org/.)

Being the patient: Journal about a time you found healing. This might be something you received from medical professionals, from the patient and ongoing care of a loved one, or something you experienced through nurturing community. What were the sources of your illness or injury? What relationships, contexts, and practices healed you? Did you feel the presence of God in this process? Can you feel it looking back? How did it make you feel to be dependent and vulnerable? How can this experience instruct you in engaging in the disciples' call to be wounded healers? How might this help us think about the injuries that we have perpetrated against the land and creation?

The spiritual exercise of assessment: Analyze the particular methods and tools of assessment that you are asked to engage in. How is your work evaluated? Are there mechanisms that assess your efficiency and productivity? Is there a software that tracks your work or that you regularly update? Are you required to write regular reports or self-evaluations? Who do you report this to? What is being measured? What sorts of values do these measures reflect? Are there explicit and implicit rewards and penalties attached to this assessment? In what ways do you monitor yourself? Do you keep a to-do list or make note of accomplishments? Do you feel the push for productivity and efficiency shaping your time at work? Your time away from work? How closely is your job performance tied into your feelings of self-worth? Do these practices nurture or undermine your relationships at work or at home? Do you feel a congruence of vision and values with the institution for which you work? Are there other institutions or communities where you feel this congruence?

Chapter 6

SCRIPTURE

Review Luke 24:13–35.

Read Luke 14:15–24.

Luke 14:15–20—What is the social status of the first set of people to be invited? Are they poor peasants or rich landholders?

Luke 14:21–22—How does the organizer of the banquet react to being snubbed? Are the poor invited first or only after rejection?

Luke 14:23–24—Is the inviter a stand-in for God? Is this an account of the messianic banquet or a counter-example about the ways of benefactors?

DISCUSSION

The Green Christ: *What does the ideal of the messianic banquet tell us about God's purposes for creation?* What does right relationship between God, neighbors, and land look like? How are the banquets of empire built upon different relationships with neighbors, land, and (often implicitly) God? What role do Jesus' experimental meals play in undermining the banquets of the kingdom and striving after the messianic banquet?

Walking the path today: *In what ways do the meals that we share with family, co-workers, friends, professional contacts, and strangers resemble the banquets of God's kingdom or the empire?* How might these meals be transformed? How might this change how we connect with the land, loved ones, and strangers?

EXERCISES

What's in a name? What titles, labels, roles, and names are or have been associated with you (mom, manager, brother, autonomous consumer, queen bee, brother, leader, loner, customer, partner, rival, entrepreneur, elder, pastor, child, criminal, benefactor, host, etc.)? Which of these inspire pride, shame, love, compassion, or anger? What names feel like they capture dimensions of being a child of God or a beloved creature? What names feel like they are obstacles toward seeing yourself or others in these terms?

When we sit around specific tables, what kinds of names do we and those with us take on (the meeting table at work, church, school, home, out at a restaurant, at a bar, at a potluck, at a party, etc.)? How could we rearrange these tables to change the roles we play and the roles that others are expected to play?

Imagining the joy of the Gospel: One classic spiritual exercise that opens our hearts to the Gospel is to imagine ourselves in the scene—picturing the landscape, listening for the noises of water, birds, or a bustling town square, and then to imagine the scene unfolding. In a similar vein, try and find the perspective of joy in a Gospel story. Has someone or something that seemed lost been found? Has someone that was chained been released? Are their people who have found a sense of connection—of love or solidarity—with their neighbors, God, or the land? Is there the glimmer of a promise, the opening to a different future, or the blossoming of hope in the story? Find this perspective and inhabit it. Imagine that you are the person encountering the joy of the story. Sit in this place, bathed in light or seeing the light peering out from under the door in a darkened room. Train your attention on this joy and familiarize yourself with it, in hopes that you can begin to see it elsewhere—in the Gospels and in your life.

Time for community and communion: What is the social cost of being busy? Do you find it hard to plan meetings, events, or even a gathering with friends or family? How often do you show up to an event exhausted? How much of your leisure time do you spend numbing out?

Write out a schedule for how you spent your time yesterday. If you are in a group compare with others looking for shared gaps, parallel patterns, or sheer complexity and difference. On this schedule: Circle what was necessary and indicate why. Put a box around what is important and indicate why. Underline what was optional and indicate why. If you were planning your day around what was joyful and just for you and your community in what ways would your day look different?

Chapter 7

SCRIPTURE

Review Matthew 6:9–15.

Read Luke 1:46–56.

Luke 1:46–49—What makes Mary lowly? What is her social status? What brings her joy in this prayer of praise?

Luke 1:50–53—Who is lifted up and who is brought low in this prayer of a peasant? What is the hope of the hungry?

Luke 1:54–55—What significance does the covenant made with Abraham about land have for the birth of Jesus?

DISCUSSION

The Green Christ: *What does it mean to pray for God's kingdom to come to earth as it is in the heavens?* How is this the prayer of a peasant? How does this relate to your previous understanding of the Lord's prayer?

Following the path today: *What habits or rituals in your life connect you to others and give you hope?* What can you do to build a community and a place that will sustain you in the long work of sustainability and social justice?

EXERCISES

On earth as it is in the heavens: Think of a neglected space in your neighborhood or town. It might be an abandoned lot, a place in your yard, a brownfield (a lot affected by environmental degradation), a neglected park, or a littered stream bed. Write a story about how this place might find healing. Can you imagine how this patch of creation could be cared for and nurtured so that human and nonhuman life might flourish here? Who are the actors and heroes of this story? What conflicts or obstacles do they face? What does a happy ending look like? How might this story be told? As a colorful children's book? A novel with hints of magic realism? A realistic documentary? A poem? A liturgy? Self-produced short online clips? A television series?

Contemplating creation: Find a beautiful place to sit and pray. Do not close your eyes. Keep them open and watch. Look for the movement and the quiet abiding of the world around you. Take a moment and listen, tease out the layers of sound and notice how they join together. As thoughts arise that pull you away—work left to do, injuries you feel, anxieties that weigh on you—breathe gently and look up to your teachers: the birds of the air who soar in the heavens, and the lilies of the field, that send themselves into the earth. Look to these creatures as your teachers and rest in their rhythms. Let them begin to shape your own. As you return to your day, say to yourself: "Give us this day our daily bread." Remember the blessings given by God, the need and generosity that animates creation, the connections you have to those around you, and the small work of this day and this time.

Bibliography

Adams, Samuel L. *Social and Economic Life in Second Temple Judea*. Louisville: Westminster John Knox, 2014.

Arendt, Hannah. *The Human Condition*. Chicago: University of Chicago Press, 1989.

Arsenault, Chris. "Only 60 Years of Farming Left If Soil Degradation Continues." *Scientific American*. https://www.scientificamerican.com/article/only-60-years-of-farming-left-if-soil-degradation-continues/.

Bahnson, Fred. "Field, Table, Communion: The Abundant Kingdom Versus the Abundant Mirage." In *Making Peace with the Land: God's Call to Reconcile with Creation*, 83–111. Downers Grove, IL: InterVarsity, 2012.

———. *Soil and Sacrament: A Spiritual Memoir of Food and Faith*. New York: Simon and Schuster, 2013.

Banks, Adelle M. "Black Church Food Security Network Brings Fresh Food to Baltimore." *Christian Century*, May 8, 2018. https://www.christiancentury.org/article/news/black-church-food-security-network-brings-fresh-food-baltimore.

Barber, William J., and Jonathan Wilson-Hartgrove. *The Third Reconstruction: How a Moral Movement Is Overcoming the Politics of Division and Fear*. Boston: Beacon, 2016.

Bass, Diana Butler. *Grounded: Finding God in the World, A Spiritual Revolution*. New York: Harper One, 2015.

Bauckham, Richard. *Living with Other Creatures: Green Exegesis and Theology*. Waco, TX: Baylor University Press, 2011.

Benton-Short, Lisa, et al. *A Regional Geography of the United States and Canada: Toward a Sustainable Future*. 2d ed. Lanham, MD: Rowman and Littlefield, 2019.

Berry, Wendell. *The Art of the Commonplace: The Agrarian Essays of Wendell Berry*, edited by Norman Wirzba. Berkeley, CA: Counterpoint, 2002.

———. *Blessed Are the Peacemakers: Christ's Teachings about Love, Compassion, and Forgiveness*. Berkeley, CA: Shoemaker Hoard, 2005.

Betcher, Sharon V. *Spirit and the Politics of Disablement*. Minneapolis: Fortress, 2007.

Bieler, Andrea, and Luise Schottroff. *The Eucharist: Bodies, Bread, and Resurrection*. Minneapolis: Fortress, 2007.

Boer, Roland, and Christina Petterson. *Time of Troubles: A New Economic Framework for Early Christianity*. Minneapolis: Fortress, 2017.

Boff, Leonardo. *The Lord's Prayer: The Prayer of Integral Liberation*. Maryknoll, NY: Orbis, 1983.

Brock, Rita Nakashima. *Journeys by Heart: A Christology of Erotic Power*. New York: Crossroad, 1988.

Brock, Rita Nakasima, and Rebecca Ann Parker. *Saving Paradise: How Christianity Traded Love of This World for Crucifixion and Empire*. Boston: Beacon, 2008.

Brown, Wendy. *Undoing the Demos: Neoliberalism's Stealth Revolution*. New York: Zone, 2009.

Brueggemann, Walter. *Isaiah 1–39*. Louisville: Westminster John Knox, 1998.

———. *The Land: Place as Gift, Promise, and Challenge in Biblical Faith*. Minneapolis: Fortress, 2002.

———. *Money and Possessions*. Louisville: Westminster John Knox, 2016.

———. *Sabbath as Resistance: Saying No to the Culture of Now*. Louisville: Westminster John Knox, 2014.

———. *Tenacious Solidarity: Biblical Provocations on Race, Religion, Climate, and Economy*. Minneapolis: Fortress, 2018.

———. "The Uninflected *Therefore* of Hosea 4:1–3." In *Reading from This Place*, Vol. 1, *Social Location and Biblical Interpretation in the United States*, edited by Fernando F. Segovia and Mary Ann Tolbert, 231–50. Minneapolis: Fortress, 1995.

Callahan, Allen Dwight. *A Love Supreme: A History of Johannine Tradition*. Minneapolis: Augsburg Fortress, 2005.

Caputo, John D. *Weakness of God: A Theology of the Event*. Bloomington, IN: Indiana University Press, 2006.

Cardenal, Ernesto. *The Gospel in Solentiname*. Maryknoll, NY: Orbis, 2010.

Carter, Christopher. "Blood in the Soil: The Racial, Racist, and Religious Dimensions of Environmentalism." In *The Bloomsbury Handbook of Religion and Nature: The Elements*, edited by Laura Hobgood and Whitney Bauman, 45–62. New York: Bloomsbury, 2018.

Carter, Warren. *John and Empire: Initial Explorations*. New York: T&T Clark, 2008.

———. *Matthew and Empire: Initial Explorations*. Harrisburg, PA: Trinity, 2001.

———. *Matthew and the Margins: A Sociopolitical and Religious Reading*. Maryknoll, NY: Orbis, 2000.

Clapp, Rodney. *New Creation: A Primer on Living in the Time between the Times*. Eugene, OR: Cascade, 2018.

Clark, David. *On Earth as in Heaven: The Lord's Prayer from Jewish Prayer to Christian Ritual*. Minneapolis, Fortress, 2017.

Cobb, John B. *Jesus' Abba: The God Who Has Not Failed*. Minneapolis: Fortress, 2016.

Cole, Luke W., and Shelia R. Foster. *From the Ground Up: Environmental Racism and the Rise of the Environmental Justice Movement*. New York: New York University Press, 2000.

Copeland, M. Shawn. *Enfleshing Freedom: Body, Race, and Being*. Minneapolis: Fortress, 2010.

Cronon, William. "The Trouble with Wilderness: Or, Getting Back to the Wrong Nature." *Environmental History* 1 (1996) 7–28.

Crosby, Michael. *House of Disciples: Church, Economics, and Justice in Matthew*. Maryknoll, NY: Orbis, 1988.

Crossan, John Dominic. *God and Empire: Jesus Against Rome, Then and Now*. New York: Harper, 2007.

———. *The Historical Jesus: The Life of a Mediterranean Jewish Peasant*. New York: Harper, 1992.

Crossan, John Dominic, and Jonathan L. Reed. *Excavating Jesus: Beneath the Stones, Behind the Texts*. New York: Harper Collins, 2002,

Daly-Denton, Margaret. *John: An Earth Bible Commentary: Supposing Him to Be the Gardener*. New York: Bloomsbury, 2017.

Darot, Pierre, and Christian Laval. *The New Way of the World: On Neoliberal Society*. Brooklyn, NY: Verso, 2013.

Dauvergne, Peter. *Environmentalism of the Rich*. Cambridge, MA: MIT Press, 2016.

Davis, Ellen F. *Biblical Prophecy: Perspectives for Christian Theology, Discipleship, and Ministry*. Louisville: Westminster John Knox, 2014.

————. *Scripture, Culture, and Agriculture: An Agrarian Reading of the Bible*. New York: Jennings Cambridge University Press, 2009.

DeLuca, Kevin, and Anne Demo. "Imagining Nature and Erasing Class and Race: Carleton Watkins, John Muir, and the Construction of Wilderness." *Environmental History* 6.4 (2001) 541–60.

Dickinson, Wilson T. *Exercises in New Creation from Paul to Kierkegaard*. New York: Palgrave MacMillan, 2018.

Douglas, Kelly Brown. *Stand Your Ground: Black Bodies and the Justice of God*. Maryknoll, NY: Orbis, 2015.

Eberhart, Timothy Reinhold. *Rooted and Grounded in Love: Holy Communion for the Whole Creation*. Eugene, OR: Pickwick, 2017.

Echlin, Edward P. "Jesus and the Earth, Walking Our Christology." *New Blackfriars* 86 (2005) 493–504.

Elizondo, Virgilio. *Galilean Journey: The Mexican-American Promise*. Maryknoll, NY: Orbis, 2000.

Elliott, J. H. "Temple versus Household in Luke-Acts: A Contrast in Social Institutions." *Hervormde Teologiese Studies* 47 (1991) 88–120.

Fiensy, David A. *The Social History of Palestine in the Herodian Period: The Land Is Mine*. Lewiston, NY: Edwin Mellen, 1991.

Fiorenza, Elizabeth Schüssler. *In Memory of Her: A Feminist Theological Reconstruction of Christian Origins*. New York: Crossroad, 1984.

Fisher, Andrew. *Big Hunger: The Unholy Alliance between Corporate America and Anti-Hunger Groups*. Cambridge, MA: MIT Press, 2017.

Food and Agriculture Organization of the United Nations. "The State of Food Security and Nutrition in the World 2017." http://www.fao.org/state-of-food-security-nutrition.

————. "Key Facts and Findings." http://www.fao.org/news/story/en/item/197623/icode/.

Foucault, Michel. *The Birth of Biopolitics: Lectures at the Collége de France 1978–1979*. New York: Palgrave Macmillan, 2008.

————. *Discipline and Punish: The Birth of the Prison*. New York: Vintage: 1995.

Freyne, Sean. *Jesus, a Jewish Galilean: A New Reading of the Jesus Story*. New York: T & T Clark, 2004.

Gonzalez, Justo L. *Luke*. Louisville: Westminster John Knox, 2010.

————. *The Story Luke Tells: Luke's Unique Witness to the Gospel*. Grand Rapids: Eerdmans, 2015.

Goodman, Martin. *The Ruling Class of Judea: The Origins of the Jewish Revolt against Rome A.D. 66–70*. New York: Cambridge University Press, 1987.

Gottlieb, Robert, and Anupama Joshi. *Food Justice*. Cambridge: MIT Press, 2010.

Green, Joel B. *The Gospel of Luke*. Grand Rapids: Eerdmans, 1997.

Guha, Ramachandra, and Joan Martinez Alier. *Varieties of Environmentalism: Essays North and South*. New York: Earthscan, 1997.

Guthman, Julie. *Agrarian Dreams: The Paradox of Organic Farming in California*. Berkeley, CA: University of California Press, 2004.

————. "Bringing Good Food to Others: Investigating the Subjects of Alternative Food Practice." *Cultural Geographies* 15 (2008) 431–45.

Hanson, K. C. "The Galilean Fishing Economy and the Jesus Tradition." *Biblical Theology Bulletin* 27 (1997) 99–111.

Harvey, Jennifer. *Dear White Christians: For Those Still Longing for Racial Reconciliation*. Grand Rapids: Eerdmans, 2014.

Heltzel, Peter Goodwin. *Resurrection City: A Theology of Improvisation*. Grand Rapids: Eerdmans, 2012.

Hendricks Jr., Obery M. *The Politics of Jesus: Rediscovering the True Revolutionary Nature of the Teachings of Jesus and How They Have Been Corrupted*. New York: Doubleday, 2006.

Hengel, Martin. *The Zealots: Investigations into the Jewish Freedom Movement in the Period from Herod I until 70 A.D*. Edinburgh: T & T Clark, 1989.

Herzog, William R. *Jesus, Justice, and the Reign of God: A Ministry of Liberation*. Louisville: Westminster John Knox, 2000.

————. *Parables as Subversive Speech: Jesus as Pedagogue of the Oppressed*. Louisville: Westminster John Knox, 1994.

————. *Prophet and Teacher: An Introduction to the Historical Jesus*. Louisville: Westminster John Knox, 2005.

Hillel, David. *Out of the Earth: Civilization and the Life of the Soil*. Berkeley, CA: University of California Press, 1991.

Hollenbach, Paul W. "Jesus, Demoniacs, and Public Authorities: A Socio-Historical Study." *Journal of the American Academy of Religion* 48 (1981) 567–88.

Horden, Peregrine, and Nicholas Purcell. *The Corrupting Sea: A Study of Mediterranean History*. Malden, MA: Blackwell, 2000.

Horsley, Richard A. *Galilee: History, Politics, People*. Valley Forge, PA: Trinity, 1995.

————. *Jesus and Empire: The Kingdom of God and the New World Disorder*. Minneapolis: Fortress, 2002.

————. *Jesus and the Powers: Conflict, Covenant, and the Hope of the Poor*. Minneapolis: Fortress, 2011.

Horsley Richard A., and John S. Hanson. *Bandits, Prophets, and Messiahs: Popular Movements at the Time of Jesus*. Minneapolis: Winston, 1985.

Howard-Brook, Wes. *Becoming Children of God: John's Gospel and Radical Discipleship*. Maryknoll, NY: Orbis, 1994.

Hughes, J. Donald. *An Environmental History of the World: Humankind's Changing Role in the Community of Life*. New York: Routledge, 2001.

————. *Environmental Problems of the Greeks and Romans: Ecology in the Ancient Mediterranean*. 2d ed. Baltimore: Johns Hopkins University Press, 2014.

Jacobs, Ken. "Americans Are Spending $153 Billion a Year to Subsidize McDonald's and Wal-Mart's Low Wage Workers." *Washington Post*, April 15, 2015. https://www.washingtonpost.com/posteverything/wp/2015/04/15/we-are-spending-153-billion-a-year-to-subsidize-mcdonalds-and-walmarts-low-wage-workers/?noredirect=on&utm_term=.0a39e46a4e80.

Jenkins, Willis. "The Feast of the Anthropocene: Beyond Climate Change as Special Object in the Study of Religion." *The South Atlantic Quarterly* 116 (2017) 69–91.

———. *The Future of Ethics: Sustainability, Social Justice, and Religious Creativity.* Washington, DC: Georgetown University Press, 2013.

Jennings, Willie James. *The Christian Imagination: Theology and the Origins of Race.* New Haven, CT: Yale University Press, 2010.

Jeremias, Joachim. *The Parables of Jesus.* New York: Scribner, 1972.

Jha, Shalene, et al. "A Review of Ecosystems Services, Farmer Livelihoods, and Value Chains in Shade Coffee Agroecosystems." In *Integrating Agriculture, Conservation, and Ecotourism: Examples from the Field,* edited by W. Bruce Campbell and Silvia Lopex Ortiz, 141–208. Dordecht: Springer, 2011.

Jha, Sandhya Rani. *Transforming Communities: How People Like You are Healing Their Neighborhoods.* St. Louis: Chalice, 2017.

Jones, Serene. *Trauma and Grace: Theology in a Ruptured World.* Louisville: Westminster John Knox, 2009.

Karris, Robert J. *Eating Your Way through Luke's Gospel.* Collegeville, MN: Liturgical, 2006.

———. "Luke 24:13–35." *Interpretation* 40 (1987) 57–61.

Keller, Catherine. *Face of the Deep: A Theology of Becoming.* New York: Routledge, 2001.

———. *On the Mystery: Discerning God in Process.* Minneapolis: Fortress, 2008.

Kierkegaard, Søren. *The Sickness unto Death: A Christian Psychological Exposition for Upbuilding and Awakening.* Volume 19, *Kierkegaard's Writings.* Edited by Howard V. Hong and Edna H. Hong. Princeton, NJ: Princeton University Press, 1980.

King, Philip J., and Lawrence E. Stager. *Life in Biblical Israel.* Louisville: Westminster John Knox, 2001.

Kinsler, Ross, and Gloria Kinsler. *The Biblical Jubilee and the Struggle for Life.* Maryknoll, NY: Orbis, 1999.

Kivel, Peter. "Social Service or Social Change?" In *The Revolution Will Not Be Funded: Beyond the Non-Profit Industrial Complex,* 129–50. Durham, NC: Duke University Press, 2007.

Klein, Naomi. *This Changes Everything: Capitalism vs the Climate.* New York: Simon and Schuster, 2014.

Langlands, Bryan K. *Cultivating Neighborhood: Identifying Best Practices for Launching a Christ-Centered Community Garden.* Eugene, OR: Resource, 2014.

Linthicum, Robert C. *Transforming Power: Biblical Strategies for Making a Difference in Your Community.* Downers Grove, IL: InterVarsity, 2003.

Lott, Melissa C. "10 Calories in, 1 Calorie Out—the Energy We Spend on Food." *Scientific America,* August, 11, 2011. https://blogs.scientificamerican.com/plugged-in/10-calories-in-1-calorie-out-the-energy-we-spend-on-food/.

Lowery, Richard H. *Sabbath and Jubilee.* St. Louis: Chalice, 2000.

Luther, Martin. *Lectures on Romans: Glosses and Scholia.* Volume 25, *Luther's Works.* Edited by Hilton C. Oswald. Saint Louis: Concordia, 1972.

Malina, Bruce J., and Richard L. Rohrbaugh. *Social Science Commentary on the Synoptic Gospels.* Minneapolis: Fortress, 1992.

McFague, Sallie. *The Body of God: An Ecological Theology.* Minneapolis: Fortress, 1993.

———. *Life Abundant: Rethinking Theology and Economy for a Planet in Peril.* Minneapolis: Fortress, 2001.

———. *Speaking in Parables: A Study of Metaphor and Theology.* Philadelphia: Fortress, 1975.

Moe-Lobeda, Cynthia D. *Resisting Structural Evil: Love as Ecological-Economic Vocation.* Minneapolis: Fortress, 2013.

Mooney, Chris. "Plastic within the Great Pacific Garbage Patch is 'increasing exponentially' scientists find." *Washington Post,* March 22, 2018. https://www. washingtonpost.com/news/energy-environment/wp/2018/03/22/plastic-within-the-great-pacific-garbage-patch-is-increasing-exponentially-scientists-find/?utm_term=.d4eb9bc657a6.

Meyers, Carol L. *Rediscovering Eve: Ancient Israelite Women in Context.* New York: Oxford University Press, 2013.

Myers, Ched. *The Biblical Vision of Sabbath Economics.* Washington DC: Tell the Word, 2001.

———. *Binding the Strong Man: A Political Reading of Mark's Story of Jesus.* Maryknoll, NY: Orbis, 2008.

———. *Who Will Roll Away the Stone?: Discipleship Queries for First World Christians.* Maryknoll, NY: Orbis, 1994.

Nembhard, Jessica Gordon. *Collective Courage: A History of African American Cooperative Economic Thought and Practice.* University Park, PA: Pennsylvania State University Press, 2014.

Norgaard, Kari Marie. *Living in Denial: Climate Change, Emotions, and Everyday Life.* Cambridge, MA: MIT Press, 2011.

Oakman, Douglas E. *Jesus and the Economic Questions of His Day.* Lewiston, NY: Edwin Mellen, 1986.

———. *Jesus and the Peasants.* Eugene, OR: Cascade, 2008.

O'Day, Gail R., and Susan E. Hylen. *John.* Louisville: Westminster John Knox, 2006.

Oketech, Johnstone Summit, and Tara Polzer. "Conflict and Coffee in Burundi." In *Scarcity and Surfeit: The Ecology of Africa's Conflicts,* edited by Jeremy Lind and Kathryn Sturman, 85–158. New Muckleneuk: Institute for Security Studies, 2002.

Patel, Raj. *Starved and Stuffed: The Hidden Battle for the World Food System.* New York: Melville House, 2007.

Peterson, Anna L. *Everyday Ethics and Social Change: The Education of Desire.* New York: Columbia University Press, 2009.

Reed, Jonathan L. *Archaeology and the Galilean Jesus: A Re-examination of the Evidence.* Harrisburg, PA: Trinity, 2000.

Rieger, Joerg. *Jesus vs. Caesar: For People Tired of Serving the Wrong God.* Nashville: Abingdon, 2018.

Ringe, Sharon H. *Jesus, Liberation, and the Biblical Jubilee: Images for Ethics and Christology.* Philadelphia: Fortress, 1985.

Robbins, Paul. *Lawn People: How Grasses, Weeds, and Chemicals Make Us Who We Are.* Philadelphia: Temple University Press, 2007.

Rogers, Heather. *Green Gone Wrong: How Our Economy is Undermining the Environmental Revolution.* New York: Verso, 2010.

Rogers-Vaughn, Bruce. *Caring for Souls in a Neoliberal Age.* New York: Palgrave Macmillan, 2016.

Rossing, Barbara. "River of Life in God's New Jerusalem: An Eschatological Vision for Earth's Future." *Mission Studies* 16 (1999) 487–99.

Rousseau, John J., and Rami Arav. *Jesus and His World: An Archaeological and Cultural Dictionary*. Minneapolis: Fortress, 1995.

Ruether, Rosemary Radford. *Gaia and God: An Ecofeminist Theology of Earth Healing*. San Francisco: Harper, 1992.

———. *To Change the World: Christology and Cultural Criticism*. New York: Crossroad, 1981.

Saad, Lydia, and Jeffrey M. Jones. "U.S. Concern about Global Warming at Eight-Year High." *Gallup*, March 16, 2016. http://www.gallup.com/poll/190010/concern-global-warming-eightyear-high.aspx.

Salvatierra, Alexia, and Peter Heltzel. *Faith-Rooted Organizing: Mobilizing the Church in Service to the World*. Downers Grove, IL: InterVarsity, 2014.

Sawicki, Marianne. *Crossing Galilee: Architectures of Contact in the Occupied Land of Jesus*. Harrisburg, PA: Trinity, 2000.

Schade, Leah D. *Creation Crisis Preaching: Ecology, Theology, and the Pulpit*. St. Louis: Chalice, 2015.

Scialabba, Nadia El-Hage, and Maria Muller-Lindenlauf. "Organic Agriculture and Climate Change." *Renewable Agriculture and Food Systems* 25 (2010) 158–69.

Schottroff, Luise. *The Parables of Jesus*. Minneapolis: Fortress, 2006.

———. *Lydia's Impatient Sisters: A Feminist Social History of Early Christianity*. Louisville: Westminster John Knox, 1995.

Schottroff, Luise, and Wolfgang Stegemann. *Jesus and the Hope of the Poor*. Eugene, OR: Wipf and Stock, 2009.

Scott, Bernard Brandon. *Re-Imagine the World: An Introduction to the Parables of Jesus*. Santa Rosa, CA: Poleridge, 2001.

Segovia, Fernando F. *Decolonizing Biblical Studies: A View from the Margins*. Maryknoll, NY: Orbis, 2000.

Shiva, Vandana. *Stolen Harvest: The Hijacking of the Global Food Supply*. Cambridge: South End, 2000.

Shove, Elizabeth. "Converging Conventions of Comfort, Cleanliness, and Convenience." *Journal of Consumer Policy* 26 (2003) 395–418.

Smith, Dennis E. *From Symposium to Eucharist: The Banquet in the Early Christian World*. Minneapolis: Fortress, 2003.

Smith, James K. A. *Desiring the Kingdom: Worship, Worldview, and Cultural Formation*. Grand Rapids: Baker Academic, 2009.

Sobrino, Jon. *Jesus the Liberator: A Historical Theological Reading of Jesus of Nazareth*. Maryknoll, NY: Orbis, 1993.

Soelle, Dorothee. *Suffering*. Philadelphia: Fortress, 1973.

Street, R. Allen. *Subversive Meals: An Analysis of the Lord's Supper under Roman Domination during the First Century*. Eugene, OR: Pickwick, 2013.

Tanner, Kathryn. *Christianity and the New Spirit of Capitalism*. New Haven, CT: Yale University Press, 2019.

Taussig, Hal. *In the Beginning Was the Meal: Social Experimentation and Early Christian Identity*. Minneapolis: Fortress, 2009.

Taylor, Mark Lewis. *The Executed God: The Way of the Cross in Lockdown America*. Minneapolis: Fortress, 2001.

Thistlethwaite, Susan Brooks. *#OccupytheBible: What Jesus Really Said (and Did) About Money and Power*. New York: Astor and Blue, 2012.

de la Torre, Miguel A. *Doing Christian Ethics from the Margins*. 2d ed. Maryknoll, NY: Orbis, 2014.

———. *The Politics of Jesús: A Hispanic Political Theology*. Lanham, MD: Rowman & Littlefield, 2016.

Trainor, Michael. *About Earth's Child: An Ecological Listening to the Gospel of Luke*. Sheffield: Sheffield, 2012.

Vitousek, Peter M., Harold A. Mooney, Jane Lubchenco, and Jerry M. Melillo. "Human Domination of Earth's Ecosystems." *Science* 227 (1997) 494–99.

Wenell, Karen J. *Jesus and Land: Sacred and Social Spaces in Second Temple Judaism*. New York: T & T Clark, 2007.

Wirzba, Norman. *Food and Faith: A Theology of Eating*. New York: Cambridge University Press, 2011.

———. *Living the Sabbath: Discovering the Rhythms of Rest and Delight*. Grand Rapids: Brazos, 2006.

———. *The Paradise of God: Renewing Religion in an Ecological Age*. New York: Oxford University Press, 2003.

———. *Way of Love: Rediscovering the Heart of Christianity*. New York: Harper One, 2016.

World Health Organization. "Obesity and Overweight Fact Sheet." http://www.who.int/en/news-room/fact-sheets/detail/obesity-and-overweight.

Wright, Christopher J. H. *God's People in God's Land: Family, Land, and Property in the Old Testament*. Grand Rapids: Eerdmans, 1990.

Made in the USA
Middletown, DE
14 March 2021